W9-AVK-102

Shakespeare's Ear

Shakespeare's Ear

Dark, Strange, and Fascinating Tales from the World of Theater

TIM RAYBORN

Skyhorse Publishing

Skyhorse Publishing books may be purchased in bulk at special discounts for sales promotion, corporate gifts, fund-raising, or educational purposes. Special editions can also be created to specifications. For details, contact the Special Sales Department, Skyhorse Publishing, 307 West 36th Street, 11th Floor, New York, NY 10018 or info@skyhorsepublishing.com.

Skyhorse® and Skyhorse Publishing® are registered trademarks of Skyhorse Publishing, Inc.®, a Delaware corporation.

Visit our website at www.skyhorsepublishing.com.

10 9 8 7 6 5 4 3 2 1

Library of Congress Cataloging-in-Publication Data is available on file.

Cover design by Rain Saukas

Print ISBN: 978-1-5107-1957-6
Ebook ISBN: 978-1-5107-1958-3

Printed in the United States of America

Contents

Introduction

The Grim and the Unusual in the History of Western Theater

We love to be shocked, and the darker the subject, the better. Let's be honest, that's the reason why so many people are fascinated by television news reports, Internet updates on various social media platforms, and any other ways of finding out about some gruesome story as it happens. Many have the same desire for the grotesque in their fiction, and theater is potentially even more enticing, being a live spectacle. Reading is lovely and the screen provides amazing escapes, but to see the morbid, the grotesque, the strange, and the violent happen in front of you? That is something truly unique that only drama can provide.

"To be or not to be, that is the question." Yes, indeed, that *is* the question that has sent shivers of horror down the backs of countless high school students in the English-speaking world and left untold numbers of theatergoers—who want to appear sophisticated and educated—totally baffled because they're still not quite sure what that whole speech is really about; who actually speaks "Shakespeare," anyway?

Drama is one of those areas that exists in a sort of side world at the edge of many people's awareness. Nearly everyone remembers having to endure the trauma of performing in school plays as children; this was followed by reading plays for their own good when they were in high school. Afterward, though, most people don't give much thought to these theatrical excursions, rather like long division and frog dissection, and that's a terrible shame—about drama, that is, not long division or frog dissection, unless you're really into those. Plays are just another of those general-education topics that are absorbed and then get stored away in the file cabinet of our brains, never to be accessed again, because far more important things take their place. Those who use Western technologies (and that would be most of us) are bombarded with movies, television programs, web series, online videos, and countless other diversions. But alongside these nonstop, 24/7 entertainments, there still exists the world of live stage shows that has demonstrated a surprising tenacity and will to survive, even in our age of endless stimulation overload.

But why? What could possibly be appealing about watching a dozen actors pretend to fight a huge war in a Shakespeare play, when you could see a CGI effects fest with a budget of $200 million exploding all over the gigantic movie screen in bloody 3-D? The thing is, countless people still prefer (or at least still go to see) the former on a regular basis. There is something highly appealing about any live performance, as music aficionados will readily tell you. You just can't beat that live sound, and for many, the thrill of seeing living actors on a stage doing what they do best can't be duplicated on a big or a small screen. There is an immediacy, a danger, and a sense of connection that only a play can provide.

So this book is an attempt to combine two of our loves: the closeness of a live performance and our endless fascination with the grotesque, the grim, the bloody, and the bleak; they blend together surprisingly well. Another surprise is how much goes on behind the scenes—in fact, the skulduggery offstage has frequently been greater than that onstage.

The book is divided into two parts, or more appropriately, acts. Act I is a historical tour, taking you back to ancient Mesopotamia and Egypt, where violent proto-dramas enacted the stories of the gods, and then continuing through the Greeks to the Middle Ages, on to the glorious Tudor and Stuart ages, and beyond into the "modern" world (whatever that means). Act II is a miscellany of topics, including some things that you really should know about Shakespeare, the zany Commedia dell'Arte, the methods for portraying blood and gore onstage throughout history (a very important topic!), and essential information on dramatic ghosts and the seemingly endless theater superstitions, as well as some miscellaneous theatrical oddities.

So who might some of our odd cast of characters be? Well, you're certainly familiar with Shakespeare, or his name, at any rate. Maybe you know a bit about Christopher Marlowe—though you may not know about his horrible (and, some say, alleged) death. You've probably heard of Sophocles and/or some of the other ancient Greek playwrights, whose tragedies were early models of over-the-top grimness. You may also recall Molière, the French writer of farces, even if you've never read or watched any of his work.

Others will likely be less familiar to you. What about Thomas Kyd or Moll Cutpurse? Or the actor William Davenant, who implied that he was Shakespeare's illegitimate son? Read on and find out.

Beyond playwrights and actors, theatrical history is bursting with odd stories. Just what exactly is a slapstick? (Hint: it's actually pretty close to what the name suggests.) What was the stomach-turning Grand Guignol in Paris and why was it so popular? Why does "the Scottish Play" have so many superstitions associated with it? And for that matter, why are there so many bizarre theatrical superstitions in general? Did people really riot over theater shows? How did a live horse end up flying off a London stage into an orchestra pit? And why do so many of the dead seem to come back to theaters to give eternal encores?

This book is a veritable auditorium of the abhorrent, a green room of the grotesque, and a curtain call of the creepy. Herein you will find all sorts of stories about playwrights, actors, theaters, companies, and audiences engaged in activities ranging from the horrible to the hilarious to the hideous, and sometimes all at the same time. You don't need any previous knowledge of theater history—or of plays in general—to enjoy this unsettling excursion. You can dip into it anywhere you like, though you might get a bit more out of it by reading it from cover to cover—but that's really just my way of trying to entice you into devouring it all! Pick a story, dive in, and prepare to be shocked and fascinated.

These days, many view the theater as a bastion of the elite, a high-brow indulgence that is expensive, out of touch, and irrelevant to most people, but for many centuries, it was *the* most popular entertainment around. In Elizabethan England, for example, admittance to a playhouse was extremely cheap (one penny, the price of a large tankard of ale), and in Georgian England, there were mass protests when one London manager tried to raise admission prices to cover the costs of building a new theater after a fire; he was forced to back down. Audiences forgave him and returned soon enough. They've been flocking to theaters ever since, not just in England but all over the world.

The sustained devotion of theatergoers throughout history suggests that plays are endlessly fascinating and speak to us in unique ways. Learning about the astonishing and often violent antics that happened behind the scenes of great dramas makes the whole genre even more fun. So, settle in and let the lights go down and the curtain rise. The play's the thing, but the rest of the theatrical world is pretty wild, too!

Act I

The Strange Lives and Odd Fates of Playwrights, Actors, Theater Companies, and More

1

The Ancient World

The origins of drama are as mysterious as the origins of music, art, and other creative outputs. The idea of taking on a role to represent someone or something else almost certainly had an important place in ancient religions and rituals. Of course, that is a convenient catch-all explanation. Whenever we don't understand something about the past, whether it be a statue, a stone circle, a burial plot, or anything else, we (rather smugly, it seems) label it as having been used for "ritual purposes," as if that really tells us anything. One wonders how many hilariously wrong attributions are out there: perhaps that little stone "idol" was actually used to grind wheat, or maybe it was set out to let others know that the primitive toilet was occupied. Or maybe it was some kind of "marital aid."

Still, it doesn't stretch credibility to suggest that some kind of primitive drama may have arisen in prehistory to enact myths, or to teach the young how to hunt, or gather, or perform any other duties essential for a group's survival. By the time that recognizable civilizations developed in the ancient Near East, they were certainly using dramatic representations in religious ceremonies. Whether they also did so for secular entertainment is another question. It does seem that, at least in the case of the Greeks, ideas about comedy and tragedy came from rituals for the wine god Dionysus, which is quite appropriate, given most entertainers' love of alcohol; we'll investigate those stories in the next chapter. For now, here is a small selection of violent ritual dramas that were played out for religious edification and possibly entertainment in some very old cultures. These don't seem to have evolved into separate performances with their own dedicated theaters, but they were an important early example of the idea of a story portrayed with costumes, masks, and declamation, if not dialogue. They may well have been early plays, but since we have little evidence about how they may have been performed, we will focus more on the stories they depicted.

Ancient Mesopotamian dramatic rituals

Sacred marriages and divine retribution

The Fertile Crescent in the Near East hosted the rise of some of the earliest civilizations over six thousand years ago. These societies became adept at everything that we tend to associate with, well, civilization: agriculture, cities, governments, taxes, hierarchical structures, temples and organized religion, and most importantly, beer production.

The Sumero-Babylonian mythologies were rich in epic content and would have made splendid tales to relay orally, or in rituals at certain times of the year. Among the most important of these was the sacred marriage between the goddess Inanna/Ishtar and her lover Dumuzi, known as Tammuz in later Babylonian myth, originally a king said to have ruled for thirty-six thousand years—talk about needing term limits! This marriage was "performed" by the current king (who was presumably much more mortal) and the high priestess of the goddess at the New Year celebration ceremony. In addition to reciting dialogue derived from the myth, the presentation probably included the whole shebang as far as marriage was concerned, including the wedding night whoopee in front of the faithful.

Despite this unusual live performance, a night's fun was not meant to signify the beginning of wedded bliss. The myths offer an unpleasant account about what happened later on. Some of these events were probably also acted out in the rituals, giving a more dramatic presentation of beliefs that helped define humanity's role in the world. In this story, Ishtar descends into the underworld, to visit her sister Ereshkigal, the Queen of the Underworld and the dead. Ereshkigal is mourning the loss of her husband, Gugalanna, who was killed by the famous heroes Gilgamesh and Enkidu; Ishtar had sent Gugalanna to fight Gilgamesh for resisting her sexual advances—which is something you just don't do to a goddess—and Gilgamesh bested him. Ereshkigal, in her anger and grief, was determined to humiliate her sister (who she felt was responsible for the whole thing), forcing her to remove an article of clothing at each of the seven gates to her dark realm. When Ishtar finally arrives, she is naked and enraged with Ereshkigal. Thereafter, Ishtar is imprisoned and all sex ceases on earth. Well, that's no fun!

The head god, Ea/Enki, hears about this sibling squabble (Ishtar had arranged for him to be notified if she were gone for more than three days, a sensible precaution) and basically tells Ereshkigal to cease and desist and let her sister go. The queen has no choice but to obey, and so Ishtar returns to the world of the living, putting on one garment at a time as she leaves. But there is a condition: someone else must take her place. She doesn't want anyone to have to make that sacrifice, but when she sees her husband Dumuzi not mourning her loss at all, she immediately chooses him, and down he goes, dragged by an entourage of demons; so much for that thirty-six-thousand-year reign.

All of this was juicy stuff to portray, and it's possible that these kinds of stories were given dramatic readings, even if they were not actually "plays" in the way we think of them. Various masks have been found that seem to represent gods and monsters, which would have made for a splendid way to convey religious teachings about the authority and power of the gods, reasons for the natural order of things, and our place in the cosmos. These temple areas, if not exactly "theaters," could certainly accommodate large and curious crowds.

Did these theatrical-like concoctions make their way out of the temple and into secular life? There isn't much evidence, but they certainly could have, even if only on a small scale. It's easy to imagine royalty being entertained by masked players telling such stories at a banquet (including the disrobing and angry demons), for example, even if no public theaters were ever built.

Ancient Egyptian dramatic rituals
Violence, dismemberment, and hippo burgers

Egypt in the ancient world was a wonder, a culture filled with mystery and fantastic myths. It has captivated the imagination of the West and the world since the beginning of modern archeology in the eighteenth century. Its buildings, pyramids, and statues inspire awe, and its culture continues to fascinate. Egypt's body of religious beliefs and rituals was immensely complex and changeable, with certain narratives and gods being melded into one another over the centuries, stories being adapted and rewritten, and beliefs being updated as the need arose.

At the heart of these, however, were certain key myths that retained their power, among them the legends of the gods Osiris, Set, Isis, and Horus. To mark the annual Nile flooding that came in spring, these tales would be reenacted at temples and shrines for the benefit of the priests and the gods they worshipped; the general public was probably not allowed to witness certain sacred dramas, while others may have been widely viewed. Given that some of these accounts were pretty violent, the dramatic portrayals could get a bit bloody, as well.

The myth of Osiris—the god of the underworld who presided over the judgment of souls, as well as of agriculture and rebirth—was well known and revered throughout Egypt. It tells of how the green-skinned god was envied by his brother, the jackal-headed god Set, who coveted his throne. Set attacks Osiris and dismembers him, cutting him into fourteen pieces (or sixteen, or forty-two, the stories vary). Osiris's wife and sister (it's complicated), Isis, recovers all of the pieces and puts him back together, Frankenstein's monster-like, but she is unable to recover his phallus. No problem! She fashions a replacement out of gold, and using an ancient spell, brings her brother back to life long enough for them to do the deed and produce a child, Horus, the god of the sky. Thereafter, Osiris becomes lord of the underworld, and the hawk-headed

Horus becomes a much-loved god who battles against his father's murderer on several occasions.

This striking series of episodes lent itself well to ritual dramas at various festivals that were performed yearly in Abydos, Heliopolis, and other cities. One wonders how the actors might have presented Osiris being chopped up and distributed about the land. They probably used a number of props and masks, and spoke dialogue derived from the written mythological accounts.

The villain of the story, the god Set, was represented on some occasions by a live hippo in the performance area (in some myths, Set took the form of a hippo). The high priest, or perhaps even the pharaoh, would kill the animal, thus representing the vanquishing of the god. Thereafter, it was carved up and portions were served and eaten as a final symbolic gesture of Set's defeat.

Sometimes enthusiasm for the ritual dramas could go too far. The Greek writer Herodotus (*ca.* 484–*ca.* 425 BCE) wrote in his *Histories* about a pageant that got out of hand:

> At Papremis . . . while some few of the priests are occupied with the image of the god, the greater number of them stand in the entrance of the temple with wooden clubs, and other persons to the number of more than a thousand men with purpose to perform a vow, these also having all of them staves of wood, stand in a body opposite to those: and the image, which is in a small shrine of wood covered over with gold, they take out on the day before to another sacred building.

> The few then who have been left about the image, draw a wain with four wheels . . . and the other priests standing in the gateway try to prevent it from entering, and the men who are under a vow come to the assistance of the god and strike them, while the others defend themselves. Then there comes to be a hard fight with staves, and they break one another's heads, and I am of opinion that many even die of the wounds they receive; the Egyptians however told me that no one died.

Sometimes these mock battles were not so mocking. The Roman poet Juvenal (late first to early second century CE) records how rivalries between towns during these ritual dramas could become fierce and lead to violence. In the towns of Ombus and Denderah, for example, there was so much enmity that they would try to disrupt each other's performances, first with fists, then with the throwing of stones, and finally with arrows! One unfortunate combatant from Denderah was left behind and apparently cut to pieces; maybe they were emulating the whole Osiris/Set thing a little too well.

The Hittites and the Anatolian Greeks

Stormy marriages, drunk dragons, and castrated gods

The Hittites occupied what is now Turkey, with an empire that reached its height by the fourteenth century BCE. They had their own unique culture and beliefs, including religious rituals that may have been acted out as dramas.

Like the Mesopotamians, they performed rituals wherein the king and queen would act out a sacred marriage between gods, in this case the weather god Tarhun (also known as Teshub) and the sun goddess Arinniti, who may have been the supreme deity in the Hittite pantheon. We say "may" because much information has been lost about their beliefs and has to be pieced together from stone inscriptions, a tedious task for which, thankfully, there are still enthusiasts. This ritual took place in Arinna, the major cultic center for Arinniti's worship. The exact nature of the ritual is not known. It may have been public, or performed in front of priests only. It may have been symbolic, or they may actually have ritually consummated the marriage. But it was undoubtedly an important dramatic ritual.

At the spring festival of Puruli, held in the city of Nerik, there was a commemoration of the sky god's defeat of the dragon god Illuyanka. The story tells how Teshub gets his butt kicked by said dragon in their first encounter. In one version, he asks Inara, the goddess of wild animals, for help, and she devises a plan to get the dragon drunk. The reptile, then quite tipsy, is done in by Teshub and other gods; not very fair. Another version records that Teshub loses his eyes and heart to the dragon after their first battle—damned inconvenient—and devises a plan for revenge by marrying and having a son who marries the dragon's daughter and asks for his father's eyes and heart back as a wedding gift. The gracious dragon agrees, and Teshub, thus restored, goes back to face him again and kills him; again, not very sporting. Some surviving texts indicate that there were directions for the ritual, implying that it was performed for an audience, but we don't know how many actually saw it, or if it was an annual enactment.

By the first millennium BCE, the mother goddess Cybele was widely worshipped in the same region, and the tragic story of her love for the god Attis was well known. Ritual representations of the tale were performed at festivals, probably in caves rather than in temples, but certainly before an audience of some kind. The later Greek version of events was very saucy, indeed. Cybele refused the advances of Zeus, a bold move which the arrogant leader of the gods was not about to take lightly. He approached her as she slept, and—for real—got himself off on her. This money shot was enough, her being a fertility goddess and all, for her to become pregnant, and at the appropriate time, she gave birth to one Agdistis, a hermaphrodite.

The gods weren't happy about this, so they cut off Agdistis's penis and buried it in the ground. From this sprang an almond tree—no jokes about "nuts." The nymph Nana became pregnant from one of the almonds—ancient Greek contraception clearly sucked—and gave birth to the beautiful Attis. Agdistis, even though technically his parent, fell in love with Attis and announced this at his wedding, which drove Attis mad. He ran into the forest, castrated himself, and bled to death (violets were said to have sprung up from his blood in the ground). His spirit entered into a tree, but Agdistis asked Zeus to preserve his body forever. In one version of the story from Ovid, Cybele is completely devoted to Attis and it is her devotion that drives him insane. In some accounts Cybele and Agdistis are combined, and Cybele seeks Zeus's help to resurrect Attis, whose festival as a reborn god is then celebrated yearly.

Can you imagine trying to act this story out? One would hope that they wouldn't want to be too realistic in depicting the details, but then again, it seems that priests of both Cybele and Attis were required to be eunuchs, and probably performed that operation on themselves as part of their initiation. That is some serious and painful devotion!

2

Ancient Greece and Rome

Drama as we like to think of it really came into its own during the Greco-Roman period, from roughly 700 BCE in Greece until at least the mid-fourth century CE in Rome. The two genres that have been most often associated with the theater—comedy and tragedy—were invented and then developed to near perfection by the Greeks. Incidentally, "tragedies" didn't have to be particularly tragic (though people died in them often enough); the term simply meant that the subject matter in a play was given a serious treatment. We will look at comedy and tragedy as the Greeks understood them in a bit more detail later in the chapter.

A key part of drama in ancient Greece was the dramatic competition, wherein playwrights would vie against one another for prizes and bragging rights, rather like a theatrical Olympics. The best example was the City Dionysia, established in Athens in the sixth century BCE. It was an annual religious festival held in March/April that included many types of performances. The most important were:

- **Dithyrambs**: These were choral works for a group of fifty men and fifty boys. Each group sang and danced in honor of Dionysus. The choruses were financed by a *choregos*, a wealthy citizen who supported their efforts as a matter of civic pride.
- **Comedies**: Originally, only three playwrights were allowed to enter;

this number was later expanded to five. Such comedies were most often set in contemporary times and poked fun at Athenians, both real and invented.

- **Tragedies and satyr plays**: Three playwrights entered the competition, each offering three tragedies and a satyr play. Satyr plays were mythological tales of the gods and heroes. The chorus of these plays was always made up of satyrs (or rather, people dressed up like them), those Pan-like, lecherous, and bawdy half men/half goats who piped and danced in the revels of Dionysus. Such plays were comic and even vulgar, and were intended to contrast with the dark themes, sadness, and death of the tragedies.

These competitive activities were funded by the city and were considered crucial to urban identity. Those who won the competition were able to feel great pride and enjoy being able to boast of their victory, as well as engage in some epic celebrations for their efforts, involving much wine and food.

Drama, of course, made its way into the Roman Empire, but those silly Romans eventually turned their attention to shows that were more, shall we say, on the naughty side. The esteemed Greek plays coexisted with hugely popular street theater that spared no one and nothing in its attempts to shock, provoke, and get a laugh, as well as a few coins. This chapter will look at some of the genres of the time, from the noblest to the lewdest, and introduce you to some Greek and Roman playwrights whose works, lives, and deaths were on the peculiar side (bear in mind that many of these biographies are a mixture of myth, legend, and fanciful invention). But first, let's start with a basic question, the answer to which may seem obvious: What are comedy and tragedy?

Comedy and tragedy

It's all Greek to me

Before we delve into the strange and unfortunate experiences of some of the ancient world's greatest playwrights, a bit of background on the genres they used is helpful. In our modern interpretations, comedy makes us laugh and tragedy makes us sad. The two masks so often seen in association with drama have one face smiling and one frowning to indicate this exact distinction. But, as you may have guessed, the truth is a little more complex than that.

So what were these kinds of tales, and why were they so popular?

Tragedy (*tragōidia*) may have had its origins in the worship of the wine god Dionysus, who later became the patron of the theater. Aristotle held that tragedy grew out of a form of hymn sung to the god. Not everyone accepts this theory, and it's a debated subject in the study of Greek drama. Even the roots of the word itself are disputed. It may derive from "song of the goats," referring to the satyrs, or it may mean "song of the harvest," also appropriate for a god of wine and vegetation. At some point, the idea of presenting mythological stories publicly took hold. Initially, there was only one actor, in costume and wearing a mask so that he could properly impersonate a god and tell his or her story without presuming to do so in mere mortal garb, thus offending said god. Eventually a chorus was added and then two other speaking actors, to allow the story to unfold in a more naturalistic manner. With these innovations came dark tales of revenge and justice presided over by stern gods who sometimes interfered in mortal affairs way too much. Sometimes the plays affected the actors themselves. In an early theatrical anecdote, Greek rhetorician Lucian (*ca.* 120/25 CE–180/200 CE) recorded how an actor portraying Ajax became so involved with the character's descent into madness, that he really went mad himself and nearly killed the actor playing Odysseus. Later, he came to his senses and was filled with remorse: "For when his partisans begged him to repeat the performance, he recommended another actor for the part of Ajax, saying that 'it was enough for him to have been mad once.'"

Comedy (*kōmōidia*) had less lofty origins and topics than its sister genre. It probably arose by the sixth century BCE, though mockery and satire in both literature and everyday life were surely far older. The word probably derives from the ancient Greek for "singer/comic poet." Comedies were more down-to-earth than tragedies and dealt less with mythology (the gods, of course, should not be mocked) and more with social commentary. Political satire, sexual humor, and the foibles of life were all fair game. Greek comedy is divided into three eras: Old Comedy (*archaia*), Middle Comedy (*mese*), and New Comedy (*nea*). The old comedies were more fantastical, but later plays focused more on real-world plots and employed stock characters, something the Romans would take over with glee; these may have influenced the later Commedia dell'Arte in Italy (we'll get to that in act II), though not every scholar thinks so. The themes of the New Comedy had a lasting impact on Western drama down to Shakespeare and beyond, since this form of comedy emphasized real life and familiar situations (especially related to love and its endless problems) instead of mythic stories.

Aeschylus (525/524–*ca.* 456/455 BCE)

Heads up

Aeschylus is one of the great tragedians (how's that for a wonderful word?) of ancient Greece. Credited as the "father of tragedy," he is said to have written as many as ninety plays, but alas, only seven of them have survived, and some believe that one of these may not be his. Still, his are among the earliest surviving dramatic works, along with those of Sophocles and Euripides. Within Aeschylus's meager less-than-ten-percent surviving output, however, are great works such as the *Oresteia* trilogy, a series of three plays that describe the bloody aftermath of the Trojan War.

King Agamemnon, the leader of the Greek army during the war, returns after the victory at Troy, but his wife, Clytemnestra, is none too happy that he sacrificed their daughter to the gods to ensure victory, so she murders him. Their son, Orestes, and daughter, Electra, vow to avenge this murder, and eventually Orestes kills Clytemnestra and her lover Aegisthus. He is then beset by the Furies, who intend to avenge the matricide and hound Orestes into the wilderness; eventually, he must stand trial before the gods, including Athena. In the vote on his guilt, they cannot break a tie and so Athena votes in his favor and he is acquitted. The rule of law is upheld and the values of Athens are extolled. Um . . . hooray? The final play of the trilogy, *The Eumenides*, was said to have been so terrifying at times that several audience members died of fright and women miscarried, though this is likely just fanciful nonsense that was written down in a later biography of the playwright.

Another of his plays was *Seven against Thebes*, which sounds rather like the title of a 1950s Western starring John Wayne. In this charming tale, the sons of the ill-fated Oedipus (more on him in a bit)—Eteocles and Polynices—agree to rule the city in alternating years, but at the end of his first year, Eteocles refuses to cede power to his brother. They quarrel. They fight in single combat. They kill each other. Everyone laments. An additional ending was added some fifty years later (*Seven against Thebes II: This Time It's Personal*), where everyone laments even more.

Aeschylus was born in Eleusis, a town north of Athens, and it seems that he was destined for greatness as a playwright from a young age. At least this is what the Greek writer and geographer Pausanias (*ca.* 110–*ca.* 180 CE) wrote when he recorded that as a young man, Aeschylus worked in a vineyard. He attracted the attention of none other than the wine god Dionysus, who visited him in a dream and told him that he should, instead of toiling among the vines, turn his attentions to writing dramatic tragedies, which were soon to become all the rage. Aeschylus obeyed the god's suggestion (really, how could he refuse?) and did just that.

He served in the wars against the Persians, which informed his earliest-surviving play, titled, appropriately enough, *The Persians*. His penchant for writing what he knew eventually led him into trouble, however. It seems that he may have been devoted to the Eleusinian Mysteries, which had nothing to do with gumshoes and murder, but was a cult based on the myth of Demeter and Persephone. The devotees of this secretive religious sect were required to keep mum about its ritual activities. Aristotle, in his *Nicomachean Ethics*, suggests that Aeschylus may have spilled the beans on at least some of these secrets in a play or two:

But of what he is doing a man might be ignorant, as for instance people say "it slipped out of their mouths as they were speaking," or "they did not know it was a secret," as Aeschylus said of the mysteries . . .

Yep, the old "it just slipped out" defense.

Apparently on one occasion, some audience members who heard such a confession were not pleased with this little faux pas, and attempted to kill Aeschylus. Some sources say that he took refuge at the altar in the theater of Dionysus; it would make sense to appeal to the god that got him into this whole business to begin with. He was brought to trial but eventually acquitted, in part because of his war service. Thereafter, he went on to achieve great acclaim, winning prizes in drama competitions and generally being cheered all around.

The Roman writer Pliny the Elder (23 CE–79 CE) claimed that a shadow hung over him, however, in the form of a prophecy that he would die from a falling object. Because of this, Aeschylus preferred to be outside to avoid any heavy objects, such as statues, falling on him while indoors. And sure enough, for a man who devoted his life to tragedies, he met his end (so legend says) in an astonishingly tragicomic way. Pliny faithfully (or not) recorded in his *Natural History*:

> [The eagle] has a clever device for breaking tortoiseshells that it has carried off, by dropping them from a height; this accident caused the death of the poet Aeschylus, who was trying to avoid a disaster of this nature that had been foretold by the fates, as the story goes, by trustfully relying on the open sky.

Apparently, the bird was confused by his bald head and saw it as a nice shiny rock on which to bash out the innards of the unfortunate tortoise. The hapless reptile fell to its doom, and took Aeschylus with it. Presumably, the bird had a lovely feast afterward, with a place setting of dead Greek dramatist. Ah well, the best-laid plans and all that.

Sophocles (*ca.* 497/96–406/05 BCE)

Out of breath, all choked up, or just plain happy

Sophocles is most remembered for the disturbing family goings-on in his three Theban plays: *Oedipus the King* (or *Oedipus Rex*), *Oedipus at Colonus*, and *Antigone*. These days, people are vaguely familiar with the plot, which kept Freud and friends busy for quite some time, but the details are still quite shocking: when Oedipus is an infant, it is prophesized that he will kill his father and marry his mother, so his parents, King Laius and Queen Jocasta, plan to murder him. However, the servant they entrust with doing the appalling deed (not being willing to do it themselves, of course) cannot go through with it, and the baby ends up with a childless couple. Oedipus grows up not knowing his heritage, but one day he learns of the prophecy and flees from his adopted parents, thinking them to be his biological ones and wanting to spare them.

He eventually meets and quarrels with—you guessed it—Laius, kills him (check box one), solves the riddle of the Sphinx (as you do), becomes the new ruler of Thebes, and marries—you guessed it—Jocasta (check box two). When the truth emerges, Jocasta kills herself out of shame, and Oedipus blinds himself and goes into self-imposed exile. However, the two had children—ew—and the legacy of the family's curse lives on in them.

Oedipus goes to the town of Colonus. He dies and his sons, Polyneices and Eteocles, quarrel, as you may remember from Aeschylus's *Seven against Thebes*. Polyneices dies, and Oedipus's daughter Antigone wants to bury him in Thebes, but because he was declared a traitor, she cannot. She resolves to do so anyway, and King Creon (brother of Jocasta) sentences her to death. Eventually, he is convinced to change his mind and spare her, but Antigone has already committed suicide. Creon's son, Haemon (Antigone's fiancé), kills himself after unsuccessfully attempting to stab Creon in revenge. Learning of Haemon's suicide, Creon's wife, Eurydice, kills herself in grief and curses her husband. Creon is left alone and distraught, but hopefully wiser. Cheery stuff.

Sophocles was born into wealth and became the most acclaimed playwright of his time. He is credited with the innovation of adding a third player to the stage (which allowed for more realistic interactions; previously only one or two actors performed onstage together) and of giving his characters more emotional depth. He allegedly lived a very long life; some sources say as long as ninety-one years. As you might expect, different accounts of his life circulated, and there are no fewer than three versions of his death, two of them quite silly and the third rather charming. One story relates that he choked on grapes at the Anthesteria festival in Athens, held each January or February in honor of Dionysus; maybe the god wasn't as impressed with Sophocles as he had been with Aeschylus. A second tale relates that he expired from trying to read aloud a long passage from his play *Antigone*; he wanted to do it in one breath for dramatic effect, but couldn't manage and died. The third story says simply that he died of happiness at winning a victory in a competition. A eulogy composed some time afterward noted that "he ended his life well without suffering any misfortune," so there may be some truth to the peaceful death story, but let's be honest, it's not as much fun as the other two.

Euripides (*ca.* 480–*ca.* 406 BC)

Gone to the dogs

Euripides was the third of the great ancient Athenian Greek dramatists, along with Aeschylus and Sophocles, yet more of his plays have survived than those of the other two combined—as many as nineteen out of more than ninety that he wrote, still a tragically small number (slight pun intended). This may have been due to the later Romans considering him to be the superior playwright and so taking care to preserve more of his works.

His tragedies are retellings of ancient myths and often focus on the dark side of human nature. They include *The Trojan Women* (which tells the sad fates of the women after the fall of Troy), *Bacchae* (an account of

Dionysus and his wild and frenzied worshippers), *Electra* (the daughter of Agamemnon who plots revenge for his murder), and *Medea* (a spurned wife takes revenge on her former husband, Jason).

His plays often dealt more with everyday concerns than mythic ones, despite the use of such myths to tell the stories. Women feature as strong individuals, another unconventional representation, and a controversial one to his male Athenian audiences, who were not used to seeing women portrayed in such a way. For many, his characters were too realistic for the time, and his tendency to represent various gods less reverently than custom dictated led some to accuse him of atheism.

There is one amusing plot device that has long been associated with Euripides. He was especially fond of the literary solution of bringing in a god to solve problems. During the performance, this was commonly done by having said god lowered by a crane (*mechane*) from the roof down onto the playing area, to the amazement and wonder of all. The appearance of such a divinity gave rise to the Latin expression *deus ex machina*, "god from the machine," and became associated with using a contrived plot device to get one out of a narrative problem that couldn't otherwise be resolved. While certainly useful, this approach was considered lazy by some. The comic playwright Antiphanes (*ca.* 408–334 BCE) was an early critic of its use: "When they don't know what to say and have completely given up on the play, just like a finger they lift the machine and the spectators are satisfied." Some have defended Euripides's use of this solution, since in his plays, the gods cause many of the problems to begin with, so it's only right that they should clean up their own messes.

Biographies of Euripides are conflicting, and his end is no exception. He may have been invited to settle in Macedonia by King Archelaus I in 408 BCE. If so, he doesn't seem to have lasted there long. Various versions of his death have circulated over the centuries. One states that he simply succumbed to the effects of a harsh Macedonian winter, which was considerably colder than those of Athens and took its toll on his old body. The more interesting account says that a woman seeking revenge, perhaps his wife, let loose a pack of dogs on him, who tore him apart. Another account says that a group of women did it, perhaps the frenzied followers of Bacchus that he had written about, which would be an ironic end, to be sure!

Philemon (*ca.* 362 BCE–*ca.* 262 BCE)

He made an ass of himself

Not to be confused with the Philemon of the New Testament, this fellow hailed from either Cilicia on the south coast of Turkey or the island of Sicily; the records are a little unsure about his origins because those place names sound pretty similar. Regardless, by about 330–328 BCE he made his way to Athens, where he showed a talent for writing comedies. He is said to have written ninety-seven dramas, of which some fifty-seven are known to us by title or at least in some surviving fragments. He won competitions and made quite a name for himself, as his brand of comedy was all the rage.

He is said to have died at the ripe old age of a hundred and one—other sources say between ninety-six and ninety-nine; if true, this was quite an accomplishment, surpassing even Sophocles. This longevity was attributed to his temperance, frugality, and desire for a simple and happy life, but in all likelihood it's just a literary fiction. Perhaps befitting one who lived so long, there is more than one version of his death. The best comes from the Roman historian Valerius Maximus (*ca.* 20 BCE–*ca.* 50 CE) and involves a donkey, fruit, and alcohol. It is retold here in a splendid account by the English dramatist Richard Cumberland (1732–1811). It sounds like a Monty Python skit. The odd letter that looks like an "f" with no crossbeam is an old form of "s." But if you want to pronounce it as an "f" just for laughs, feel free. "Fuffocated by a fudden fit" does sound pretty sunny, er, funny:

> [Maximus] tells us Philemon was fuffocated by a fudden fit of laughter upon feeing an afs, who had found his way into the houfe, devour a plate of figs, which his page had provided for him; that he called out the boy to drive away the afs, but when this order was not executed

before the animal had emptied the plate, he bade his page pour out a goblet of wine and prefent it to the plunderer to complete his entertainment; tickled with the pleafantry of this conceit, and no lefs with the grotefque attitude and adventure of the animal, Philemon was feized with a fit of laughing and in that fit expired.

There is probably a lesson to be learned in all of this, but exactly what that might be is not clear; maybe all will be revealed after drinking a bit more wine.

Seneca the Younger (*ca.* 4 BCE–65 CE)

To bleed or not to bleed

Lucius Annaeus Seneca was a Roman philosopher, statesman, and dramatist during the turbulent decades of the first century, when Rome seemed to be ruled by one crazy, incompetent emperor after another—seriously: Tiberius, Caligula, Nero; what the hell? Even if you've only seen the TV production of *I, Claudius*, you'll have a pretty good idea of how nutty and scary these guys were (at least according to their biographers).

Born in Córdoba, Spain, but raised in Rome, Seneca later had the less-than-enviable responsibility of being tutor and then advisor to Nero, the famously tyrannical ruler who fancied himself a master musician (let's just say he wasn't) and who may or may not have had a hand in the fire that devastated the city in 64 CE.

Seneca was a gifted writer of tragedies, and his surviving plays had great influence during the Middle Ages and Renaissance. His style, especially in the form of the revenge tragedy, was quite popular in Elizabethan England, when such blood-soaked tales were in great demand. His plays may or may not have been acted in his own lifetime. Some have argued that they were merely intended for private recitation, since public theaters at the time didn't usually stage "serious" tragedies. But they do work well onstage and have been successfully presented in modern times, so perhaps he did hope for them to be performed.

In his role as an advisor to Nero, Seneca may have had some success in limiting the young man's excesses in the first year of his reign, but he was later criticized as being a hypocrite for denouncing tyrants while remaining in the service of one. He seemed to enjoy his life of extravagance as well, as historian Cassius Dio (*ca.* 155–235 CE) wrote:

> Though finding fault with the rich, he himself acquired a fortune of 300,000,000 sesterces; and though he censured the extravagances of others, he had five hundred tables of citrus wood with legs of ivory, all identically alike, and he served banquets on them.

Undoubtedly, living amid luxury tainted him over time, and Nero's insane activities probably bothered him less than they should have. But realistically, what choice did he have? He couldn't just denounce the young man, hand in his two weeks' notice, and apply for the position of advisor to another emperor somewhere else. He walked a fine line in the service of a dangerous and unstable youth, and it ultimately came back to haunt him.

At first, it seemed like he would escape this precarious situation intact. The one thing he could and did do when he wanted out was offer to go into retirement. Surprisingly, Nero agreed, and they apparently parted on good terms. This post-tyrant life went well for a few years, but in 65 CE, a certain statesman named Gaius Calpurnius Piso hatched a plot to assassinate Nero (who by now really was getting out of hand) and have himself declared emperor. The plan was foiled, but Seneca was implicated as a conspirator; whether he had actually been involved is unknown.

Of the more than forty people accused, nearly half were ordered by Nero to commit suicide, a clever form of execution that saved him the time and effort. Besides, refusing to do so would mean being arrested and executed anyway; at least with a suicide, the victim could choose how they would die. Seneca was one of those ordered to die by his own hand, and he complied with the imperial command. He had his veins opened and prepared to bleed to death. However, according to the historian Tacitus, Seneca's age and poor diet meant that he did not bleed quickly, and that the process was painful. He ingested poison, but this likewise failed to do the trick. He then had himself immersed in a bath, which allowed the blood to flow more freely and was considered a painless way to pass on. Ultimately, he probably suffocated on the thick steam from the bathwater.

Seneca's reputation as a philosopher was such that he was brought into the Christian fold. Some early Christian writers believed that he had converted to Christianity before his death; some even held that his death in the bath was a kind of baptism. This clever interpretation of the facts allowed for his works to be preserved and exert great influence in Western Europe over the next 1,500 years and more. Nero wasn't so lucky, being seen as a crazy monster.

Atellan farces and Roman mimes (*ca.* 391 BCE–third century CE and later)

A mad extravagance

Atellan farces, or *fabulae Atellanae*, were rustic comedies imported to Rome from southern Italy around 391 BCE, though the writer Livy (*ca.* 59 BCE–*ca.* 17 CE) records that they were first performed in Rome in 363 BCE as a means of appeasing the gods and combating a pestilence that was ravaging the area. I guess that makes sense; there's a terrible disease, so let's make the gods laugh and maybe they'll do something about it.

These farces were vulgar plays with low-brow humor that poked fun at everything—politics, myths, contemporary issues—and contained a good amount of improvised humor and off-the-cuff remarks, so that no two shows were ever quite the same. The players (most often from the lowest classes of society) wore masks and portrayed a series of stock characters: the mean and sneaky Macchus, the obese and simple Bucco, the greedy and arrogant Manducus, the elderly and foolish Pappus, and the agile, clown-like Samnio. The similarity between some of these fellows and those in the later Italian Commedia dell'Arte has long been recognized, and the Commedia may represent a survival in folk tradition of these earlier Roman originals, though not all scholars accept this lineage. Essentially, the farces presented the lower classes in comical and even insulting ways, which was a reflection of how the upper classes viewed them.

By the early first century BCE, two Roman dramatists, Lucius Pomponius and Quintus Novius, created written plots for the Atellan farces, giving them a literary format and more respectability. Special actors were hired to perform these new comedies, which were presented at the end of tragedies, presumably to give the audience something lighter before they went home. It was rather like the cartoons shown at the beginning of movies back in the day, only in reverse.

Despite this respectable new incarnation, the plays were controversial and had detractors among older, more conservative Roman citizens and those who held power. According to Tacitus, Emperor Tiberius, who was lampooned by one such farce for his legendary lechery, responded to complaints with the following proclamation, a classic pot-kettle-black situation:

> [The farces] had often . . . sought to disturb the public peace, and to bring disgrace on private families, and the old Oscan farce, once a wretched amusement for the vulgar, had become at once so indecent and so popular, that it must be checked by the Senate's authority.

The plays were banned in Italy by 28 CE, but obviously, this prohibition did not last very long, since who can resist a good naughty satire? Indeed, such a ban probably only increased their appeal. Imperial resistance was only temporary, anyway; we know that Emperor Hadrian (76–138 CE) enjoyed them at banquets, and was presumably the one who arranged for them to be performed in the first place.

The other great dramatic tradition of Rome was mime. This word may call to mind images of Marcel Marceau or annoying men in white face paint creeping out people in local parks, but Roman mimes had many qualities that were different from those of their contemporary counterparts. There were two different types of performers, the mime and the pantomime.

Mimes were generally itinerant players who could set up a makeshift stage anywhere where there was a paying audience. Their routines included singing, dancing, juggling and other acrobatics, and performing short skits with humorous and vulgar themes: satires of public figures and institutions, physical comedy, and burlesques were popular. Stories were often improvised, but might focus on mocking country life and its ways, or even lampooning the gods, always a controversial and risky choice. Needless to say, these performers were among the lowest of the low in social class, but over time they did gain limited respectability, and some mimes were even employed by wealthy and noble families.

The pantomime was on another level of quality and esteem, and has a bit more in common with our modern concept of mimes. Such performers always worked solo, remained silent, and took on every role in the production. This involved the wearing of different masks and being something of a quick-change artist with costumes. They were accompanied by musicians and a chorus, who recited or sang the story (usually with tragic or mythic themes), while the pantomime acted and danced out the events and characters in silence. It was a curious blend of drama and a kind of primitive ballet, and was highly prized, worlds away from the street theater of the mimes. Emperors such as Nero and Domitian enjoyed these performances; one can imagine Nero wanting to take part, since he was enamored of all things musical and dramatic.

Mimes persisted for several centuries as everyday entertainment for the lower classes and a guilty pleasure that the rich liked to indulge in once in a while. The emperor Aurelian (214/15–275 CE) is said to have taken "a strange delight in mime," while the truly horrible Emperor Carinus (*d.* 285 CE) was reported to have filled his palace with mimes, singers, and prostitutes. The wonderfully named Emperor Heliogabalus (*ca.* 203–222 CE) apparently decided that mimes' simulated sexual activity during shows simply would not do, so he ordered them to actually *have* sex onstage while performing. Well, I suppose it's a job perk. However, Roman biographies of Heliogabalus are notoriously suspicious. In his short, eighteen-year life, he was said to have married and divorced five women, as well as one man, but his portrayal as a degenerate may have been a political hatchet job by his enemies after his assassination. Regardless, the mimes of the time were undoubtedly only too happy to incorporate him into their future farcical performances, live sex acts notwithstanding.

3

The Middle Ages and Renaissance

Things didn't go so well for the Romans beginning in the third century. All the usual culprits of a civilization's failure gradually came into play: poor leadership, economic problems, population issues, food shortages, and so on. The empire watched as its borders gradually shrunk; increasingly worried Romans also noticed that there were quite a few angry people on the other side of those borders— "barbarians" they called them—that were eager to have a bit of the Roman good life, whether by assimilating into the empire or taking it by force.

Even Rome's gods weren't safe, as a new religion, Christianity, took root, especially among the poor and dispossessed. While offering a more egalitarian vision of life and simpler religious rituals devoted to a single deity, this new belief was quite a bit stricter about personal conduct. Its adherents didn't like what they saw everywhere: moral laxity, violence, corruption, vulgarity, and general nastiness. Pastimes like popular music and drama were natural targets for indignant Christian attacks; fart jokes and public shagging simply weren't going to be okay in this new worldview.

Christian writers such as Tertullian (*ca.* 155–*ca.* 240 CE) believed that the very practice of acting was devoted to the creation of lies, and therefore was hated by God:

Will God be pleased with the man who alters his appearance with a razor [mimes frequently shaved their heads], betraying his own face. . . . Again I ask whether this business of masks in fact pleases God, who forbids the making of any likeness . . . when in his law he ordains that the man who wears female dress is accursed, how will he judge the pantomime actor who sways around in imitation of a woman?

Despite this opposition, and even as Christianity grew in political power over the next two hundred years, actors continued their activities, entertaining the masses and being praised for their talents. With the fall of the Western Roman Empire and the advances of barbarian tribes into the former Roman territories of Italy, France, and Spain, one would think that players and entertainers of all kinds would be the last thing on people's minds; fleeing from large, unwashed men with big, sharp weapons would tend to become a priority. But this image of the "Dark Ages" is incomplete and inaccurate. Various archeological digs have revealed that at least some areas seem to have seen little violence. Towns were often fortified and then apparently carried on as they always had. The barbarian tribes did not so much want to destroy Rome as claim it for themselves, and eventually a succession of Germanic tribal leaders were proclaimed Roman emperors.

It's an interesting thought that the need to be entertained does not subside even in the face of tragedy. A modern example would be how Hollywood boomed during World War II; people wanted an ever-increasing supply of movies to take their minds off the grim events of the world, even if just for a few hours. It probably would not have been all that different in the decades and centuries after Rome's fall. Those who could make people laugh, wow them by juggling and tumbling, or take them to a fantastic place with a story or a drama would probably have been highly valued, regardless of any religious opposition. Such performers probably couldn't travel around a lot, and certainly didn't make much (if any) money, but they must have existed in some form.

This is not to say that music and drama flourished in the early Middle Ages; the records are too sparse for us to have a clear picture. But there are probably ancient Roman elements to later forms of medieval and Renaissance entertainments, and it's highly unlikely that these diversions died out only to suddenly spring back to life several centuries later.

Entertainers were described by many different words in early medieval writings, but these were not used with any consistency, so it's difficult to tell if the writer is speaking of musicians, jugglers, players, or some combination. Much of the evidence that we do have comes in the form of religious prohibitions; always look for what was banned to find out what was popular! For instance, the Council of Rome in 382 warned English clergy not to permit celebrations and plays (*ludos*), while the Council of Clovesho in 747 warned that monasteries should not host traveling performers of any kind. An account from about the year 835 mentions that Emperor Louis I (778–840), despite being nicknamed "the Pious," was entertained by *mimi* (mimes) at a banquet. King Edgar of England (943–975) noted with some irritation that the *mimi* of his time mocked monks and religion openly during their shows in marketplaces. This sounds very similar to a mime performance in Rome from nearly a thousand years earlier.

So some forms of dramatic entertainment seem to have persisted in the long centuries after Rome. These were not the serious, well-plotted dramas of the Greeks and high-brow Romans, but certainly they were the popular entertainments that the common people would continue to flock to, regardless of political circumstances, what religion they were told to obey, or what invader was knocking at the doors.

Speaking of religion, one important genre of medieval drama was the liturgical play. As the name implies, these plays were church-sanctioned performances of biblical scenes presented in churches and usually given at specific feasts and holidays (Christmas, Easter, and so on). Though performed in Latin, these plays were obviously of great use for instructing the largely illiterate populace (rather like the images in stained glass), and they grew over time to become lavish productions, with their own sets, costumes, props, and music.

Religious dramas found their way into the streets as well, in the form of mystery plays. These weren't religious whodunnits, but rather depictions of scenes from the Bible, staged during religious feast days at various times of the year in vernacular languages for the benefit of the common people. In England especially, they were hugely popular, being presented on pageant wagons that became portable stages, hauled out into the streets for all to see. A series of plays is known as a cycle, and different cities each had their own versions of these cycles, which were based around biblical stories, such as the nativity and the passion. They were typically scenes from the Bible with extra dialogue added in. A number of town craft guilds were responsible for various stagings of the plays, which could be elaborate and detailed. The term "mystery play" probably derives from the Latin *ministerium,* meaning "occupation," which links the plays to the guilds. These performances were a matter of civic pride, and the cycles flourished in England (with varying degrees of Church approval) up until the Reformation.

Given the nature of the plays performed in this period—street theater improvised by unlettered players and liturgical dramas written anonymously for the glory of God—the identities of specific medieval playwrights are mostly unknown, though there are some exceptions as the Middle Ages progressed into the Renaissance. We will look at a few of these individuals in this chapter, along with some of the key medieval genres and forms, and the requisite revolting, violent, and funny stories that frequently went with them.

Jacopone da Todi (*ca.* 1230–1306)

Saddled up

Jacopone was a Franciscan monk who had been born into a wealthy noble family. He studied law at the University of Bologna and then began a successful practice of screwing clients, thirteenth-century style. He married a noble lady, Vanna, and seemed to have it all, except that his wife wasn't so impressed with his amoral behavior and took to wearing an itchy hair shirt in an attempt to hurt herself to atone for his sins. Sometime shortly after they were married, she died at a tournament when the stand where she was situated collapsed. Jacopone rushed to help her but found her dying and discovered her less-than-fashionable underwear.

Realizing that she was doing this on his behalf, he eventually gave away all of his possessions and became a wandering ascetic, gaining a reputation for being quite mad; in fact, "Jacopone" is a nickname basically meaning "crazy James." He tried to live up to it, once crawling around the square of his hometown on all fours while wearing a saddle on his back and a bridle in his mouth. On another occasion, he showed up at his brother's wedding covered head to toe in tar and feathers. Once, someone asked him to carry two capons (castrated roosters) to his home, but Jacopone took them instead to the man's family tomb, telling him that this was his true home. Ah yes, dear old crazy James, always good for a laugh!

After a decade of this nonsense—during which no one apparently did much about him—he was able to gain admission to the Franciscan order; they apparently weren't overly worried about his brand of crazy. In the next few decades he wrote a large number of *laudi*, Italian religious songs. These vernacular poems evolved into dialogues that took on the form of dramatic interaction between different speakers. They were effectively early Italian religious plays. One in particular, *Donna de Paradiso*, is all dialogue and concerns the passion of Christ. Some of his other *laudi* include *Que fai, anema predata*, a conversation between a poet and a dead nun who laments that she has been damned, causing the poet to worry about his own fate (this might be a good plot for a horror story), *Audite una entenzone*, wherein the rich converse with a poor and elderly man, and *O Christo pietoso*, a drama about the Last Judgment featuring a cast of Christ, Satan, and various angels. Such works were performed first behind the closed doors of the order, but value was seen in bringing them to the people, and instead of only being sung, they were sometimes recited, laying the groundwork for early Italian drama. Jacopone's minidramas, along with other *laudi*, helped it all happen when wandering Franciscans took them to towns and popularized them by performing them for laypeople.

He didn't fare so well in other areas, however. Being part of an extreme branch of the Franciscans that practiced absolute poverty and asceticism—the Spirituals—he denounced Pope Boniface VIII and was promptly imprisoned and excommunicated. Though released in 1303, he was broken and died only a few years later.

The fabliaux: scandalous minidramas (*ca.* 1200–*ca.* 1340)

All the naughty bits, and then some!

Obscene, irreverent, violent, scatological, offensive—and these were just the good points! The fabliaux had them all and much more. These wonderfully scandalous and comic stories in poetic form circulated widely in medieval France and were enjoyed by everyone from the humblest peasant to the snootiest noble (even though they weren't supposed to like such things). They could be heard anywhere from market fairs and street corners to the dining halls of the wealthy and powerful. The heyday of the fabliaux was in northern France during the thirteenth and fourteenth centuries, but their themes and plots would influence writers like Boccaccio, Chaucer, Rabelais, and Molière for centuries to come.

Written versions survive in many manuscripts, but the real fun would have been in hearing them performed live. Jongleurs (medieval poets and musicians) and out-of-work clerks included these tales in their repertoires and recited them for whoever would listen. They might have played an instrument like a fiddle at various points for added effect. But these recitals wouldn't have been bland poetry readings. A number of scholars now believe that fabliaux poems were in fact miniplays, with the narrator taking on different voices for different characters, acting out scenes of humor and violence, and generally bringing these earthy fancies to vivid life. It's also entirely possible that more than one performer may have been involved, with each taking one or more character roles, thus turning the stories into true plays.

So what about them was so shocking? Oh, plenty. Even by modern standards, some of these tales will make a listener blush. Rather than recounting the heroic deeds of ancient superheroes or the endless relationship problems of the upper classes, the fabliaux are firmly set in the real world of working people, but not in a sympathetic way. Peasants are crude and stupid, husbands are jealous fools, wives are deceitful and prone to adultery, the clergy and monks are lustful and greedy, and those who attempt to rise above their social stations fail and are severely punished. These negative portrayals obviously amused those with more money and standing, but they were also popular with the peasantry, who didn't appreciate their fellows trying to improve their lot in life. The poems weren't just for entertainment, though; they always had a moral and showed how those who indulged in greed, corruption, and sin were made to pay for it.

The language was uncensored; the equivalent of the word for "fuck" appears in at least twenty-five poems; "cunt" is equally popular. One story was known as "The Knight Who Made Cunts Talk," and the plot was exactly about that! These words were probably not particularly offensive at the time and only became so later on as tastes changed. Sexual activity appears frequently, though in a controlled way; the missionary position is predominant, oral sex hardly ever happens, and any descriptions of homosexual behavior are accidental encounters between two ignorant male characters, used for comic effect.

Violence in the form of mutilations was also popular, with castration being a source of much mirth. One story, "The Crucified Priest," tells of how said priest is having an affair with a woman whose husband is a carver of crucifixes. The husband comes home while the adulterous couple are eating (a common setup in these stories for later sex), so the already-naked priest runs and hides in the carver's workshop before he is discovered, but the husband knows what's up. He goes to his work area and sees the priest, motionless and stretched out on a cross, pretending to be a large crucifix. The husband expresses dismay that he has made such a fine Christ figure but accidentally added genitals to it, so out comes the knife and off come the priest's "three hanging ornaments." The priest runs away, but is caught and brought back, and forced to pay money to the wronged husband. So the story ends, and much amusement was had. The moral was that clergymen need to keep to themselves, or they will lose much more than their dignity. The corrupt priest is such a common stock character in these stories that many believe they were a real and common problem.

Another tale worth knowing is a ridiculously ribald fantasy about the gullibility of peasants and the duplicitous nature of their wives, "The Four Wishes of Saint Martin." In this poem, a farmer in Normandy is devoted to Saint Martin, who appears to him and rewards him with four wishes for his faithfulness. The man rushes home in excitement to tell his wife that their troubles are over and that they will soon be rich, as they can wish for anything. The wife asks that he let her make one of the four wishes. He reluctantly agrees, and the lustful wife then wishes that he be endowed with penises everywhere, so that she may take pleasure in them all. With her words, the transformation begins,

> with pricks appearing on his beak
> and springing from his mouth and cheek
> attenuated pricks and burly,
> large pricks, stubby pricks, pricks curly,
> bent pricks, sharp pricks, pricks immense;
> on every bone, however dense,
> pricks sprouted up with startling ease
> a prick leaped up on both his knees . . .

Needless to say, the man is not at all happy with this, and so uses one of his wishes to have his revenge, asking that his wife be covered with the female equivalent:

> She found, within a moment's space,
> two cunts were now upon her face,
> and on her brow, four, side by side.
> in front, in back, cunts multiplied
> and there were cunts of every kind
> and cunts before and cunts behind
> cunts sinuous and straight, cunts brushy
> hairless cunts, cunts piled and plushy . . .

Needless to say, the wife is not at all happy about this, either, and immediately demands that he use the third wish to remove all of these genitalia; at least they'll still have one wish left and can make themselves rich. He does as she asks, but lo and behold, this wish takes away *all* of their bits, so they have none. They have no choice but to use the final wish to bring back one each. Ultimately, their greed and foolishness leave them no better off than they were before.

You can imagine how these kinds of stories could have been acted out, with different comical voices and hilarious miming of the action. The fabliaux were a sharp contrast to the morality plays and liturgical dramas that permeated medieval theater, but in their own way, they offered moralizing teachings, which is probably why religious officials more or less tolerated them. Through the use of vulgarity and hilarity, the fabliaux entertained, amused, shocked, and warned about the consequences of one's actions.

Elaborate and ridiculous medieval stage sets (fourteenth and fifteenth centuries)

Burning men and Death in a onesie

Medieval plays were not just performed in churches and outside for commoners. The upper classes took an increasing interest in drama of all kinds as the years and centuries rolled by, and they began to devise new and over-the-top ways of presenting stories in dramatic form, while adding extra bells and whistles to flesh them out. By the fourteenth century, the props and sets for plays, banquet entertainments, and other diversions were becoming ever more elaborate and, at times, almost ludicrously complicated.

An example of the crazy extravagance can be seen in the Twelfth Night celebrations of December 1378 for King Charles V of France, held in Paris. The spectacle was a dramatic recreation of the taking of Jerusalem by crusaders in the year 1099, because nothing says Christmas cheer like a good, wholesale slaughter of infidels! Props included a ship with a mast and sails, presumably pulled in on wheels, and a miniature of Jerusalem itself (!), complete with towers and even a makeshift mosque minaret, from which a hapless actor dressed as an Arab made a pitiful attempt at mimicking the Islamic call to prayer. Actors dressed as crusaders disembarked from their "ship" and made an assault on Jerusalem, climbing ladders and eventually "taking" the city and killing its inhabitants. *'Tis the season, Fa la la la la, la la, la, la.*

In 1389, a similar production was mounted, this time retelling the story of the fall of Troy—who knows, maybe they even recycled some of the sets? Apparently, this ship could hold up to one hundred "Greek" soldiers, but after the battle began, the fighting had to be called off, because the heat and the commotion were upsetting many of the guests.

At a coronation party for Ferdinand I of Aragon (1380–1416), the banquet included a fire-breathing gryphon that preceded the dishes as they were carried in—maybe more modern restaurants should try this?— and a multilevel structure representing heaven. Musicians dressed as angels and wearing wings sat on these levels and played music as they rotated, while a child representing the Virgin Mary sat in majesty at the top. Best of all, however, was the actor portraying Death. He wore a tight yellow leather outfit that made him look thin and gaunt. The mask had no eyes, which added to his frightening visage. He would gesture to the guests and beckon them, an ugly reminder of the final fate that awaited them all. At another performance, the court jester was a victim of a noble prank, when they bound him with rope and had Death descend and then haul him back up the structure. The poor fellow was terrified and accidentally urinated on the heads of certain guests, which apparently amused the young king greatly.

Chaucer seems to have been aware of these extravagances, which he notes in his "Franklin's Tale":

> For often at feasts have heard it said
> That magicians within a large hall
> Have made water and a boat come in,
> And row up and down in the hall.
> Sometimes a terrible lion has seemed to appear;

And sometimes flowers grow as in a field;

Sometimes a vine, and white and red grapes;

Sometimes a castle of mortar and stone . . .

The most outrageous example of entertainment taken too far was the infamous *Bal des Ardents*, or "Ball of the Burning Men," an unfortunate performance that went horribly wrong. On January 28, 1393, a masquerade ball with lavish entertainments was held at the court of King Charles VI to celebrate the wedding of the queen's lady-in-waiting. Charles had become king at the age of twelve but suffered from mental illness and psychotic episodes, which meant that the affairs of state were mostly run by his advisors.

Despite his troubles and the fact that he was mostly a king in name only, this celebration was meant to be lavish. All manner of entertainments, disguises, loud music, and shenanigans ensued, but one nobleman, Huguet de Guisay, concocted the idea of having several courtiers—including himself and the mentally unstable king—dress up as "wild men," a popular mythic image common in medieval art used to represent the wildness of nature, in contrast to the order of a civilization devoted to God.

They donned masks and costumes made of linen and coated in resin, to which they attached flax to give them a wild and shaggy look. At the festivities, they proceeded to dance in and put on quite the show, improvising dialogue, howling obscenities, and challenging the amused attendees to guess their identities. It was just the kind of thing that young hotheads in any age would revel in doing. But things soon went wrong. Charles's brother, the Duc d'Orléans, entered late to the goings-on, and he was already drunk and carrying a torch. You can see where this is going. In an effort to guess the wild men's identities, he held the flame too near (or maybe even tossed it at one of the wild men), a spark fell onto one of them, and the costume flared up like a matchstick. The fire quickly spread to the others, and the king was only saved by the quick thinking of Joan, Duchess of Berry, who threw her large skirt about him and saw to it that he was ushered to safety.

For the others, the outcome was grim indeed. Some in the audience tried to save the burning men, but they too were injured. The Monk of Saint-Denis (*ca.* 1350–*ca.* 1421) wrote, "Four men were burned alive, their flaming genitals dropping to the floor . . . releasing a stream of blood." Actually, only one wild man died immediately, while three others, including the instigator Huguet, lingered for a few days in agony before perishing. The remaining performer, the Sieur de Nantouille, had the good sense to jump into a vat of wine to extinguish the flames and so survived.

The fallout from this sordid affair was a bit surprising, in that the common people of Paris were roused to great anger over nearly losing their king in such a stupid way. They threatened to depose and murder his advisors if nothing was done in response, and the court took this warning seriously. The nobles made a penitential walk through Paris, and the duke, who was blamed for the whole affair, made a large donation to build a new chapel at a monastery. He had a bad reputation already, and his deadly mishap only made it worse. Chroniclers accused him of practicing sorcery and cited this incident as a plot to murder the king. He was eventually assassinated in 1407 on these same charges, but his death only led to a civil war, which lasted for decades. And all because some courtly performers got a bit hot under the collar.

Arnoul Gréban (*ca.* 1420–1473/86) and Simon Gréban (mid-fifteenth century)

Plays for days

Arnoul was a canon at the church of Le Mans, and at one point seems to have been organist at Notre Dame Cathedral in Paris; he may have lived his last years in Florence. Simon was a monk of St. Riquier and secretary of Charles of Anjou, Count of Maine (Arnoul may have served him, as well). The Gréban brothers were no doubt very serious in their faith, as can be seen from their devotion to writing mystery plays. But they weren't concerned with writing dozens of them—oh no. They wanted each one to have the maximum impact, so they focused very intently on a small select few—one each, in fact.

In the early 1450s, Arnoul wrote his play, *Mystère de la Passion* ("The Mystery of the Passion"), which, as the title suggests, was a passion play, with all of the usual events and theological instructions that such dramas were meant to provide. But Arnoul wanted extensive detail and extra material, probably just to be sure that the message was clear. His play ran for almost thirty-five thousand lines and featured something like two hundred and forty characters. It was intended to portray everything from the fall of humanity and lectures by allegorical figures to the complete life of Christ, culminating in his passion, death, and resurrection. It was designed to run over at least four days, and presumably the audience was expected to return for each day, if they knew what was good for them.

Simon did his brother one better in the 1470s, when he penned *Le Mystère des Actes des Apôtres* ("The Mystery of the Acts of the Apostles"), a dramatization of Acts. Acting under the patronage of King René of Anjou, Simon may have been assisted by Arnoul, who already had experience in creating a butt-numbing biblical epic. His play ran for over sixty thousand lines and contained an astonishing cast of some five hundred roles, covering the events of Pentecost up until the suicide of Nero. Nothing like it has ever been attempted since in Western theater. Take that, Cecil B. DeMille! The play was performed over the course of at least nine days and was staged several times in the later fifteenth century and into the sixteenth; one source claims that it was shown at least once in 1539 and lasted for thirty days!

It undoubtedly tested the audience's patience to the breaking point, and if its intent was to make suffering for the faith a genuine experience shared by all, it did a magnificent job.

Onstage agony: accidents and otherwise (fourteenth to sixteenth centuries)

Burning the devil's butt, a real execution, and almost killing Christ

With these elaborate mystery plays getting ever lengthier and more involved, it was only natural that sometimes things would go badly wrong, and a few splendid examples from the fourteenth and fifteenth centuries illustrate this clearly.

In Paris in March 1380, one Jehan Hemont attended a passion play and offered to help his friend in preparing a truly special effect for the day, a set of cannons that fired and simulated claps of thunder at the death of Christ. But the drama became all too real for Jehan when one of the cannons misfired, striking him in the leg and causing a serious wound that ultimately killed him. Four years later, a certain Perrin le Roux was assisting in another passion play, with similar "cannonical" effects, when one misfired, hitting him in the eye and killing him as well. Was there a passion play curse?

Well, in Metz in 1437, one Father Nicholas de Neufchâtel was playing the role of Christ and was left hanging for so long that he passed out and was near death; he had to be taken down hastily and revived. In the same play, Father Jehan de Nissey took on the unenviable but necessary role of Judas. The scene where he hangs himself in shame and guilt apparently went on for far too long, as one account records: "But because he was hanging too long . . . he lost consciousness and was almost dead, because his heart failed. For that reason, he was taken down in great haste and taken to a nearby place so that he could be rubbed with vinegar and other things to ease his pain."

Satan fared no better during a performance of the *Mystère de Saint Martin* ("The Mystery of St. Martin") in Seurre (south of Dijon) in 1496. Old Nick was up to his usual tricks, but the hellfire and brimstone were a little too real for comfort: "Fire broke out on his clothes near his buttocks, so much so that he was seriously burned. But he was rescued quickly, undressed and redressed, that, as if nothing had happened, he came back to play his role; and later went back home."

A few years earlier in 1485, another devilish legend had circulated, again in Metz. What was up with that place? The story said that a player who took the role of a devil had a desire to know his wife while still wearing his diabolical costume—some early role-playing sexy-time, apparently. She wasn't thrilled with the idea, but eventually gave in and as a result, became pregnant. The problem was that the child was born looking half human and half demon, though curiously, it was the upper half that apparently resembled the devil. They were not allowed to baptize the baby, "until a trip had been made to Rome in order to determine what was to be done with it."

This little fable was obviously a reflection of the medieval fear that taking on a demonic role could accidentally invite real demons into one's life, with all the resulting misfortune they would bring. Some legends spoke of such actors going mad after playing devils and then behaving like them in their real lives. And fear of onstage appearances by Old Nick persisted from the Middle Ages into the Renaissance, and flared up in relation to Marlowe's play about Faust (see the next chapter). As recently as 1824, there were reports that in an English pantomime called *The Sorcerer*, twelve devils dancing onstage were joined by a mysterious thirteenth, though it seems that this extra demon was quite human, being a producer's joke rather than an incursion from the infernal regions.

Something more bloody than a burned butt, baptism dilemmas, and demonic possession was on the minds of two play producers in Tournai in Belgium. According to legend, in 1549, they concocted a grisly theatrical entertainment for Prince Philip II of Spain, who was touring the area. The play included a scene where the biblical Judith decapitates the Assyrian general Holofernes as he sleeps in a drunken stupor, thus saving her city. The producers allegedly decided that it would be hugely entertaining to have a real execution onstage, substituting a condemned murderer and heretic for the actor portraying Holofernes; another condemned man would be substituted for Judith and would strike the blow. Something similar occasionally happened during old Roman plays (see chapter 3 in act II), so this was just an update for the Renaissance! According to the story, the execution went off without a hitch, said heretic was beheaded, the crowd went wild, and Philip arrived just in time to see the moment of death. Apparently he was mostly unmoved, but remarked to his entourage: "Nice blow."

Of course, the skeptical reader might already be thinking that this story sounds a bit off. Would a condemned man really go along with this, pretending to be asleep so that he could willingly have his head cut off? Would another condemned man be able to swing the sword so well on the first try that the head would fall off perfectly in one blow? Well, the source insists that the heretic accepted the execution instead of terrible torture and the would-be executioner accepted the task when offered a pardon. But other sources make no mention of this event at all, which leads many to suspect that it was invented for political purposes—a warning to heretics or a way of showing the young Philip's power, for example. We'll probably never know, but it's nothing to lose our heads over.

Pietro Aretino (1492–1556)

Porn and laughing too much

Aretino was a writer of plays, poetry, and satire, much revered and feared in his day for the power of his words. He had a stormy beginning, being born an illegitimate child in Arezzo and later being banished from the city. He took up residence in Perugia before finding his way to Rome, but even there, he was quite prepared to mock the establishment. When Pope Leo X's pet elephant, Hanno, died in 1516, Aretino wrote "The Last Will and Testament of the Elephant Hanno," a scathing satire of the upper classes and the pope himself. He soon gained a reputation for this kind of work, and it seems that wealthy nobles and even kings gave him money to escape the worst of his vicious words.

Indeed, he overstepped and went too far in his mockery, probably more than once. While in Rome, he was the target of an attempted assassination by Bishop Giovanni Giberti in July 1525. Giberti had been the subject of one of his satires and wanted revenge. Further, Aretino had already been in trouble before when he provided *Sonetti Lussuriosi* ("Lust Sonnets") to *I Modi* ("The Ways" or "The Positions"), a collection of drawings depicting sixteen sexual positions that were completely explicit and potentially pornographic, even by modern standards. The collection caused outrage, and the Catholic Church managed to destroy most copies of the first printing. English translators have ever since been embarrassed about rendering Aretino's sonnets literally from Italian, and often give less earthy approximations, such as this one, but the meaning should still be fairly clear:

> My fingers are but stragglers at the rear,
> Who go a-foraging for what they find;
> And they are not ashamed to lag behind,
> Since there's no foe in front they need to fear.
> They've wandered through a tufted valley near.
> And you yourself have said they were most kind.

As a result of these not-insignificant infractions, Aretino fled Rome and settled in Venice in 1527, a place that he proudly declared was the "seat of all vices." Venice was profoundly antipapal and far more tolerant of outcasts than anywhere else in Italy.

This was good news for Aretino. He was bisexual and proud in an age when such a declaration was extremely dangerous. One of his comedies, *Il marescalco* ("The Equerry"), contains a scene where the leading character learns that the woman he is engaged to is actually a page in disguise, and he is delighted. This was bold storytelling at a time when such thoughts (never mind actions) could land one in jail or worse. In Venice, however, he was sought out by other men who wanted advice in pursuing their own desires, and he was happy to provide such information and assistance, for a price, of course. This price included his promise to keep quiet about their activities—he was quite a skilled blackmailer.

For all of his scandalous and satirical writings, his plays were relatively straightforward and avoided the satire and earthiness of his other works. Aretino lived large and enjoyed the benefits and freedoms that his adopted city offered. He grew very wealthy and never ceased his scathing attacks and controversial actions. Accounts of his death say that he was told a dirty joke by his sister and laughed so hard that he either couldn't breathe or became apoplectic. He fell backwards in his chair and crashed to the floor, dying instantly.

His words have never lost their power to shock. As recently as 2007, contemporary composer Michael Nyman set some of his sonnets from *I Modi* to music in a work called *8 Lust Songs*. At a performance at Cadogan Hall in London in 2008, the printed program containing the lyrics in English translations was withdrawn over charges that the words were obscene. When a recording of the piece was released in the United States, the compact disc carried the "Parental Advisory: Explicit Content" sticker on it, an unusual fate for a classical recording. Aretino would probably have been delighted at the controversy, and likely would have found a way to blackmail someone over it all.

Miguel de Cervantes (1547–1616)

Much more than tilting windmills

Cervantes is, of course, best known for his work *Don Quixote*, considered by some to be the first truly "modern" novel. But Cervantes also wrote a considerable number of plays. In fact, he was so keen to be a successful playwright that it overshadowed his attention to his other works; even *Don Quixote* was not a work that he valued as highly as he did his dramatic output.

He was the son of a barber-surgeon (those that cut hair and also performed bleedings and bone settings among other painful practices), but his early life is a bit of a mystery. We know that at some point he journeyed to Italy, either as a student or possibly fleeing the law—perhaps for having wounded someone in a duel. But whatever the reason, he eventually found a purpose in the military in 1570, joining the Infantería de Marina (Spanish Navy) stationed at Naples. In 1571, he was on board the *Marquesa*, which sailed as part of the fleet against the Ottoman Turks, engaging and defeating them in the Battle of Lepanto in October of that year. This was a huge tactical and moral victory for

Western Europe, which had for decades been dealing with the Eastern Mediterranean as an "Ottoman lake." This victory showed that the Turks were not invincible.

The battle was a triumph for the Spanish and Italian forces, but not for Cervantes. He was already ill at its start, but insisted on remaining at his post, reasoning that it was better to die in battle then cower below deck. In his weakened state, he was shot three times, twice in the chest and once in the arm. Incredibly, he survived and recovered, but the arm wound made his left hand largely unusable for the rest of his life. He was philosophical about his injuries, remarking that he "lost the movement of the left hand for the glory of the right." He also noted later:

> If my wounds have no beauty to the beholder's eye, they are, at least, honorable in the estimation of those who know where they were received; for the soldier shows to greater advantage dead in battle than alive in flight.

This was not the end of his military exploits. Determined to show that a mere three gunshots would not keep him down, he recovered and was again stationed at Naples, where he was active in naval service from 1572 to 1575. In September 1575, his ship sailed for Barcelona but was attacked by Ottoman pirates, and this time, he was not so fortunate. He was taken prisoner and sent to Algiers, where he was held captive as a slave for the next five years. He tried to escape several times but failed. Eventually, his parents paid a ransom and he was able to return home to Madrid. He would later claim that the idea for *Don Quixote* came to him during his captivity, and his years in slavery inspired two plays, *El trato de Argel* ("Life in Algiers") and *Los baños de Argel* ("The Dungeons of Algiers").

Once home, he hoped to make a splash in the world of theater, but found that, like so many other artistic types, he needed the dreaded day job to make ends meet. His plays simply weren't successful enough to provide him an adequate income. They focused on allegorical figures as characters and often had a strong moral tone that made them less popular than, say, the works of Lope de Vega (see chapter 5). He also used the "Aristotelian unities," so called because they derived from theater rules set down by Aristotle himself, in constructing his plays—an approach popular with conservative Spanish playwrights:

- Unity of action: there should be only one main story, with few subplots.
- Unity of time: the story should take place over twenty-four hours or less.
- Unity of place: the setting and the stage should only represent one physical place.

Obviously, this approach was very limiting (i.e., boring), and it's easy enough to see why sticking to this structure made his work less appealing than the plays of those who broke these rules.

In the 1580s, he took on such enviable jobs as collecting taxes and helping to oversee the ill-fated Spanish Armada, but eventually fell afoul of creditors and ended up in prison twice, in 1597 and 1602. He lived until 1616, possibly dying of complications from diabetes. Interestingly, Cervantes and Shakespeare died only one day apart, Cervantes on April 22, 1616, and Shakespeare on April 23, 1616.

He was buried at the Convent of the Barefoot Trinitarians, in Madrid, but his bones disappeared after the convent was rebuilt in 1673; apparently, said bones were sent somewhere else and later brought back, but the details are sketchy. In early 2015, it was announced that some of his remains were identified, right back at the convent where he was interred, so it seems the story was true after all.

4

The Tudor and Stuart Ages: A Golden Age of English Theater

In the mid to later sixteenth century, England saw a "renaissance" in drama that changed its language and literature forever. English reached previously unseen heights of poetry and beauty in the hands of a group of master playwrights. It was a time of such importance that it deserves its own separate chapter.

Theater fairly exploded in Elizabethan England, due in no small part to the fact that Queen Elizabeth herself was very fond of plays and became a patron to playwrights and companies. What was fashionable among the nobility (i.e., enjoying plays) found its way down to the lower classes, where such productions became a welcome diversion from the drudgery of daily life.

Traveling groups of English players had long enjoyed varying degrees of popularity (or infamy) in inn yards and halls, but things changed beginning in the 1560s, as permanent theaters rose up where none had been before. Indeed, these new structures were the first such buildings dedicated solely to drama since Roman times. And don't think that moralists didn't notice. One of the first things that Puritans and religious conservatives did was brand these new playhouses as pagan shrines attempting to bring back the days of pre-Christian society. While this accusation was untrue, theaters did quickly become places where the less savory elements of society would congregate, as we will see. But they were also attractive to all the other classes in Elizabethan society, from peasants and workers to merchants and nobles, who eagerly paid the small cost to be entertained for a few hours, to be transported away to fantastical locations where love, adventure, laughter, and murder abounded. Once plays really caught on, no amount of condemnation could keep the crowds away.

The first of these new structures, the Red Lion, was built in 1567, financed by a wealthy grocer named John Brayne. It doesn't seem to have been in use for long, being situated too far out in farmlands for easy access by the public. However, less than ten years later, Brayne, assisted by his brother-in-law, James Burbage, an actor under the patronage of the powerful Earl of Leicester (and one of Queen Elizabeth's favorites), contributed to the construction of a much longer-lasting structure. This new building, called simply the Theatre, opened in 1576; it would stand the test of time, or at least for the next twenty-one years. It was built on the south bank of the Thames—just out of the jurisdiction of the City of London. This was a wise move since many (especially of a more religious bent) within London objected to playhouses being built in the city itself and the city had its own laws regulating performances. The Theatre was subject instead only to the laws of the queen, who, as we have seen, happened to adore plays, and so it prospered and flourished. Thanks to this royal approval, other theaters started popping up with some regularity over the next few years: the Curtain in 1577, the Newington Butts theater in about 1580, the Rose in 1587, the Swan in 1595, and, of course, the legendary Globe in 1599, among others.

All of these theaters needed plays, and plays needed playwrights to write them, actors to act in them, and monarchs to behold the swelling scene. And so, despite religious protests, civic protests, closures during plague months, and a host of other obstacles, the play really was the thing for more than a half century, and English drama grew into a literary art form that has stood the test of time. But with that success came the inevitable dark side, so this chapter gleefully examines a sampling of stories that show that there was something rotten not only in the state of Denmark.

Tudor and Jacobean playhouses: dens of iniquity

With the establishment of dedicated permanent theaters, the professional lives of actors took a—wait for it—dramatic turn. Instead of consisting of traveling players—which still existed, of course, more on them below—a company could now reside, at least at certain times, at a semi-permanent home and attract repeat customers. The problem was that having fixed locations put plays into the same category as more unsavory entertainments, such as bear-baiting rings, cock-fighting dens, gambling establishments, and brothels. Concern about the potential for crime and disorder led to a law banning theaters in the city of London itself, so they tended to be built on the south side of the Thames, outside of London proper at that time. This relegated playhouses to the neighborhoods containing said brothels and animal-baiting pits, along with prisons, asylums for the insane (such as Bedlam), and smelly trades such as dyeing and tanning. The Common Council of London issued a statement in 1574 noting:

> [The] great disorder rampant in the city by the inordinate haunting of great multitudes of people, especially youth, to plays, interludes, namely occasion of frays and quarrels, evil practices of incontinency in great inns having chambers and secret places adjoining to their open stages and galleries, inveigling and alluring of maids, especially of orphans and good citizens' children under age . . . [The] uttering of popular, busy, and seditious matters, and many other corruptions of youth and other enormities . . . From henceforth no play, comedy, tragedy, interlude, not public show shall be openly played or showed within the [limits] of the City.

Plays attracted large crowds from all walks of society, which frequently meant those from the criminal underworld who had more on their minds than seeing the latest history play or tragic bloodbath. Cut-purses and petty thieves were rampant at these afternoon gatherings, and one could easily have one's coins removed in such a crush of people.

Unlike modern productions, these spectacles were not viewed in reverent silence, but were loud and boisterous. Audience members might yell out at the actors, make jokes, or otherwise be disruptive, no doubt testing the patience of those onstage. Of course, if things got too rowdy or violent, the troublemakers could be forcibly ejected, but it wasn't uncommon to see groundlings using a portion of the stage as a makeshift table for gambling with dice and playing cards, right in front of the actors. So it's understandable that in all of this confusion and noise, crime flourished.

Playhouses were also convenient meeting places for would-be criminal masterminds that had more ambitious plans than just relieving an unsuspecting merchant of his week's earnings. Plots for burglary, smuggling, and even murder were hatched in the dark back spaces and some of the side rooms adjacent to the main stage.

Nevertheless, theaters became so popular that they surpassed churches in attendance. In 1586, one Maliverny Catlyn, an agent of Francis Walsingham (more on him below), noted with disgust that "the play houses are pestered when the churches are naked; at the one, it is not possible to get a place; at the other, void seats are plenty."

Perhaps the most notorious feature of theaters, and the one which Puritans railed against incessantly, was that some were attached to brothels. Noted theater owners and producers such as Edward Alleyn and Philip Henslowe both owned houses of ill repute and made a significant amount of money from them. So, they reasoned, why not combine them with playhouses and increase the earnings?

The Curtain Theatre—where many of Shakespeare's plays would be performed in the 1590s—opened in 1577. By 1579, satirist and playwright Stephen Gosson noted of the patrons:

> To celebrate the Sabboth, flock to Theaters, and there keepe a generall Market of Bawdrie: Not that any filthynesse in deede, is committed within the compasse of that grounde, as was doone in Rome, but that euery wanton and his Parmour, euery man and his Mistresse, euery

John and his Joan, euery knaue and his queane, are there first acquainted and cheapen the Merchandise in that place, which they pay for elsewhere as they can agree.

These early theaters were places for hooking up, but by the later Elizabethan period, some theaters connected directly to brothels, which only added to the already dim view that many moralizers held of them. Still, their popularity couldn't be denied, and as long as the plays themselves were not deemed seditious or blasphemous—the government banned politics and religion as main topics in plays, fearing that they were too dangerous, given all of the religious strife that still existed in the country—they were allowed to operate. All plays still had to be licensed by a Master of Revels—what a wonderful job title—who determined if they were suitable for a public audience.

These restrictions did little to dampen the enthusiasm that the public had for plays. In spite of censorship, religious opposition, and an unsavory reputation, the theater thrived, provided that a nasty little inconvenience like plague didn't spring up. In that case, the theaters were closed and the players went on tour. Road trip!

Traveling players: liars, vagabonds, and ne'er-do-wells

Every so often, something would cause the London playhouses to be closed. Usually it was the outbreak of some disease. At that point, the actors and companies had no choice but to pack up, leave town, and try to make some cash by presenting their latest dramas elsewhere. There was a problem, though. Being a wandering minstrel—or a wandering anything, for that matter—was technically a crime, one that could be severely punished if said wanderers did not adhere to some pretty strict guidelines. The intent was to deter beggars, thieves, and con men, but unfortunately, artists of all kinds got screwed too.

Up until the time of Henry VIII, wandering entertainers could usually be assured of a welcome (if not always warm) from the hundreds of monasteries that dotted the English countryside; monastic houses were generally open to travelers that obeyed their rules and respected their wishes. When Henry did away with those and confiscated their wealth in the 1530s, however, it cut off a valuable source of hospitality, rather like having a major hotel chain shut down. The new Church of England was not as generous (or at least as tolerant) toward secular entertainers. By 1572, the Act for the Punishment of Vagabonds was put into effect, basically banning the activities of all traveling entertainers who were not either under someone's patronage or servants in a lord's household. This meant that players were scrambling to obtain such patronage and identifying marks (such as clothing in specific colors or livery) that would associate them with a given noble, which allowed them to carry on their work. Of course, they were not always honest about this.

One report about the splendidly named highwayman Gamaliel Ratsey (who was hanged in 1605) noted that he once met a group of traveling players who said they were attached to a certain noble. A week later, he encountered them again in a different location; he was wearing a disguise, so they didn't recognize him. At this point, they claimed to be associated with a different noble patron, one who was better known in that particular area; this switch would no doubt improve their takings. Ratsey asked them for a private performance, paid them handsomely, and robbed them the following day, presumably with weapons drawn, while giving them a stern lecture about their lack of honesty!

Despite these hardships, traveling players left London during times of plague and took to the countryside, plying their entertainments in whatever towns would have them. They still had to operate under government censorship, but comedies, tragedies, and histories all proved popular with regional audiences. It's probable that the young William Shakespeare saw such groups in his youth in Stratford and was inspired by their seemingly romantic lives to take up acting and penning his own works. Without the bubonic plague, the greatest playwright in English might never have found his own voice!

Thomas Kyd (1558–1594)

I deny everything

Kyd was arguably the first of the great Elizabethan dramatists, writing in the 1580s, nearly a full decade before Shakespeare was active. During that time (probably in 1586–1587), he wrote a splendidly named play, *The Spanish Tragedie containing the Lamentable End of Don Horatio and Bel-imperia; with the Pitiful Death of Old Hieronimo*; nothing like spoiling the plot in the main title! Actually, the name was usually shortened to *Hieronimo*, which was obviously way more suited to playbills. This work was destined to be among the most popular plays of the Elizabethan era, eclipsing many other works now far better known—*Romeo and Juliet*, anyone? The play was a bloody revenge tale that drew on the style of the Roman writer Seneca, and it influenced a number of other prominent works such as Shakespeare's delightfully appalling *Titus Andronicus* and that little-known drama *Hamlet*. Kyd's play led the way in making these gory tales popular in Elizabethan and Jacobean playhouses.

The Spanish Tragedie is a rather complex story, beginning straight off with the death of Andrea, a Spanish officer, who returns as a ghost to seek revenge on his killer, the Portuguese Prince Balthazar. Of course, Balthazar falls in love with the daughter of the Duke of Castile, Bel-Imperia, who had been Andrea's love—awkward—and through a series of unfortunate events, the king of Portugal becomes convinced that marrying these two will bring about peace between his country and Spain. Meanwhile, Bel-Imperia hooks up with Horatio, Andrea's friend—again, awkward—and when Balthazar and his cronies find out about this, they hang him and imprison her. Horatio's father, Hieronimo, finds his son's body and goes mad, but conveniently recovers to begin plotting revenge.

Through all of this, Lorenzo, the king's nephew, has been trying to help Balthazar by permanently silencing anyone who could spill the beans about Horatio's murder. Hieronimo and Bel-Imperia concoct a plan to take revenge on all of them, performing a play for the guests of a royal entertainment, inviting Lorenzo and Balthazar to act with them. In the course of the show, Hieronimo stabs Lorenzo to death and Bel-Imperia kills both Balthazar and herself. Hieronimo explains to the audience that these deaths were not faked and reveals the whole sordid story. He then bites off his own tongue so as not to implicate Bel-Imperia as his co-conspirator (and so tarnish her name) and successfully kills the Duke of Castile and himself. The ghost of Andrea, seeing that vengeance has been served, is satisfied and departs, reflecting on the carnage:

> Ay, now my hopes have end in their effects,
> When blood and sorrow finish my desires:
> Horatio murder'd in his father's bower;
> Vild Serberine by Pedringano slain;
> False Pedringano hang'd by quaint device;
> Fair Isabella by herself misdone;
> Prince Balthazar by Bellimperia stabb'd;
> The Duke of Castile and his wicked son
> Both done to death by old Hieronimo;
> My Bellimperia fall'n, as Dido fell,
> And good Hieronimo slain by himself:
> Ay, these were spectacles to please my soul!

Wow.

This kind of crazy drama of blood and revenge would become all the rage in London over the next twenty years. The play-within-a-play device and the ghost of the wrongly murdered man would both feature in *Hamlet*, for example. In 1602, additions were made to *The Spanish Tragedie*, with some 320 new lines being penned for it. Some scholars have put forth pretty convincing evidence (based on textual similarities) that Shakespeare himself may have been the author of these new lines. Updates of older works were common at the time.

In any case, Kyd's life would see its own share of bloody drama, and he was destined for a tragic and violent end. Between 1587 and 1593, Kyd was in the service of a nobleman who has never been identified, and at this time, he also crossed paths with the notorious Christopher Marlowe (more on him below), who may have also been in the service of said unknown lord. Marlowe, as we will see, was very possibly up to his ears in spying and intrigue, but it was his personal life that got him, and by association Kyd, into trouble. Marlowe, allegedly being both a homosexual and an atheist, was guilty of two serious crimes that could carry the death penalty.

Though Kyd did not seem to share Marlowe's views or his orientation, he may have had some of Marlowe's writings on both topics in his possession. It seems that an informer turned him in, and he was arrested in May 1593. The papers in question denied the divinity of Christ. Thereafter, Kyd was tortured and insisted that the works belonged to Marlowe, who, he said, also believed that Christ himself was homosexual. Marlowe was summoned to answer these charges but met a violent end on May 30, 1593, before a decision could be rendered, as we will see.

Kyd was released eventually, but he never recovered from his injuries, and he was no longer welcome in his lord's service. The cloud of suspicion hung heavy over his head, and many probably thought that he was a nonbeliever, as well.

This may all seem strange to the modern reader, when we are accustomed (at least in theory) to a live-and-let-live philosophy, but in those days, having an "improper" set of religious beliefs could be a matter of life and death. England had gone through a great deal of social upheaval since Henry VIII had broken with the Catholic Church in 1534. His son Edward VI strengthened the Protestant position as England's official religion after gaining the throne in 1547, while Henry's daughter, Mary Tudor (the infamous "Bloody Mary"), reinstated Roman Catholicism immediately after Edward's untimely death in 1553. Finally, Elizabeth I put Protestantism back in place with her accession in 1558, and the Anglican Church replaced the Catholic Church permanently. This topsy-turvy change of official beliefs meant that adhering to the "correct" faith was more than a matter of personal preferences; it concerned political survival, national security, and keeping order. Those who continued to adhere to Catholicism in Protestant England were, at least initially, tolerated, but they came to be viewed increasingly with suspicion and prejudice. Those who held no beliefs at all were effectively enemies of the state, which held that it obtained its authority from God.

Kyd was an example of how a deep thinker could get swept up into things beyond his control and could suffer the consequences of daring to entertain dangerous ideas, even if not adhering to them. He seems to have died in the summer of 1594, at only thirty-five years old. In December of that year, his parents renounced administration of his estate, probably because he had debts. As a final indignity, even though *The Spanish Tragedie* was immensely popular in his day and the decades immediately afterward, he was forgotten as an author for a remarkably long time. It was only in the later eighteenth century that his name was rediscovered in association with the play and he was able to again achieve recognition as the author of one of the most influential English plays of the age.

Robert Greene (1558–1592)

A Groats-Worth of Wit

Greene was a highly educated writer of pamphlets, prose, and plays, having received degrees from both Oxford and Cambridge. He was acutely aware of his fine education and had no problem lording it over those with fewer advantages than he, in particular, William Shakespeare; more on that momentarily. However, Greene's credentials didn't mean that he wanted a scholar's life or, even worse, one attached to the Anglican Church; far from it. He reveled in debauchery and lived a bohemian lifestyle. He was so fond of making up stories about his exploits and adventures that it's difficult to know what actually happened and what was just his invention. He claimed to have traveled to Spain, Italy, Germany, Poland, and France, a remarkable achievement, but no definitive evidence for these journeys has been found. He further said that he married a gentleman's daughter but, "forasmuch as she would perswade me from my wilful wickednes, after I had a child by her, I cast her off, having spent up the marriage-money which I obtained by her." He proceeded to seek new fortunes in London. Again, evidence for this account is inconclusive.

His version of what happened on his way to London also may or may not be true. He alleges that he met a player who told him that there was great potential for scholars to become playwrights, and so he joined this actor, took residence in a brothel, and began making money writing plays. He took a mistress (sister to a famous leader of a gang of thieves, later hanged) and together they had an illegitimate child. Thereafter, he drifted from inn to inn and tavern to tavern, always finding a way to cheat and lie his way out of things, and somehow avoid paying his debts, bragging that "nothing rested in him almost but craftiness."

In the *Repentance of Robert Greene* (published after his death in October 1592), a work thought to be autobiographical, Greene claims:

> Now I do remember (though too late) that I have read in the scriptures how neither adulterers, swearers, thieves nor murderers shall inherit the kingdom of heaven. What hope then can I have of any grace when (given over from all grace) I exceeded all other in these kind of sins?

> Young yet in years, though old in wickedness, I began to resolve that there was nothing bad that was profitable, whereupon I grew so rooted in all mischief that I had as great a delight in wickedness as sundry hath in godliness, and as much felicity I took in villainy as others had in honesty.

> From whoredom I grew to drunkenness, from drunkenness to swearing and blaspheming the name of God; hereof grew quarrels, frays, and continual controversies which are now as worms in my conscience gnawing me incessantly.

> I was beloved of the more vainer sort of people, who being my continual companions came still to my lodging, and there would continue quaffing, carousing and surfeiting with me all the day long.

There probably is truth in these stories, though how much he embellished to make himself look even more rakish is unclear. His enemies denounced him as a liar, cheat, thief, and scoundrel, and decried his wasted degrees and his leaving a good wife behind. More than once, Greene claimed that he felt called to repentance and wanted to make a new start, but he always slid back into his grifting ways.

Despite his failings, he was the central figure in a group of London writers (including Christopher Marlowe and others) who were penning works for the stage as well as poetry and pamphlets. It was this group that Shakespeare eventually attached himself to when he arrived in the big city. Not having their university degrees, he was an odd man out, despite his talent, and some resented him for it; for many of them, Shakespeare was merely a player, not a true writer. For Will's part, it seems that while he was content to share their company, he was not the debauched sort of man they had hoped for and he did not engage in their criminal or other unsavory activities, though their lifestyles undoubtedly gave him ideas for future characters.

In August 1592, after a meal of too much Rhenish wine and pickled herring, Greene became ill (as would just about anyone!). Having no lodgings, he was taken in and looked after by a shoemaker and his wife, of all people. One of Greene's enemies records that he had pawned even his clothing for money, and knowing that he had little time, he asked the wife to place a wreath of bay leaves on his head, so that he could die resembling a poet laureate (i.e., one of the esteemed poets of ancient Greece, Rome, or Renaissance Italy crowned with a laurel wreath on the head in honor of their literary work). This episode seems pretty silly, and may be another invention, but Greene's ego makes it possible that the story is true.

His most notorious work appeared after his death. Titled *Greene's Groats-Worth of Wit*, it included scathing commentaries about several of his fellow writers, including this famous passage:

For there is an upstart Crow, beautified with our feathers, that with his Tygers hart wrapt in a Players hyde, supposes he is as well able to bombast out a blanke verse as the best of you: and being an absolute Johannes Factotum, is in his owne conceit the onely Shake-scene in a countrey.

Scholars have generally agreed that this was an attack on Shakespeare for daring to presume that, as an actor, he could claim to be the equal of those university-educated slackers and ne'er-do-wells, when in fact all he was doing was shamelessly imitating them. Some at the time and now believe that the pamphlet was actually authored by another dramatist, Henry Chettle (*ca.* 1564–*ca.* 1606), using Greene's name as a way of hiding his own attacks. Debate about this has gone back and forth; the work may actually have been a kind of collaboration between the two, with Chettle filling in and embellishing Greene's words. Chettle actually denied having anything to do with writing the scurrilous attacks on his fellow playwrights, as did Thomas Nashe (1567–*ca.* 1601), a writer and satirist who, so rumor claimed, ghostwrote part of the work. Nashe in particular liked a good scrap, so why he was so vehement in his public denial of any connection (calling it a "lying pamphlet") is mysterious. One possibility is that he was paid a visit by a representative of the Earl of Southampton (soon-to-be patron of Shakespeare and dedicatee of the sonnets), who was not at all amused at such slanderous words.

Regardless of Greene's attack (assuming he wrote the work), his plays probably had some influence on the bard; Shakespeare seems to have modeled Falstaff in part on Greene, for example, and two of Greene's own plays, *The Scottish History of James the Fourth* and *Pandosto*, may have influenced the content of *A Midsummer Night's Dream* and *The Winter's Tale* respectively. Greene probably wouldn't have appreciated the tribute.

Christopher Marlowe (1564–1593)

A poke in the eye

Marlowe was an undoubted genius, the greatest of the playwrights of that circle of college-educated writers that lived in London in the late

1580s. Noted for such dramas as *Tamburlaine*, *Edward II*, and *Doctor Faustus*, Marlowe possessed remarkable skill and his works were triumphs of craft and words. He no doubt had a significant influence on another playwright who was almost his exact contemporary, William Shakespeare. It's entirely possible that he would have eclipsed Shakespeare as the age's greatest dramatist, if not for the inconvenient fact that he died violently when he was not yet thirty years old. The circumstances of that death and the controversial life that led up to it make him one of the most fascinating figures in the history of the theater.

Marlowe was born in Canterbury in February 1564—the exact date is not certain, we only have a baptism date of February 26. He was the son of a shoemaker who saw to it that his son received a good education. So the young Christopher was able to gain a scholarship to attend Corpus Christi College in Cambridge, where he took his bachelor of arts degree in 1584. He continued to study for a master of arts degree, but already controversy surrounded him. In fact, Cambridge University was reluctant to grant Marlowe this degree in 1587 because there were rumors that he had converted to Catholicism, not exactly the best career choice a few decades after Queen Mary burned Protestants alive and tried to roll back England to being a Catholic nation. One rumor said that Marlowe intended to leave England and go to the college at Rheims in France and take ordination as a priest.

Then the Privy Council (the queen's government) intervened and insisted that the degree be granted, because of Marlowe's service to said government. Why would this important body care about an otherwise unknown student? This question has led to a lot of speculation, but it may well be that Marlowe was already being employed in the business of espionage for Sir Francis Walsingham (Elizabeth's spymaster) or others. Writers, artists, musicians, and their kind made very good spies because they could travel, their art allowed them to cross borders, and they were often in close company with nobility and government officials. Was Marlowe going undercover to Rheims, posing as a convert but actually there to gather information? He was known to take long absences from the college and to spend more money than he could have had as a humble student with poor parents. So, was he on some spymaster's payroll? It's certainly possible, and he may have been pretending to be a priest-in-training to learn what he could about conspiracies against Elizabeth's government.

In 1592, he was arrested in the Netherlands for being involved in coin counterfeiting, a serious infraction, but when he was returned to England to face investigation and possible trial, no charges were brought. He may have been taking part in some botched spy mission during which he got caught and the English government preferred to hush the whole thing up.

In any case, Marlowe was also a major figure of the London theater scene, writing his masterpieces and allegedly living a bohemian lifestyle. It has long been supposed that he might have been homosexual or at least preferred dalliances with other young men, an offense in Elizabethan England that could have serious consequences, even if many tended to simply look the other way when confronted with the possibility.

He and Shakespeare seemed to enjoy the friendly competition of writing plays, using each other's works as inspiration for their own. They may have even tried to one-up each other with each new work they wrote in response to the other's. Certainly, Marlowe's plays influenced certain plots and ideas of Shakespeare, even years later: *The Jew of Malta* influenced *The Merchant of Venice*, *Edward II* influenced *Richard II*, and *Faustus* influenced *Macbeth*. Meanwhile, Shakespeare's *Henry VI* plays probably prompted Marlowe to write *Edward II* to begin with.

Today, Marlowe is best remembered for his *Tragical History of the Life and Death of Doctor Faustus*, the story of a man who summoned demons and sold his soul to the demon Mephistopheles for earthly rewards. Since Puritans were already railing against plays as being satanic, you can imagine how this plot feature must have gone over, particularly when the actor playing Faustus performed faux black magic rituals in front of the astonished audience, summoning a "demon" who would arrive in a puff of smoke through the trap door in the stage. At a time when most people fervently believed such magical feats were possible in real life, this must have been almost too much. Some claimed that they saw more than one devil onstage during performances of the play, and that the second one looked decidedly real. The scene wherein Faustus commands Mephistopheles to take the offer of his soul to Lucifer is quite striking:

> Go bear these tidings to great Lucifer:
> Seeing Faustus hath incurr'd eternal death
> By desperate thoughts against Jove's deity,
> Say, he surrenders up to him his soul,
> So he will spare him four and twenty years,
> Letting him live in all voluptuousness;
> Having thee ever to attend on me,
> To give me whatsoever I shall ask,
> To tell me whatsoever I demand,
> To slay mine enemies, and to aid my friends,
> And always be obedient to my will.
> Go, and return to mighty Lucifer,
> And meet me in my study at midnight . . .

It's remarkable that Marlowe was able to get such a work past the censors.

It did not help that his reputation was already under question; the most persistent rumor insisted that Marlowe was an atheist, a serious charge given the state's reliance on the idea of divinely ordained rule.

In 1593, Marlowe was questioned for unorthodox beliefs and behavior. Richard Baines (*fl.* 1568–1593), a double agent, accused him of a number of charges, especially heretical views:

> This Marlowe doth not only hould them himself [atheist beliefs], but almost into every Company he Cometh he persuades men to Atheism willing them not to be afeard of bugbeares and hobgoblins, and vtterly scorning both god and his ministers . . .

In other words, Marlowe was charged with viewing religious beliefs as superstitions, a very serious accusation. He was accused of saying that the fear of hell, demons, and other such terrors (including folk beliefs like fairies) was foolish, and those who promoted these ideas were worthy only of disdain.

This controversy started because of an inflammatory note put up on the Dutch Church in London, a warning about Protestants coming from France and the Netherlands. It was written in Marlowe's style, alluded to his plays, and was signed "Tamburlaine." Marlowe probably had nothing to do with it, but if his enemies were trying to frame him, they did a good job. He was investigated, which was how the authorities were led to Thomas Kyd, and the dangerous papers in his possession.

Kyd, as we saw, also accused Marlowe of a lack of belief, though this may have been to save his own neck. He and another who had spied on Marlowe testified that Marlowe believed that Jesus was a bastard (in the literal sense), that Mary was a prostitute, that Moses had cleverly deceived the Jews, that the existence of the Native Americans disproved the Old Testament, and that Jesus and John the Baptist were homosexual lovers, among other blasphemies. It was claimed in another document that Marlowe was so well able to argue for atheism that he could confound theologians and prove the lack of a god better than they could prove the existence of one. With this kind of reputation, it seems almost inevitable that he would make powerful enemies who would wish to do him harm, and that is probably exactly what happened.

Of all the mysteries surrounding Marlowe, his death in 1593 is the greatest, and has spawned countless conspiracy theories. The timing was certainly suspicious, for as we saw with Kyd, Marlowe was under investigation and was ordered on May 20 to stay nearby and report to the council daily. On May 30, he was at an inn in the company of three other men: Ingram Frizer, Nicholas Skeres, and Robert Poley. All three had been at one time or another involved with the Walsingham family, which pretty much guarantees that they were engaged in espionage of some sort; further, the building they were in was noted for being used by spies. According to their testimony, a dispute over the food and drink bill arose, and Marlowe stabbed at Frizer with a dagger, slightly wounding him. Frizer fought back, and in the ensuing struggle, stabbed Marlowe in or just above his right eye, killing him. The inquest ruled that Frizer's actions were self-defense and he was pardoned a month later. Marlowe was buried in an unmarked grave and there the matter rested. Or did it?

The problem was that all three men were of dubious character, to say the least, being involved not only in spying, but also in various scams and criminal activities in the ever-growing Elizabethan underworld. Their testimonies could hardly be considered truthful or reliable, especially since this put a convenient end to a man with allegedly dangerous ideas just when he was under investigation. So, what happened? We don't know, but there are many theories:

- The glittering courtier Sir Walter Raleigh arranged his murder, because he shared Marlowe's lack of religious belief and feared that Marlowe would incriminate him.
- Lord Burghley (Lord High Treasurer and chief advisor to Elizabeth) had him murdered because Marlowe was secretly promoting Catholic propaganda.
- Various members of the Privy Council conducting the investigation had him murdered, because they shared his views and feared that he might expose them as fellow nonbelievers.
- Queen Elizabeth ordered his murder because of his subversive activities.
- He was killed as a result of involvement in criminal dealings.
- His murder was faked so that he could be sent abroad to continue his spy work under a new name.
- His murder was faked so that he could continue a secret relationship with the courtier Sir Thomas Walsingham.

Any or none of these could be true, and some are more plausible than others. A few believe that the faked death scenario allowed him to continue to write plays, which he sent to London and consented to have published under the name of—you guessed it—Shakespeare (see the Shakespeare chapter in act II for more on the so-called authorship controversy). A government-ordered assassination seems likely, especially given how quickly his killer was let off the hook.

What actually happened that day was known only to a few, and they took that knowledge to their graves. Just as importantly, a remarkable talent was removed too early and English literature was robbed of many fine works yet to come. But of course it's fun to speculate, and an unrepentant, bohemian, shocking genius like Marlowe would probably revel in the attention that his death (or lack of it) has been given over the centuries.

Ben Jonson (1572–1637)

Rule of thumb

Jonson is the third of the great "trinity" of Elizabethan and Jacobean playwrights, standing alongside Marlowe and Shakespeare. He was born in London; his father died before his birth, and his mother then married a bricklayer. Jonson was fortunate to be able to attend the well-regarded Westminster school, where he developed a love for a variety of subjects, such as history, language, and literature. He was set to attend Cambridge University, but this plan was interrupted, apparently by his being made to apprentice to his stepfather, which must have seemed a terrible anticlimax to his scholarly pursuits. He left this position sometime afterward, joining the military and going to the continent, where, he later said, he killed an enemy soldier in hand-to-hand combat and took his weapons and armor as trophies; it would not be the last time that violence found its way into Jonson's life.

On his return to London, he began to work as an actor, taking roles such as the tongue-biting Hieronimo in Kyd's bloody *Spanish Tragedie*. As a younger contemporary of that first wave of playwrights that included Marlowe and Shakespeare, he wasn't in their company, but pursued his career separately. His first great work was his comedy *Every Man in His Humour* from 1598, which established Jonson as a genuine talent. Part of a genre known as the "comedy of humors," it represents each of its characters as exhibiting one or more traits associated with the humors, the four personality types believed since ancient Greek times to make up a human being. The plot tells how the practical Edward Knowell spies on his son, concerned about his moral character and his interest in poetry. However, Knowell's attempts are hindered by his servant, Brainworm, who is employed as the spy but deliberately screws up his master's commands. Other characters bring in their own foibles and much fun ensues.

It wasn't as fun for Jonson offstage, however. Shortly after the play's production, he was arrested and brought to trial for killing Gabriel Spenser. Spenser was an actor who had been in trouble himself in 1596, also being charged with killing a man. However, Spenser wasn't punished, so he must have defended himself admirably in court. The following year, he was also charged with acting in a seditious play, *The Isle of Dogs*, which was cowritten by Jonson and Thomas Nashe. A "lewd" play that may have even satirized the queen, it was suppressed and no known copies survive. Several people involved in it were arrested, including Spenser, who spent nearly two months in prison, but Jonson seems to have only spent a brief time under arrest.

Maybe Spenser resented the fact that the playwright was spared. In any case, he seems to have challenged Jonson to a duel, which was fought on September 22, 1598. While Spenser had a longer sword and wounded Jonson, Jonson struck the fatal blow, a deep stab wound. Regardless of who started it, the authorities were not pleased; duels had been outlawed by Queen Elizabeth in 1571. Jonson had no real excuse and confessed freely to killing Spenser.

This should have been enough to have him executed, but he found a convenient, if strange, way out of it. He claimed something called "benefit of clergy." This was a legal loophole used by the literate. If you could prove that you could read Latin (specifically the Bible), you could legally be classified as part of the clergy and therefore not subject to secular law, but rather to ecclesiastical, which had no death penalty. And if you were not literate? You were basically screwed. Even the literate perpetrators did not get off completely scot-free, however. Jonson was branded on the thumb and his possessions were confiscated. He was then released; but such offenders only received one pass. If they committed any further offenses, the hand of the law would smash them as harshly as anyone.

While Jonson was in jail awaiting his painful fate, he secretly converted to Catholicism, a bold and astonishing move, given the country's hostility toward the older faith. Maybe he figured that he had nothing to lose at that point. Regardless, he was released and would live on well into the reign of King Charles I. His conversion lasted a little over ten years. In 1610 he reconverted to the Anglican faith after the assassination of King Henry IV of France, a Catholic monarch who had been tolerant of Protestants but was murdered by a Catholic fanatic, François Ravaillac. Perhaps sensing new danger to Catholics in England in the form of a backlash, Jonson declared his renewed Protestantism by defiantly drinking wine from a communion chalice, something normally reserved for the Catholic priest alone.

Despite his long life, tragedy and controversy continued to dog him. His son died of bubonic plague in 1603, and he was embroiled in another controversy between 1599 and 1602, the so-called "War of the Theatres," a literary battle between Jonson and two other playwrights, who satirized each other in their plays, sometimes very harshly. Jonson claimed that his rivals were plagiarists and hacks, inferior and bombastic. He in turn was attacked as being full of pride and a cuckold.

As if this conflict weren't enough, Jonson just couldn't seem to stay out of trouble. In 1605, he was briefly imprisoned for cowriting a play, *Eastward Hoe*, that contained some anti-Scottish references. This was not the brightest idea when the new king, James I, was from Scotland. Jonson, also of Scottish heritage, claimed that he voluntarily offered to go to prison to atone for this offense, and this action may have led to his avoiding the punishment of having his ears and/or nose cut off. Once again, fortune favored him, and he escaped a dreadful punishment.

Jonson had a temper and was rather vain, probably at this point thinking that he could pretty much get away with anything. Though he was a friend of Shakespeare, he may have resented the older man's genius. Scottish poet William Drummond wrote of Jonson:

> He is a great lover and praiser of himself; a contemner and scorner of others; given rather to losse a friend than a jest; jealous of every word

and action of those about him, (especiallie after drink, which is one of the elements in which he liveth).

He suffered a series of strokes in the 1620s, but continued writing plays and lived on until 1637. He was interred in Westminster Abbey, with a curious condition: his grave is a mere eighteen-inch square, meaning that he was buried standing up. This may have been for financial reasons; longer graves were more expensive to obtain, though it would seem that an equal amount of work was required to dig down that much deeper. He may have been much poorer by this time, and seems to have asked the king for this size of grave, though given that he still had a good reputation, it does seem odd that no one ponied up some extra cash for a proper horizontal burial. Maybe there was some sort of private joke, or he was trying to make one last point, but if so, he took the meaning with him to his tiny grave.

Moll Cutpurse (*ca.* 1584–1659)

A.k.a. Mary Frith, a.k.a. Mary Markham, a.k.a. the Roaring Girl

"Moll Cutpurse" was the popular name of Mary Frith, one of the most remarkable and notorious women of early-seventeenth-century England. She was famous for her connections to organized crime, for dressing as a man and smoking a pipe, for swearing frequently and unapologetically, and for being one of the first women to appear onstage in the London theaters of the 1600s. Her notoriety was such that she became a very popular figure with the common people; she was even the subject of a play, *The Roaring Girle* (published in 1611), a fictionalized and sensationalist account of her life. She also appeared as a character in the comic play *Amends for Ladies* (1618), concerning (among other things) a husband testing his wife's fidelity, and she may have been the subject of an earlier lost pamphlet, "The Madde Pranckes of Merry Mall of the Bankside" (1610).

From her beginnings as a humble pickpocket to being something of a celebrity in the London underworld, Moll always seemed able to elude capture, or least any severe punishments. She was first indicted in 1600 for stealing a small sum of money and her lack of interest in being a law-abiding citizen only increased afterward. She admitted to being present on the stage at the Fortune theater, where, dressed in a man's clothing, she delivered bawdy monologues, sang dirty songs, and played the lute, no doubt to the great amusement of the audience, if not the authorities. She admitted to making "some other immodest & lascivious speaches" in this stage show, which occurred, it seems, after a performance of *The Roaring Girle*, with the full consent and cooperation of the players and playwrights, and delighted the audience, despite (or perhaps because of) its illegal nature.

She flaunted her lifestyle and almost dared the law to do something about it. She was arrested at the end of 1611 on charges of being dressed improperly (i.e., as a man) and being involved in prostitution (most likely as a pimp). She was forced in 1612 to do penance at St. Paul's Cross, next to the great cathedral in London. However, one observer, John Chamberlain, noted that her sincerity about the whole thing was decidedly lacking:

> Moll Cutpurse, a notorious baggage that used to go in man's apparel, and challenged the field of diverse gallants, was brought to [St. Pauls' Cross], where she wept bitterly and seemed very penitent; but it is since doubted, she was maudlin drunk, being discovered to have tippled of three-quarters of sack before she came to her penance.

Her defiant behaviors continued, and it seems that in the 1620s, she was in the habit of finding young male lovers for bored middle-aged housewives, for a fee, of course. She operated an ingenious pickpocketing racket, wherein her cutpurses would steal coins, those robbed would come to Moll for help, she would then have the thieves return the money to her, and she would keep a "fee" for recovering the items and handing them back to the relieved victims.

She was still active during the English Civil War, in which she was a strong Royalist, and thought nothing of resorting to highwayman behavior to add to her wealth. One legend says that she waylaid Thomas Fairfax, the Parliamentarian general, robbed him, and shot him in the arm. It was said that she was pursued, arrested, and sentenced to hang for this, but got out of it by paying a £2,000 bribe, at least £320,000 in modern money, an enormous sum in those days that shows just how profitable her profession was. Despite her scandalous activities, she survived and thrived, finally dying of dropsy in 1659, just before the restoration of the monarchy. That women were finally allowed to act after this momentous event would no doubt have pleased her greatly.

The fiery end of the Globe Theatre (June 29, 1613)

All good things must come to an end

The Globe was the playhouse most associated with Shakespeare and his company. Built in 1599 from the materials of an earlier playhouse (the Theatre), which, according to legend, were dragged across the frozen Thames secretly at night, the new building played host to the staging of Shakespeare's most memorable works, performed by the greatest actors of the time. Ben Jonson's plays and other dramas were also shown there.

Since these theaters had no roofs and were open to the elements, it was necessary to perform plays during daylight hours. The shows went on regardless of the notoriously unpredictable English weather, which was actually a bit colder then than now. The problem with these structures was that they had no building codes or provisions for safety at all. They were just large square or circular constructions made of wood with thatched roofing around the sides (think of a small sports stadium, but with a stage). They were often put up in relative haste in an attempt to lure as many customers as possible (competition between theater companies was fierce), which could number a couple of thousand in a day. There were no safety regulations or plans for evacuation in the event of an emergency; they were basically disasters waiting to happen.

And just such a disaster did happen on June 29, 1613, during a performance of *All is True*, later retitled *Henry VIII*, a play that Shakespeare cowrote with John Fletcher (1579–1625). One of the Globe's special effects was a large cannon that would fire during appropriate moments in plays, such as royal processions, depictions of war, and other dramatic moments. It was dangerously situated in a hidden attic near the roof and was loaded with gunpowder. Amazingly, it had been used for years without incident, so why would this day be any different? Except that it was. For whatever reason, sparks from the cannon flew into the thatch in the roof and quickly caused a fire. Sir Henry Wotton was in attendance and provided an eyewitness account of the ensuing chaos, and of one unfortunate fellow with burned britches:

> Now King Henry making a Masque at the Cardinal Wolsey's house, and certain cannons being shot off at his entry, some of the paper or other stuff, wherewith one of them was stopped, did light on the thatch, where being thought at first but idle smoak, and their eyes more attentive to the show, it kindled inwardly, and ran round like a train, consuming within less than an hour the whole house to the very ground. This was the fatal period of that virtuous fabrick, wherein yet nothing did perish but wood and straw, and a few forsaken cloaks; only one man had his breeches set on fire, that would perhaps have broyled him, if he had not by the benefit of a provident wit, put it out with a bottle of ale.

Thank goodness for good old English ale! Amazingly, no one else seems to have been hurt, and even though the building only had two doors, evacuation apparently went smoothly enough. In the absence of any kind of organized fire brigade, the whole structure went up in flames and was completely destroyed in less than two hours. In those flames were costumes, props, and possibly original manuscripts for plays. The players were undaunted, however, and the Globe was rebuilt the following year. It thrived until 1642, when it was closed by the Puritans, and in 1644 or 1645, it was torn down to make room for new housing. In 1997, the new reconstructed Shakespeare's Globe opened for business, sitting on the approximate location of the original and designed in the style of its predecessor. It has been wildly successful in bringing the feel and atmosphere of Tudor and Stuart theater back to life, though presumably the cannon is a lot safer this time around.

Richard Burbage's very brief epitaph (1567–1619)

Brevity is the soul of wit

Burbage is considered by many to be the first great English actor, one who brought genuine emotion to his roles, rather than just declaiming his lines. He was also a friend and partner of Shakespeare, a theater owner, and a skilled painter—some think that the Chandos portrait presumed to be of Shakespeare was painted by Burbage.

He excelled at tragedies and played the main roles for most of his friend's great characters—Hamlet, King Lear, Othello, Macbeth, and Richard II, among others. He was popular and successful, but not nearly as shrewd a businessman as the bard, and so not as wealthy.

He died somewhat unexpectedly in 1619, though unlike Shakespeare, he never retired from the stage and continued acting right up till the end. He was so popular that his death threatened to overshadow that of Queen Anne (James I's wife), who had died only a few days before him on March 2, 1619; because of her death, the theaters were closed in official mourning.

Tributes to the actor poured in, such as this one from an anonymous poet who wrote of him in a funeral elegy:

> He's gone, and with him what a world are dead,
> Which he reviv'd, to be revived so
> No more: young Hamlet, old Hieronimo,
> Kind Lear, the grieved Moore, and more beside,
> That liv'd in him, have now forever died.
> Oft have I seen him leap into a grave,
> Suiting ye person, which he seem'd to have,

Of a sad lover, with so true an eye

That then I would have sworn he meant to die.

Oft have I seen him play his part in jest

So lively that spectators, and the rest

Of his sad crew, whilst he but seem'd to bleed,

Amazed, thought even then he died in deed.

The poem goes on for quite some time, praising his skill, his many roles, and his speech.

But perhaps the best epitaph was the one said to have been carved on his gravestone, a reminder of his long devotion to the stage, captured perfectly in only two words:

"Exit Burbage."

5

The Seventeenth Century

The seventeenth century was a mixed bag for theater. In England, it began with a golden age of drama that produced some of the finest plays ever written in the English language. That flowering was gutted by the events of the English Civil War and the Puritan years of no fun that followed it in the middle of the century. Theaters were finally reopened when Charles II returned to claim his crown in 1660, but with some fundamental changes, most dramatically (pun intended), the introduction of women to the English stage. This was something that would have been unthinkable to Shakespeare and his contemporaries.

In France, women had always been allowed to act, but after 1600, the French preference came to be for comedies and farces, perhaps to stave off the horrors of the wars that the country seemed to find itself perpetually engaged in throughout the century. Molière was the greatest name in French drama, but he was not universally loved, certainly not by religious authorities, as we will see. His farces drew from a variety of sources, especially the Italian Commedia dell'Arte, which by the same time was flourishing as never before (see act II for a whole chapter devoted to this zany, anarchic, and fun genre). French theater thrived under the patronage of the extravagant and decadent Sun King, Louis XIV, while Spain entered into a golden age of literature and drama, though not without its own share of controversy and violence.

As you might imagine, it's a bit of a tricky thing giving a chapter a title like "The Seventeenth Century," because some people featured here were born in the sixteenth and lived into the seventeenth, or were born in the seventeenth and made it successfully into the eighteenth. This problem also holds true for the rest of the chapters in act I, but obviously they have to be divided up *some* way. So how does one classify such individuals, who were so damned inconsiderate as to exist in more than one century? Mainly, it's based on when they did their best or most famous work, or when the most interesting (and awful) things happened to them. With that in mind, let's look at some of Europe's more intriguing theatrical escapades in the decades after Shakespeare, both in England and beyond.

Lope de Vega (1562–1635)

Affairs, exile, and an armada

Vega was a key figure in early seventeenth-century Spanish literature and drama. In addition to his other works—including about three thousand sonnets—he is credited with writing at least five hundred plays (some sources say over two thousand), an amazing output when you consider that Shakespeare wrote fewer than forty (that we know of). The quality of Vega's output varies, which may have to do with how quickly some were produced. He noted that over a hundred of his plays were performed within a day of his conceiving and writing them down!

He claimed to have written his first play at the age of twelve, and that he could already read and translate Latin by then. In his long career he helped to define Spanish theater by creating a new sense of realism in characters and establishing the Spanish comedy with a definitive three-act form. He is considered Spain's greatest literary talent after Cervantes.

After enrolling in the University of Alcalá, north of Madrid, he intended to study for the priesthood but fell for the charms of a young lady and realized that the whole celibacy thing was not going to be an option. In fact, it was *so* not going to work for him that he spent his life engaging in one scandalous affair after another. After a stint in the navy in the early 1580s, he returned to Madrid to begin a career as a playwright, and also started an affair with an actress, Elena Osorio, who was estranged from her husband. When that ended badly a few years later (she left him for someone else), he wrote rather viciously against her and her family, stating that her brother knew nothing of his profession (a doctor) and implying that her "services" were available for money. These accusations landed him in hot water for libel, which led to his being banished from Castile for two years. This punishment was made easier by the fact that he took his new lover, sixteen-year-old Isabel de Alderete y Urbina, with him. Obviously, her family was not thrilled, and they probably forced him to marry her, along with making him enlist in the navy again in 1588.

Ah, 1588—that would be the year of the famous Spanish Armada, the one that sailed to England to try to depose Queen Elizabeth I. Yes, poor Lope took part in that ill-fated venture, where the Spaniards were thumped by the disagreeable English and the even more disagreeable English weather. Fortunately for him, he survived and sailed back, tail-between-legs, with his comrades. Once home, he and Isabel moved to Valencia and then Toledo, where he wrote plays for wealthy patrons. She died in childbirth in 1594, so he finally returned to Madrid and remarried, but continued to indulge in affairs.

The first decades of the seventeenth century saw him reach his creative heights in the employment of the Duke of Sessa. After the death of his second wife, Vega finally decided to become a priest in 1614, but whatever his original intentions, he quickly determined that this little hiccup need not put an end to his affairs. Indeed, he also made the effort to introduce fine young ladies to the duke, which may be one reason that his unpriestly indiscretions were overlooked. He wrote to the duke on one occasion: "I believe I would not have had myself ordained had I believed that I should have to cease serving your Excellency in anything, and especially in those matters in which you take so much pleasure." Late in life, his son (also named Lope) died in a shipwreck and his daughter ran off with (or was abducted by) and was then abandoned by a nobleman, so unhappiness haunted him, regardless of his literary reputation. He seems to have felt he deserved it after a lifetime of scandals.

William Davenant (1606–1668)

Son of a b[ard]?

Davenant was a rare example of an actor and playwright who had a successful career during the reign of King Charles I, navigated through the Cromwell years, and picked up again late in life to attain more success during the reign of Charles II. He wrote a number of comedies, tragedies, masques, and poems, as well as opera texts (somewhat unintentionally; see below). Along the way, several crazy and not-so-great things happened to him, including contracting syphilis, losing part of his nose, being accused of treason, and being sentenced to death, all of which he weathered and survived long enough to die at a relatively advanced age.

Before we look at those things, we can start with a mystery concerning Davenant's birth. Born in Oxford in 1606, he was (allegedly) the son of Jane Shepherd Davenant and John Davenant, who was the proprietor of the Crown Inn and the mayor of Oxford. It was said that William Shakespeare was his godfather, which made for a rather illustrious beginning. Shakespeare, you see, knew the Davenants because he would stop in Oxford on the way to Stratford from London and stay at their inn, at least according to writer and antiquarian John Aubrey (1626–1697). Aubrey recorded that the poet Samuel Butler (1613–1680) commented on the rumor of something more going on. So this account is quickly becoming a "friend of a friend said this" kind of thing, but the story is interesting enough to quote Butler at length:

> Mr. William Shakespeare was wont to go into Warwickshire once a year, and did commonly in his journey lie at this house [the Crown Inn] in Oxon, where he was exceedingly respected. . . . Now Sir William [Davenant] would sometimes, when he was pleasant over a glass of wine with his most intimate friends—e.g. Sam Butler, author of

Hudibras, etc., say, that it seemed to him that he writ with the very spirit that did Shakespeare, and seemed contented enough to be thought his Son. He would tell them the story as above, in which way his mother had a very light report, whereby she was called a Whore.

The insult to Mrs. Davenant notwithstanding, the story is intriguing. Will almost certainly had not been faithful to Anne Hathaway, and who knows what he might have gotten up to in his travels? If John were away, anything was possible. Perhaps Jane had a dalliance with Will on one of these stopovers and didn't know for certain who her son's father was.

It seems that the rumor circulated in William Davenant's lifetime and that he did little to discourage it, despite the damage it could have done to his mother's (and his own) reputation. One story records that, after being knighted by Charles I in 1644, he boldly declared: "Know this, which does honor to my mother—I am the son of Shakespeare." Some have suggested that he was merely saying that he was "a son of Shakespeare" in the sense of being an heir to the great man's literary legacy, but this poetic association could have also been a way of concealing the truth. Of course, this story may just be an urban legend.

Regardless of his uncertain origins, he went on to lead a colorful and rather unsettling life. Sometime in 1630, his adventurous spirit led him to contract syphilis, and either the treatment or the disease itself caused his nose to become disfigured, marring his appearance (a terrible fate for an actor) and leaving him open to ridicule by cruel rivals and critics. One such mockery drove Davenant into a rage. The tormentor, a tapster named Thomas Warren, angered Davenant so much with his insults, that Davenant drew his rapier and stabbed the man, mortally wounding him. Davenant fled to Holland, being accused of murder, but the king eventually pardoned him. In fact, his poetry impressed Charles so much that Davenant was made a poet laureate in 1638 after the death of Ben Jonson (though the title would not become official for a few decades), a tweak on the nose—er, a poke in the eye—to his enemies.

Davenant was an ardent Royalist and supported the king during the Civil War of the 1640s. Before the war began, he was a part of the Army

Plot of 1641, a plan by Royalists to use the army to crush dissent in Parliament and occupy London, as the two sides clashed and prepared for conflict. You may recall that Charles considered himself to be king by divine right, and as such, believed that no one, not even Parliament, could tell him what to do. This didn't go over too well with a lot of people and directly caused the civil war that followed.

Davenant was implicated as a conspirator in the plot by those in Parliament loyal to Cromwell. He was accused of treason and had to flee to France. He rather bravely returned during the war, was knighted, and as we saw, may have declared himself to be Shakespeare's son—maybe it was a patriotic or provocative gesture, given the Puritan dislike for plays? After the king lost the war (and later his head), Davenant once again made a hasty retreat to France. During this stay, he converted to Catholicism; perhaps this was the ultimate act of defiance against the English Puritans now in control of the government?

Regardless of his religious affiliation, he entered the service of the exiled king-in-waiting, Charles II, who made him lieutenant governor of the Maryland colony in 1651. However, Davenant was captured at sea by English forces, returned to England, and sentenced to death. He languished in the Tower of London, but apparently the poet John Milton (of *Paradise Lost* fame) spoke up for him, and the Puritans were content to release him in 1652. Among those in the upper classes who opposed Cromwell, there was still a demand for plays, and not one to stay out of trouble, Davenant converted a part of his home into a private theater (since all public playhouses were closed) where he and his colleagues could perform their works to private audiences who were willing to appreciate them.

He also devised a clever means of producing some works in the 1650s by disguising them in music. Perhaps surprisingly, the Puritan government was more favorably inclined toward music (Cromwell was quite fond of dancing), so by collaborating with composers and basically turning plays into operas, Davenant was able to obtain official permission to show them. One such work, *The Siege of Rhodes* (recalling the Ottoman Turkish attack on the island in 1522), is generally regarded as

England's first true opera. Another musical play, provocatively titled *The Cruelty of the Spaniards in Peru*, was actively supported and encouraged by Cromwell and the Puritans as anti-Spanish (and thus anti-Catholic) propaganda. The irony that it was written by a Catholic playwright—two things they detested—was apparently lost on them.

He was pretty much able to stay out of trouble, but in 1659, he supported an uprising against the government after Oliver Cromwell's death. He was imprisoned, but amazingly, yet again nothing happened to him and once free, he was able to go back to France; all in the days before the Channel Tunnel. He returned to England for good when Charles was restored to the throne in 1660. With the theaters reopened, Davenant could at last shine once more. He was even granted, along with Thomas Killigrew (more on him next), a monopoly on playhouses and public theater performances; in other words, they had control over what was produced. During his last years, he was noted for reviving, adapting, and producing many of Shakespeare's plays, and he seemed to make no effort to discourage whatever rumors still circulated about his uncertain parentage. He died rather suddenly in 1668 and was buried in Poets' Corner at Westminster Abbey, a fitting resting place for a man who may have been the son of England's greatest playwright. Or not.

Thomas Killigrew (1612–1683)

Possessed nuns and insults to a king

English playwright and theater manager Thomas Killigrew was the son of Sir Robert Killigrew, a courtier of King James I, so he had a privileged start in life, including becoming a page to King Charles I, but rather than pursuing higher education, he wanted to write plays; so much for respectability. He had a love of the theater from a young age and volunteered as an extra at the Red Bull Theatre in London to be able to view its plays for free. But later on, he took advantage of family money to travel to the continent, gaining life experiences and attempting to write his own plays, including *The Prisoners*, a tragicomedy about the adventures of a pirate.

One of Killigrew's most interesting early experiences was as a witness to the so-called possessed nuns of Loudun, in Poitou, France. This strange affair involved an entire convent of nuns who in 1632 accused a Catholic priest, one Urbain Grandier, of bewitching them, seducing them, and sending demons to them. Now, Grandier had a notorious reputation for womanizing and had even written against clerical celibacy. In doing so, he earned the enmity of the all-powerful Cardinal Richelieu, whom you may remember as a villain from *The Three Musketeers*.

In all likelihood, the nuns were faking, having been persuaded to do so by the local bishop or some other clergy in an effort to denounce Grandier; some may have fallen under the influence of mass hysteria and genuinely believed they were being assaulted by diabolical forces. The afflicted did many of the usual things that those possessed by demons are said to do, such as fly into rages, writhe, speak in tongues, scream and shout, and other antisocial activities. Thousands of curious people came to see the allegedly possessed nuns and their exorcisms, and Killigrew left a lengthy account of his visit in 1635. He described one young woman being freed of her demon, and how a name appeared on her arm as it departed:

> On her hand I saw a colour rise a little ruddy, and run for the length of an inch upon her vein, and in that a great many red specks; and they contracted into letters which made a distinct word; and it was the fame she spake, "Joseph." . . . This, as I live, I saw; nor could I find the least argument to question the reality of this miracle. The priest then told us, that the Devil would have wrote his own name when he went out, but that he enjoined him to write "Joseph;" for to that saint the priest had addressed himself with a vow, to have his aid in the expelling of him.

Grandier was interrogated by an ecclesiastical tribunal but acquitted. This was not satisfactory for Richelieu, who brought him to trial again and produced new "evidence," including a remarkable contract, written backwards in Latin and "signed" by various devils, including Satan himself. It read in part:

We, the influential Lucifer, the young Satan, Beelzebub, Leviathan, Elimi, and Astaroth, together with others, have today accepted the covenant pact of Urbain Grandier, who is ours. And him do we promise the love of women, the flower of virgins, the respect of monarchs, honors, lusts and powers.

It continued by noting that Grandier was obligated to defile holy things and as a result, would live happily for twenty years before joining them in hell. Each demon had his own elaborate signature and the whole thing was completely ridiculous, but it was enough for Grandier to be burned at the stake in 1634.

Killigrew seems to have been pretty unsettled by the whole affair, but surprisingly, it never formed the basis for a play, which would seem a natural thing to do. The subject matter may have been distasteful in Protestant England, or perhaps it had something to do with the Civil War, which erupted during the next decade.

Killigrew was a Royalist and subject to the Puritan crackdown on plays during their tenure as stewards of the nation. He followed the future Charles II into exile in 1647 and traveled extensively, apparently writing a new play in each city that he visited.

With the Restoration, Killigrew got in good with the returning King Charles II and was appointed Groom of the Bedchamber (a kind of valet). He was also given a royal license to reform and manage the King's Company, which was Shakespeare's former company. Samuel Pepys records that Killigrew had been given the position of the king's court jester in 1668:

Tom Killigrew hath a fee out of the Wardrobe for cap and bells, under the title of the King's Foole or jester; and may with privilege revile or jeere any body, the greatest person, without offence, by the privilege of his place.

This was not some silly position ("cap and bells" notwithstanding) but rather a tremendous honor, one that allowed Killigrew almost free rein to say whatever he liked in the context of political commentary; what writer wouldn't envy that? He is even reported to have said directly to the king that he (the king) was "Charles Stuart—who now spends his time in employing his lips and his prick about the court and has no other employment." Well, that's actually kind of true.

In the theatrical world, Killigrew may have been one of the first to hire an actress for one of his productions, and he also brought in foreign performers, including castrati from Italy. One of his plays, *The Parson's Wedding*, was written way back in the late 1630s in Switzerland but enjoyed a revival, with some rewrites, in the Restoration era. It was a bawdy comedy, and many thought it was fairly vulgar, which only enhanced its popularity. Female wantonness is a major theme in the play, such as in the description of the character of Lady Freedom, a female surgeon who represents those women who helped during the civil war. Jolly, a courtier, observes that her motives are more for sexual gratification than rendering assistance: "She converses with naked men, and handles all their members, though never so ill-affected, and calls the Fornication Charity."

As an experiment, he had the play performed with an all-female cast more than once, something that would have been unthinkable when it was first written, but which was received with much amusement by audiences eager to see the novelty of actresses. The comedy even makes a note of this at one point, challenging the restrictions of the preceding eras:

Now, to oppose the humour of that Age,
We have this day, expell'd our Men the Stage.
Why cannot we as well perform their Parts?

The play goes even further, recalling the earlier practice of boys taking women's roles—and the Puritans' fear that this practice could incite homosexual lust in male audience members—and suggesting that men took boys as lovers:

When boys play'd women's parts, you'd think the Stage
Was innocent in that untempting Age.

No: for your amorous Fathers then, like you
Amongst those Boys, had Play-house Misses too . . .

Despite commercial successes, Killigrew's attempts at theater management were not always successful, and there were quarrels over
ownership issues (he lost control of his theater to his son in 1677) and
issues with actors showing up on time. Killigrew attempted to correct
the latter problem by hiring a company prostitute as an incentive to
good attendance. Despite his business and personal problems, he was regarded highly enough to be buried in Westminster Abbey when he died
in March 1683, a testament to his value to the decadent king who, when
not busy employing his prick, entrusted Killigrew with helping to revive
English theater.

Molière (1622–1673)

The not-so-imaginary invalid

Born Jean-Baptiste Poquelin but preferring his stage name, Molière was
the greatest French playwright of the seventeenth century and one of the
greatest masters of theatrical comedy who ever lived. He elevated comedy to a respectable art form and was much in demand, despite the controversies that surrounded him. He was proficient with farce, producing
comic masterpieces such as *Tartuffe*, *The Misanthrope*, and *The Imaginary
Invalid*.

He was the son of a furniture merchant and upholster to the king;
his father's official title was "valet of the king's chamber and keeper of
carpets and upholstery"—how's *that* for an unusual job description?
Molière studied classics and law, but turned away from both his father's
profession and an academic life to embrace the world of the theater. He
created a company, the Illustre Théâtre, in 1643 and took as his mistress
the young actress Madeleine Béjart; her brother and sister also became
collaborators in the company. Yes, they were all set to show the world
what they could do, and what they did do was fail, so much so that they
ran up huge debts. Molière spent a day in prison before his debts were

paid, possibly by his father. He may have adopted his stage name about then, to spare his family the shame of having an actor using their name.

With their Paris venture a failure, they went off on a short tour of the provinces that ended up lasting for twelve years. During that time (1646–1658), Molière honed his skills to a considerable degree, acquired wealthy patrons, and moved away from being influenced by the Commedia dell'Arte to create works that stood the test of time. When the company eventually returned to Paris and began performances there, his reputation was solid.

However, he also made enemies and inspired controversy. He was not above satirizing his detractors, and many in the clergy felt that his work was lampooning them, as well, especially among the adherents of Jansenism, a Catholic theological movement that was at odds with the Jesuits and even the Church itself at times over the Jansenists' rigid teachings. However, he was able to survive their challenges because he had found favor with King Louis XIV, who had the last word on the subject.

Still, he was attacked from various sources. One major accusation concerned his personal life. In 1662, he married Armande Béjart, supposedly the much younger sister of his former lover, Madeleine. However, some accused Molière of in fact marrying his own illegitimate daughter, saying that she was his and Madeleine's child, and that Madeleine was only pretending to have a sister. The actor Montfleury was a particular devotee of this conspiracy theory, since Molière had mocked his large belly in one of his farces, and he had taken great offense over it. Montfleury was destined for a dramatic death of his own, as we will see in "The Bloody Theater" chapter. In any case, the king seems not to have taken this charge seriously, and Molière escaped punishment. The truth will probably never be known.

He was in for more trouble with his play *Tartuffe*, produced in 1664. The story concerns the plight of Orgon and his mother, who are being badly influenced by Tartuffe, a vagrant, con man, and now their boarder. Tartuffe outwardly appears pious but is actually a fraud, and he schemes to become Orgon's sole heir. Other members of Orgon's family try to free him from Tartuffe's influence and ultimately succeed. On the surface, the play is a comedy, but it has many darker satirical elements, and the religious authorities were not at all pleased. Tartuffe represents religious hypocrisy; his outward shows of piety and underlying immorality are intended as a critique of the then-current religious establishment. Tartuffe notes, for example, when he speaks of possibly inheriting money:

The treasures of this world I quite despise;
Their specious glitter does not charm my eyes;
And if I have resigned myself to taking
The gift which my dear Brother insists on making,
I do so only, as he well understands,
Lest so much wealth fall into wicked hands.

He puts on a show of being a holy man not desiring wealth, when in fact he has been scheming for it all along. The implication is that this is exactly what the religious hierarchy in France does, flaunting wealth while claiming to have no interest in it except to put it to good use for the church.

It isn't only money that Tartuffe is after. He lusts for Orgon's wife, but foolish Orgon thinks he is simply watching out for her, the typical mark of a cuckolded fool:

His interest in my wife is reassuring,
She's innocent, but so alluring.
He tells me whom she sees and what she does.
He's more jealous than I ever was.
It's for my honor that he's so concerned.

When Orgon eventually learns of Tartuffe's deceit, he angrily denounces him, pointing to the contrast between his façade and his behavior:

Ah! Ah! You are a traitor and a liar!
Some holy man you are, to wreck my life

Marry my daughter? Lust after my wife?

Though the play was performed at Versailles and the king enjoyed it, the archbishop of Paris was not pleased by these kinds of accusations. He came down hard on it, issuing an edict that threatened excommunication for anyone viewing or acting in the play, or even reading it. This was a serious charge, and it was probably only the king's protection that kept Molière from being excommunicated. Molière tried to defuse the situation by rewriting certain sections to make them less offensive, but such appeasements almost never work, and they didn't in this situation. The play remained effectively banned from public performance (private shows still took place) for some years, until the king gained the upper hand in power over the French clergy and allowed it to be shown again.

By the 1660s, Molière was showing signs of a serious lung condition, pulmonary tuberculosis, which he may have contracted many years earlier, perhaps during his brief stay in prison. It was a condition that would lead to his dramatic (quite literally) death. In 1673, ironically while performing in his play *The Imaginary Invalid*, he collapsed in a fit of coughing, but insisted on finishing the show. He somehow managed to carry on, but collapsed again after the play was over and was taken to his home. His condition was not so imaginary after all.

Two priests were summoned to deliver last rites, but given his reputation and the sour history between him and the Church, they refused to come. A more compassionate third priest did agree to perform the rites, but he arrived too late, and Molière was already gone. Thus, the great satirist passed without reconciliation with the Church he had only lightly mocked, and which had taken far more offense that it should have at his ingenious farces. It was said that he was wearing the color green at the time of his death, and some suppose this to be the origin of the theatrical superstition about green's unluckiness (see the chapter "An Abundance of Superstitions, Curses, and Bad Luck"). Under the law at the time, mere actors were not allowed to be buried in a cemetery's holy grounds. However, Armande convinced the king to allow his body to be buried in a portion of the cemetery reserved for unbaptized infants, which was something of a compromise. In 1804, Molière's remains were transferred to the more fitting Père Lachaise Cemetery in Paris; in fact, he was one of the first to be interred in the new grounds, receiving the respect he deserved but didn't always get in life.

The spectacle of English female actors during the Restoration (1660 onward)

Breeches, breasts, bawdiness, and 'bout time

With the restoration of Charles II to the English throne in 1660 after Cromwell's grim, no-fun years, the theaters were opened again. The hedonistic new king thought it would be quite the smashing idea to introduce a novelty into the plays, one that would set them apart from their forebears and quite possibly also as an added kick to the groin of the Puritans he had just ousted. He decreed that women would henceforth be allowed to act and share stages with their male counterparts. Charles had spent time in exile in France at the court of Louis XIV, where women had already been players for a long time, and he wanted his court to imitate the splendor of the French model. And to ogle lots of young actresses.

The idea wasn't completely, stunningly new even in England. English women had always been permitted to perform in masques, which were a blend of dialogue, poetry, music, and dance for courtly audiences at various festivals. As the name implies, the performers wore disguises (masks and opulent clothing) and their audiences were private and upper-class only (unlike the public and often lower-class playhouses), so participation in such festivities was considered an acceptable indulgence for a noble lady.

But a woman's appearance in the playhouses was something entirely different, unthinkable during the Elizabethan and Jacobean eras, to say nothing of the silent years under Cromwell. The Puritans certainly didn't like the idea of women actors, but almost just as bad to them was the practice of boys playing women's roles, because, as we have seen, this situation could tempt some actors into "unnatural" activities that might occur as a result of having to perform love scenes. That's why they just wanted to shut it all down and be done with it.

Anyway, with the Restoration, women reveled in their newfound freedom and took to the stage with relish and joy. A whole generation of talented actresses sprang up, freed from the constraints previously imposed on them. Undoubtedly, many women had acted in secret before, but now they could openly share the stage with men and play actual female roles, even the classic ones written a half century before.

For better or worse, many actresses used their newfound fame as a way to ingratiate themselves to wealthy men who came to see the new comedies and other theatrical entertainments. The most famous of these was Nell Gwyn (1650–1687), who became King Charles's mistress from 1668 (some sources say as late as 1670), ultimately beating out a fellow actress, Moll Davis (*ca*. 1648–1708), for his attention. There were rumors that Gwyn had conspired with female playwright Aphra Behn (*ca*. 1640–1689) and administered a strong laxative into Davis's cakes shortly before her evening tryst with the king; well, that's one way to spoil the mood!

As you might expect, working conditions were hardly ideal for equality. Women were paid less, treated poorly, and often written into plays as sexual objects rather than true characters. Plays began to feature "couch scenes," wherein women would lie, feigning sleep for a given act, often in a state of at least partial undress. More distasteful were the new rape scenes, which were justified by the idea that they allowed a female character to retain her virtue (i.e., she had not consented) but still be titillating. Women really didn't have the liberty of protesting these kinds of exploitative scenes, if they wanted to keep their jobs.

One curious turnabout was the "breeches role," in which women had the chance to cross-dress as men; this was usually a part of the story, with a woman secretly pretending to be a man while pursuing some goal. Obviously, this had long been done the other way around, since boys played the major female characters, but these new parts were specifically written as such and appeared in nearly a quarter of all Restoration comedies. The idea of seeing "real" women in these roles was part of the humor, and there was undoubtedly a thrill for both genders in seeing women wearing tight-fitting trousers that clearly showed off their legs and even buttocks, something that was otherwise forbidden. Sometimes these actresses would let loose their hair, or even expose one breast onstage as a part of the reveal that their characters were women pretending to be men, which further added to the novelty and scandal.

These roles were so popular that they were sometimes apparently added to older plays to bring them more up to date. Of course, some older works, such as Shakespeare's *Twelfth Night*, already have such a plot device worked in—a female character pretending to be a boy before revealing that said boy was really a woman all along. But in accordance with the "no women onstage" laws of that earlier time, the role was played by an actual boy onstage, pretending to be a woman . . . pretending to be a boy. The mind boggles.

Charles Rivière Dufresny (1648–1724)

A washed-up marriage

Dufresny was a French dramatist who was born into privilege but encountered troubles after that promising start. His plays are not regarded as masterpieces, but in his time they were popular enough. He was said to be the great-grandson of one La Belle Jardinière d'Anet ("the Beautiful Garden of Anet"), who was a mistress to King Henri IV of France (1553–1610), and people remarked that he bore a certain resemblance to that royal personage. As such, he found favor with King Louis XIV, who made him a *valet de chambre*, named him comptroller of the royal gardens, and even gave him a patent on the manufacture of looking glasses.

He really couldn't have asked for much more—and that's the problem. His extravagant tastes, aided and abetted by the lavish lifestyle that his positions afforded him (feasting, drinking, costly clothing and furnishings, all the usual excesses of too much wealth), meant that he tore through money like a hot knife through butter; even Louis had a difficult time replenishing his losses. Dufresny had a liking for the finer things in life and spent far more than he should have. According to one source, he also "inherited from his great-grandfather a taste for numerous experiments in love." Take that however you will. Nevertheless he married, but it was unhappy and at his wife's death in 1688, he moved to Paris, rented a good number of rooms, and indulged in gambling while writing new plays for the Parisian public. He collaborated with fellow playwright Jean-François Regnard (1655–1709) on Italian-style comedies, but the pair ran into a problem: Italian comic actors at the time were prohibited from acting onstage in France (protectionism and such), and so the venture wasn't nearly as successful as he'd hoped. King Louis still granted him an annual salary, but his extravagance had to take back seat to practicality, which annoyed him greatly.

A possibly urban legend records that he reached a state where he could no longer afford to pay his washer woman for her services, so he offered to marry her instead and, surprisingly, she accepted. True or not, this scenario was comic gold for the satirists, and Jean-Marie Deschamps (*ca.* 1750–1826) wrote a play about the incident and Dufresny's reduced circumstances: *Charles Rivière Dufresny, ou le marriage impromptu* ("Charles Rivière Dufresny, or the Impromptu Marriage").

He lived on in this humbler manner, but his liking for the trappings of wealth remained with him until the end. A friend once tried to comfort him by offering that poverty was not a vice, to which he replied, "It is much worse."

Nathaniel Lee (*ca.* 1645/53–1692)

Voted into Bedlam

Lee was a talented young dramatist born after the end of the English Civil War. He eventually excelled in writing bloody tragedies in the grand Jacobean tradition, including *The Rival Queens, or the Death of Alexander the Great, Caesar Borgia,* an adaptation of *Oedipus,* and *The Massacre of Paris.* Filled with violence and blood, his works often questioned divine right and held that tyrants should be overthrown. His early successes earned him much praise, but he soon fell in with the Merry

Gang, the notorious social circle of John Wilmot, Second Earl of Rochester (1647–1680). Wilmot, a poet and devoted libertine, took advantage of Charles's decadent Restoration court to live life to the fullest, especially when it came to excessive drinking and womanizing. Wilmot was involved in the theater and promoted his mistress, Elizabeth Barry (1658–1713) as an actress; he also once punched Thomas Killigrew, earning himself a temporary banishment from the court by the king.

Lee the debauched playwright seemed eager to join the earl in a squalid life. He was skilled as a dramatist, but his drinking was excessive, and he may have been suffering from mental problems. By 1684, he was declared mad due to his erratic behavior and confined to the infamous Bedlam hospital for the insane, where he was kept for five years before being released. He humorously observed about those who had worked to have him committed: "They called me mad, and I called them mad, and damn them, they outvoted me."

His time in the asylum had obviously not done much good—such was the state of mental health treatment on those days—and he returned to drinking, dying a few years later after an especially heavy bout, but his collected works were deemed important enough to be published in 1734.

Jeremy Collier (1650–1726)

The Profaneness of the Stage

Collier was one of many late seventeenth-century theologians who fumed at the perceived immorality of the new Restoration stage. He wasn't the first or last, or even the loudest, but he is probably the best known because of his 1698 pamphlet, the descriptively titled "A Short View of the Immorality and Profaneness of the English Stage." "Short" is obviously a subjective term, as the text runs to nearly three hundred pages and discusses everything he saw as being wrong with the theater of his day (and there was a lot of it), as well as what to do about it.

He wasn't just an agitator against plays. He was part of a cantankerous group of clerics who refused to recognize the new monarchs, William and Mary, who had displaced the previous king, James II, younger brother of King Charles II, in 1688. James had caused quite a bit of controversy by being a Catholic. It was one thing to toss out the Puritans, as Charles II had done, but turning the monarchy over to someone loyal to Rome (for the first time since Mary Tudor in the 1550s) was going too far for many. James was sent into exile, and many rejoiced when the Dutch (and Protestant) William and Mary were offered a coregency in what came to be known as the Glorious Revolution.

However, many Anglican clerics could not or would not swear an oath of allegiance to these two, feeling that James had been unlawfully displaced, regardless of his religion. This created a schism and quite a bit of controversy in the English and Scottish Churches that was not resolved until nearly the end of the eighteenth century.

In the meantime, Collier had a lot to say about the stage; quite a lot. His pamphlet railed against all of the immoralities being played out in comedies and against those playwrights that indulged in writing such things. The work is a remarkable bit of crabbed polemic that lets the reader know right away what its intentions are:

> Being convinc'd that nothing has gone farther in Debauching the Age than the Stage Poets, and Play-House, I thought I could not employ my time better than in writing against them.

One of Collier's biggest gripes was that comedies in particular let some of their awful and rakish characters get away with all sorts of mischief and never get punished for it. In chapter after chapter, he lays out his claims and attacks everything imaginable, offering up such apoplectic section titles as:

> The Immodesty of the Stage; The Ill Consequences of this Liberty; The Stage faulty in this respect to a very Scandalous degree; Swearing in the Play House an Un-Gentlemanly, as well as an Un-Christian practice; A Second Branch of the Profaness of the Stage, consisting in their Abuse

of Religion, and the Holy Scriptures; The Stage Poets make Libertines their Top-Characters, and give them Success in their Debauchery; The Stage guilty of down right Blasphemy.

These things, he believed, set a terrible example for impressionable viewers, especially young ladies, who, as delicate little flowers, needed to be shielded from the horrid goings-on of a given play:

Obscenity in any Company is a rustick uncreditable Talent; but among Women 'tis particularly rude. Such Talk would be very affrontive in Conversation, and not endur'd by any Lady of Reputation. Whence then comes it to Pass that those Liberties which disoblige so much in Conversation, should entertain upon the *Stage*. Do the Women leave all the regards to Decency and Conscience behind them when they come to the *Play-House*? Or does the Place transform their Inclinations, and turn their former Aversions into Pleasure? Or were Their pretences to Sobriety elsewhere nothing but Hypocrisy and Grimace? . . . To treat the Ladys with such stuff is no better than taking their Money to abuse them.

This was all the more true because the scandalous new "actresses," he and other critics thought, were frequently ladies of a less-than-sterling reputation, and so not to be emulated by the innocent.

Many of the playwrights whose works were singled out in his attacks responded pretty fiercely, some with pamphlets of their own, thus starting a war of words that went back and forth periodically until at least 1726, the year Collier died. Some playwrights, actors, and theater managers accused Collier of just being upset because their plays tended to portray clergymen as foolish, and that by his actions he was proving them right. John Dryden's *Don Sebastian*, for example, states:

——Churchmen tho' they itch to govern all,
Are silly, woful, awkward Polititians,
They make lame Mischief tho' they mean it well.

Wasn't Collier trying to govern, and so making himself look silly? Many of his critics thought so.

So what was the outcome of this war? Some have seen Collier's not-so-short work as a major nail in the coffin for bawdy Restoration comedy, which disappeared after the turn of the eighteenth century and was replaced by more serious and reverent material. There even appeared societies dedicated to preserving morals and honor on stages. On the other hand, while the pamphlet certainly gave more ammunition to those who already hated these plays, the genre was already winding down and declining in popularity by the 1690s. Tastes were changing, and the coregents seem to have had little interest in racy comedies, being far more straightlaced than the ribald Charles II and his anything-goes mentality. A conservative backlash against those loose-and-free years was already taking hold, and Collier was simply a soldier in an ongoing culture war rather than its instigator.

Anne Bracegirdle (*ca.* 1671–1748)

A rakish plot foiled

Anne Bracegirdle was one of the most esteemed stage actresses of the generation of restored English theaters. She was likely brought up by actors and made her debut in productions beginning in the later 1680s. She was fond of playing breeches roles (see the earlier discussion of female actors during the Restoration), but quickly added characters such as Desdemona from *Othello* and Lady Anne from *Richard III* to her repertoire. These were major dramatic parts, and soon she was winning acclaim and an increasing swarm of admirers. This, unfortunately, was not necessarily a good thing. A fellow actor remarked on her stage appearances: "Her Youth and lively Aspect threw out such a Glow of Health and Chearfulness, that on the Stage few Spectators that were not past it could behold her without Desire."

One such admirer was the unsavory Captain Richard Hill, whose infatuation got out of hand; in modern terms, we would call him a stalker. Bracegirdle was polite and cool toward him, but he convinced himself that underneath her virtuous exterior was a passionate woman waiting to be let out, and he was, of course, just the man to do it. There was one problem, though. He decided that she might very well already be in love with another man, the talented young actor and playwright Will Mountfort. She had performed in a few of his plays and they had acted several love scenes together. The captain decided that if this was the case, Mountfort would have to die. He even cursed the actor's name in front of her, declaring him to be an unworthy rival.

So Hill approached his friend, Charles Mohun, fourth Baron Mohun (*ca.* 1675–1712). Mohun was a notorious jerk who loved causing trouble, getting into duels, and gambling to try to support his lavish lifestyle. He was the perfect coconspirator in Hill's awful plan. On December 9, 1692, their scheme was put into effect. They hired six ruffians to abduct Bracegirdle, but she fought back valiantly and drew a crowd, chasing the would-be abductors off; good for her! Okay then, on to plan B. Hill and Mohun stepped up and offered to escort the actress home. She agreed somewhat reluctantly, but they did as they promised. However, once safely inside her house, she noticed that they were now loitering in the street outside, obviously up to something.

Recalling that Hill hated Mountfort, she dispatched a messenger to the actor, to warn him that the two men were plotting something. Since he lived nearby, he immediately (and in retrospect, foolishly) rushed to her aid. Coming upon Lord Mohun, Mountfort at first thought he was greeting an ally and embraced him (the two knew each other well enough), whispering words of warning to him about Hill. But as Mohun held him, Hill stabbed Mountfort with a sword, fatally wounding him. Another account says that Mohun stood nearby while Hill stabbed Mountfort in the chest. In either case, the deed was done. Hill realized that the whole thing had gone wrong and fled the country. Mohun was actually arrested and brought to trial in the House of Lords, but lucky him, he played the "get out of jail by virtue of being a nobleman" card and was acquitted; the verdict was widely condemned.

The loss of Mountfort was indeed tragic. He had much literary promise and was probably not yet thirty years old; it is believed that he coined the phrase "Be still my beating heart" in his play *Zelmane*. For her part, Bracegridle was deeply saddened by his death and felt guilty for it for the rest of her life. She probably wasn't even in love with him. In fact, many suspected that she was secretly married to (or least involved with) another playwright, William Congreve (1670–1729), whose comedies were very popular at the time, and in whose plays she acted. He is credited as the true source of two famous quotes (often misattributed to Shakespeare) from his play *The Mourning Bride*: "Musick has charms to soothe a savage breast" and "Nor hell a fury like a woman scorned."

In any case, Bracegirdle's warning had accidentally led to Mountfort's doom. She continued to act, retiring in 1707 at the height of her career, but lived on until 1748, thankfully not having to put up with any other such ridiculous advances from presumptuous and sexist Baroque jackholes.

6

The Eighteenth Century

In England, the eighteenth century saw the beginning of a backlash against the more outlandish excesses of the Restoration period, when everyone was so thrilled to be out from under the Puritan yoke that things often took on an "anything goes" vibe that thrilled many and shocked more than a few. It wasn't just that women were onstage, it was that some of them were—gasp—wearing trousers! The plays became increasingly licentious and naughty, as if in a direct flip-off to the Puritans who had tried since the 1570s to curtail them and keep the public from seeing them at all. Still, by 1700, some people were starting to feel like they had had enough.

Further, this newfound freedom also led to increasing political jabs and pointed opinions that openly criticized and mocked the government, despite all plays still technically being censored to remove overly controversial content. Things got so out of hand—reaching the stage of mocking the king's large backside—that a new act laid down the law as to what could and couldn't be said onstage. This basically watered down theater and made it far less fun and interesting, at least for a while; in response, the English novel began to flourish.

France was in some turmoil as well, as you'll recall. Louis the Sun King ended his days in 1715—you could say that the sun set on his life and reign—and some years of political intrigue followed. As the century progressed, there was increasing criticism of the very out-of-touch elite, while the masses only saw their conditions getting worse. Eventually, people started losing their heads over the whole thing.

In a century of changes, Italy seemed to have the perfect response—more Commedia, because when in doubt about the uncertain state of the world, slap someone on the butt with a prop!

Joseph Addison (1672–1719)

Inadvertent inspiration for a revolution?

Addison was an English essayist, politician, and playwright, also known for his contributions to newspapers. In 1707, he contributed the libretto to the opera *Rosamond*. The music was composed by the violinist Thomas Clayton (1673–1725), no less than a member of the King's Musick, a private orchestra for royal entertainment. Whatever Clayton's credentials and Addison's skill, the opera failed miserably, prompting one observer to say, "*Rosamond* mounted the stage on purpose to frighten all England with its abominable musick." Critics have been bringing the snark for centuries, it seems.

Wisely leaving the opera world behind, Addison instead turned his attention to the play that he is most famous for—*Cato, a Tragedy*. Set in Roman times, the work discusses the end of the republic and the beginning of Caesar's dictatorship. Cato, a devotee of the old conservative ways, is a determined foe of Caesar and ultimately commits suicide to hold on to his belief in the republic. The work is a meditation on tyranny that would have implications that Addison could never have imagined.

While very popular in the British Isles, the play also later found favor in the American colonies. As the government of King George III began to seem ever more tyrannical to some colonists, they began to draw inspiration from the plight of Cato in facing what seemed like increasingly unreasonable demands. Though the work did not "cause" the American Revolution, many of those revolutionaries drew inspiration from its dialogue.

For instance, Patrick Henry's famed words, "Give me Liberty or give me death!" seem to refer to act II, scene 4: "It is not now time to talk of aught / But chains or conquest, liberty or death."

Nathan Hale's alleged declaration "I only regret that I have but one life to lose for my country" could have been in reference to act IV, scene 4: "What a pity it is that we can die but once to serve our country."

George Washington wrote to Benedict Arnold (obviously before the latter turned traitor): "It is not in the power of any man to command success; but you have done more—you have deserved it." This echoes act I, scene 2: "'Tis not in mortals to command success; but we'll do more, Sempronius, we'll deserve it."

Washington was almost certainly referencing the play deliberately. He was a great fan of the work and made use of it many times. Congress had passed a resolution stating that public officials should not attend plays, owing to a belief that they were too closely associated with "Britishness," but Washington still ordered *Cato* to be performed at Valley Forge, possibly as a morale booster to the troops, since Cato's supporters also rallied at a time of great hardship.

When some military officers threatened mutiny over Congress repeatedly failing to pay them (money was hard to come by in those early days of a potential new nation), Washington defused the situation in his speech to the officers by again using Cato's tactics from the play: he rebuked the author of the call to mutiny (who had bravely opted to remain anonymous), appealed to the potential mutineers not to dishonor themselves by turning against the republic, and asked for personal respect based on his own past services. He also quoted from the play to make his points. Clearly it was a very meaningful work for Washington, and if not directly responsible for the revolution, its defense of liberty in the face of tyranny certainly was a model for colonists who wanted a nation of their own.

Cato was admired in Europe as well, where antimonarchist, republican sympathies grew ever stronger during the eighteenth century. The play offered role models for virtuous behavior and adherence to the ideals of liberty, both of which had enduring appeal—versions of *Cato* circulated well into the nineteenth century.

Addison himself probably would have been horrified to think that his work would inspire sedition against the British government, but he had more immediate concerns. Over the next few years, he entered into an unhappy marriage with Charlotte, Dowager Countess of Warwick, whose son from her previous marriage was Edward Rich, seventh Earl of Warwick, who, according to many, was a rakish, obnoxious little jerk. Political rivalries abounded. Addison's health failed him and he died at the young age of forty-seven, never knowing how influential his Roman play would eventually become.

Charles Macklin (1690/99–1797)

A poke in the eye II

There is some dispute about just how long Macklin lived. Either way, ninety-seven or well over a century, was hugely impressive for the time. Born in Northern Ireland, where records were not always accurate, he maintained that he had been born "in the last year of the last century," but biographers have found some evidence that he may have made his debut almost a decade earlier.

Macklin was a renowned stage actor and dramatist, best known and praised for his portrayal of Shylock from Shakespeare's *Merchant of Venice*. Shylock had previously been portrayed as a comic relief character (it was an age of freely adapting and reinterpreting old plays, even Shakespeare's), more akin to someone from the Italian Commedia. Instead of merely following stereotyped conventions from the time, Macklin actively sought out Jews in London and learned about their clothing, customs, and manners. He brought a level of seriousness to the role that had not been seen before, and it was a huge hit. Shylock became his signature character (though he played hundreds of other roles), and Macklin portrayed him for decades, ceasing only a few years before his death as his memory faded.

Macklin advocated for a more naturalistic way of acting, one that made the characters into real people, rather than just figures reciting lines to the audience in a declamatory manner, as was often the practice at the time. He taught this new realism to his students and was responsible for a change in acting techniques.

Unfortunately, Macklin had a number of run-ins with the law (most often legal disputes), the most notorious being the accidental murder of another actor, Thomas Hallam. The incident happened at the famed Theatre Royal, Drury Lane, in London. The two quarreled over a costume wig, of all things, backstage during a performance of a farce called *Trick for Trick*. Hallam was wearing it, and Macklin wanted it. In a fit of anger, Macklin struck at Hallam with his cane. The object hit Hallam in the face, pierced his eye, and entered his brain. Macklin was immediately remorseful and called for a doctor, but the damage was done, and Hallam died the next day. Macklin was brought to trial for murder and acted as his own lawyer. His genuine remorse and skillful oratory (he *was* an actor, after all!) resulted in the sentence being reduced to manslaughter. Normally, he would have been branded on his hand with a letter "M," but he also seems to have escaped this punishment.

An interesting story about his death is also worth noting, but may be nothing more than fanciful legend. It is said that on his last day (which may have also been his birthday), he awoke and took a bath in warm brandy, as you do. He then changed clothes and bed linens, and retired again to bed later. At some point he turned to his wife and said, "Let me go," and so he died, whether or not she had any say in it.

Voltaire (1694–1778)

Pissing off the establishment

Voltaire is best known as a philosopher and writer, perhaps the embodiment of French Enlightenment ideals. He is famous for his satirical novel *Candide*, but he was also a prolific playwright, penning more than fifty dramas during his long life. His biography would fill a volume or four, so here we will just look at his dramatic activities and a few of the more unusual highlights from his life.

Voltaire was born François-Marie Arouet. His father wanted him to become a lawyer, but he resisted and pursued writing instead; typical young rebel. His acid tongue and wit soon landed him in trouble. He satirically suggested that the country's regent, Philippe II, Duke of Orléans, who oversaw the minority of the young King Louis XV, had an incestuous relationship with his own daughter, and this got him promptly sent off to the charming Bastille for an eleven-month vacation, er, imprisonment between 1717 and 1718. This was a miserable confinement in a windowless cell. However, he emerged otherwise unscathed and was able to salvage his reputation by writing the play *Œdipe* ("Oedipus"), a new version of the ancient Greek tragedy. Incest also features in this play, of course, but Voltaire wisely downplayed the theme somewhat after his prison experience.

At this time, he also adopted the pen name "Voltaire," though its exact meaning is unclear. It may be a Latinized version of "Arouet," or perhaps a play on his childhood nickname, *le petit volontaire* ("the determined little thing"). Voltaire explained that he used it so as not to be confused with another similarly named poet.

Over the next few years, he wrote a mixture of drama (mainly tragedies, with varying degrees of success), as well as poetry and prose, always eager to mock society's many faults. In 1726, he ran afoul of the Chevalier de Rohan-Chabot, who then paid some hired hands to beat him up. Enraged, Voltaire challenged the nobleman to a duel, but instead he was arrested and once again thrown into the Bastille. He feared that since he had not been tried, he might be detained indefinitely, so he offered to go into exile in England instead, and this was permitted. While in London, he was a hit, and he mingled with the best and most prominent figures in society.

Voltaire was able to return to France less than three years later and in 1729, hatched a scheme with mathematician Charles Marie de La Condamine to work the national French lottery in their favor. This lottery was meant to collect money and hand out prizes as a way for the government to pay for its debts and services (then as now), but La Condamine and some professional gamblers were able to exploit it to win often, and Voltaire walked away with as much as a million French livres. This set him up for life so that he could pursue writing exclusively. All writers should be so lucky!

He continued to write plays and produced his *Letters Concerning the English Nation*, published in London in 1733. The work lauded the British government for its forward-looking views on human rights, religious toleration, and limited monarchy. A French version was published the next year, but it was never approved by the censor, and so all hell broke loose for Voltaire once again. The work was condemned, banned, and burned; Voltaire had to flee Paris for eastern France. This would be a recurring pattern for him, and he frequently lived with the fear of arrest.

In 1742, he wrote *Mahomet*, a play that on the surface seems to be purely a critique of Islam and its prophet, but underneath, it condemns the actions of the Catholic Church and religious hypocrisy in general. Voltaire was a committed Deist and believed in religious toleration, but condemned what he saw as superstition and excess peddled by adherents of all religions: "Mahomet, I know, did not actually commit that particular crime which is the subject of this tragedy . . . but what is not that man capable of, who, in the name of God, makes war against his country? . . . Above all it was my intention to show the horrid schemes which villainy can invent, and fanaticism put in practice."

This criticism of religion, especially Christianity, never abated. Many years later, he expressed an admiration for Muhammad in contrast to Jesus: "Mahomet had the courage of Alexander . . . your Jesus sweated blood and water as soon as he was condemned by his judges."

Such attitudes obviously didn't go down well with some leaders, religious or secular. In an effort to be free of such interference, he settled in Ferney on the Swiss-French border. Here he wrote *Candide* and spent much of the rest of his life. He also established a successful watchmaking business and befriended Benjamin Franklin by correspondence. He finally returned to Paris in February 1778 to see the production of one of his plays, became a Freemason at Franklin's request in April, and died a month later—there was no connection between these two events, so no conspiracy theories, please. Stories of his last days differ; his enemies said that he was reconciled with the Catholic Church and received Last Rites, while his supporters denied that any such thing had happened. He was denied a Christian burial in any case, but in 1791, the National Assembly of France had his remains interred in the Panthéon in Paris, regarding him as a forerunner to the French Revolution.

Carlo Goldoni (1707–1793)
The last laugh?

Goldoni was an Italian playwright who specialized in comedies. Some credit him with nothing less than the renewal of Italian comedy in the eighteenth century—he altered and improved the Commedia dell'Arte, using Moilère as a model. He did away with the traditional masks worn by the stock characters, allowing for greater emotional and comic expression. He is perhaps best known for *The Servant of Two Masters*, which, as the title suggests, follows the adventures of the always-hungry Truffaldino (a variant of Harlequin) in trying to serve two different employers at once, without the other knowing. The highlight of the play comes when both are staying at the same inn and Truffaldino dashes back and forth between them to provide his services, trying to make sure that each never learns of the other. It is a masterpiece of physical comedy, everything that the Commedia excels at, featuring high-energy running about the stage, jumping and acrobatics, throwing food and other objects, and desperately trying to avoid detection by the opposite master.

While Goldoni was a man with a funny reputation in front of crowds, his personal life was often less humorous. From a young age, he had been attracted to drama, though in his youth, he wrote a libelous poem about some of the local nobility, and/or visited a brothel with friends, which caused him to be expelled from Ghislieri College in Pavia in northern Italy. So he went on to study law instead. Still, his first love was the theater, and he ultimately wrote a huge number of plays. Not all of his countrymen were thrilled with his changes to the structure of their beloved Italian comedy, however. His first effort had been a tragedy, *Amalasunta*, which he submitted to an opera director. When told that it did not properly take into account the needs of the performers, Goldoni thanked him, took the manuscript home, burned it, ate a hearty meal, and slept a good sleep.

Maybe it was because of this failure that he decided that comedy was more his thing. Regardless of his chosen genre, he was always very self-critical. Even when one of his plays was successful, he would tell himself, "Good, but not yet Molière." Now that's a phrase that needs to be revived in modern theater!

In 1757, he was embroiled in a bitter feud in Venice with Carlo Gozzi, a playwright who favored the older Italian styles and deeply resented Goldoni's Frenchified updates. The rivalry became bitter, but Gozzi gained the upper hand, with audiences preferring his approach over Goldoni's, at least at that time. Goldoni was so disgusted that he left Venice and Italy forever, settling in Paris in 1761, ironically being put in charge of Italian theater, but now writing his plays in French. He was given a generous pension by the king, and everything seemed set.

Oh, except that little hiccup known as the French Revolution. The burgeoning revolutionary government was suspicious of everything and everyone tied to the Old Regime, and Goldoni was no exception. He was deprived of his income by the Convention in 1789, and he struggled terribly afterward, dying in poverty in 1793. To show that they weren't heartless monsters, however, the government voted to restore his pension . . . the day after he died.

Pierre Beaumarchais (1732–1799)

Multitalented wife murderer?

Pierre-Augustin Caron de Beaumarchais was a remarkable polymath. At various stages in his life, he was: a playwright and writer, musician, watchmaker, inventor, spy, diplomat, and supporter of revolutions (both the French and the American), among other things. As far as drama is concerned, he is most remembered for his Figaro plays: *Le Barbier de Séville*, *Le Mariage de Figaro*, and *La Mère coupable* ("The Guily Mother"). Mozart, of course, set *The Marriage of Figaro* to music as a splendid opera, and Rossini's operatic version of the *Barber of Seville* is unsurpassed.

Beaumarchais rose to prominence in King Louis XV's court as a music teacher (harp for Louis's daughters), and later worked in espio-

Attis, looking remarkably calm in the face of horrid castration and death. (Wikimedia Commons.)

A bust of Aeschylus, showing him sometime before his head became a makeshift mortar to a bird's pestle. (Wikimedia Commons.)

Roman actors, preparing to get up to all sorts of debauched things by the look of it.
(Wikimedia Commons.)

Nineteenth-century depiction of a medieval mystery play from fifteenth-century Flanders, with some folks looking rather distracted and bored.
(Wikimedia Commons.)

Wild men accidentally catching fire in the *Bal des Ardents* ("Ball of
the Burning Men"). One finds relief in a vat of wine.
(Image courtesy of the British Library.)

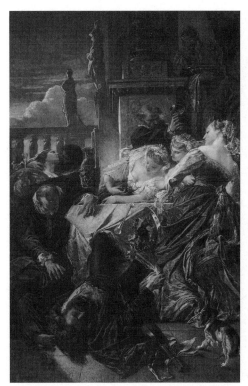

The scandalous Pietro Aretino laughs
himself to death, in a painting by
Anselm Feuerbach (1829–1880).
(Wikimedia Commons.)

A period sketch of the Swan Theatre in 1596, giving important insights into Elizabethan theater designs. (Wikimedia Commons.)

Ben Jonson, the gifted English playwright with some anger issues. (Image courtesy of the British Library.)

The title page of *The Roaring Girle*, a play about the scandalous life of the cross-dressing Moll Cutpurse; her actual life was even more interesting. (Archive.org.)

The diabolical pact of Urbain Grandier. The demons' signatures (Satan, Leviathan, Astaroth, and others) look like heavy metal band logos. (Wikimedia Commons.)

JEAN BAPTISTE,
Poquelin de Moliere

Molière, the French genius who angered many but wrote the best comedies of his age.
(Image courtesy of the Rijksmuseum, Amsterdam.)

Moll Davis, an early English actress who may have had some continence issues in her quest for royal patronage.
(Image courtesy of the National Library of Portugal, Lisbon.)

Madame Davis

The Golden Rump of King George II (as a satyr) in all its glory;
rumors of said play led to a crackdown on English theater.
(Image courtesy of the Wellcome Library, London.)

Goldoni, famous for reinventing the
Commedia dell'Arte and getting
into feuds.
(Image courtesy of the Österreichische
Nationalbibliothek in Vienna.)

Voltaire, the controversial genius who had more than a few unpleasant things to say about religion, politics, and society.
(Image courtesy of the Rijksmuseum.)

Alexander Pushkin, who couldn't stomach his final duel.
(Wikimedia Commons.)

The title page of *The Vampire*, but said vampire looks less like a creature of the night and more like a kilted hipster. (Image courtesy of the HathiTrust digital library.)

Alfred Jarry, unofficial pioneer of the Theater of the Absurd, whose own life often bordered on absurdity. (Wikimedia Commons.)

Tennessee Williams, who got a bit bottled up at the end. (Library of Congress, Washington, DC / Wikimedia Commons.)

Camus, who didn't see the forest for the trees. (Library of Congress.)

Titus Andronicus prepares to lose a hand, and all for nothing. (Wikimedia Commons.)

Sir Francis Bacon, one of many that some claim secretly wrote Shakespeare's plays; take a number and get in line, pal. (Image courtesy of the Wellcome Library.)

Pantalone from the Commedia dell'Arte, in the early seventeenth century, looking grotesque and greedy.
(Image courtesy of the Rijksmuseum.)

An eighteenth-century Punch and Judy show. Violent puppet shenanigans were a spin-off from the Commedia, and not especially child-friendly.
(Image courtesy of the Wellcome Library.)

The horrific Bluebeard prepares to kill his bride. His onstage death by the hand of a murdered wife's corpse thrilled nineteenth-century audiences.
(Image courtesy of the Rijksmuseum.)

One of the endless horrors of the Grand Guignol: "The man who killed death."
(Wikimedia Commons.)

The three witches, in thunder, lightning, and rain. Is "the Scottish Play" cursed? (Image courtesy of Michael John Goodman, The Victorian Illustrated Shakespeare Archive.)

A ghost light, kept on to illuminate the way for restless spirits and wayward janitors. (Wikimedia Commons.)

Joseph Grimaldi the mime, whose disembodied clown head is said to float about, haunting the Drury Lane Theatre in London . . . Sweet dreams! (Wikimedia Commons.)

Olive Thomas, who charmed audiences and died tragically, but now playfully haunts the New Amsterdam Theatre in New York. (Wikimedia Commons.)

Acclaimed actor David Garrick, posing with bust of Shakespeare; no bewigged dogs in sight. (Image courtesy of the Rijksmuseum.)

THE ASSASSINATION OF PRESIDENT LINCOLN.
AT FORD'S THEATRE WASHINGTON, D.C. APRIL 14TH 1865.

John Wilkes Booth (with strangely short limbs) assassinates Abraham Lincoln. Nearly a century later, one gentleman recounted seeing it all happen. (Wikimedia Commons.)

nage; he was involved in the smuggling of arms and supplies to the Americans during the revolution, financed by the French and Spanish governments, who were only too eager to stick it to the British. So important was this work that the United States might not exist without his help. He was also valued as an inventor, having apprenticed with his father, a watchmaker, and devised new ways to make timepieces into reliable instruments, rather than expensive fashion accessories.

A ten-month visit to Spain in 1764 would inspire his dramatic works and a lifelong love for the country. He hoped to become consul to Spain, but he was rejected for this post. He began to devise ways of writing about the country, which culminated in his entertaining but controversial works about Figaro. He may actually have thought up the title character during his stay, and there are autobiographical qualities in these stories. In fact, if one looks at one name by which Beaumarchais was known, *fils Caron* ("son of Caron"), pronounced roughly as "fee Karoh," the origin of the name "Figaro," suddenly becomes obvious.

The first of the Figaro plays, *The Barber of Seville*, is a farce in the Commedia dell'Arte tradition. It tells of a certain Count Almaviva, who falls in love with a young woman named Rosine and tries to think up ways to woo her. He disguises himself as a poor student, Lindor, and schemes to get into her house, where she is being held against her will by Bartholo, to whom she is engaged against her will. Almaviva runs into a former servant, Figaro, now working as a barber, who helps him with his plan. They eventually succeed, and the happy couple wed at the play's end.

All of this would seem innocuous and even charming, but Beaumarchais laced his narratives with satire and commentary that were critical of the established order. Indeed, an earlier appearance by these two characters in the play *Le sacristain* ("The Sacristan") upset King Louis XVI and he would not allow it to be performed. Further, *The Marriage of Figaro* initially passed the censor in 1781, but the king was not pleased by the content and banned it. Marie Antoinette did not find it as offensive and asked her husband to relent, but he refused. The story of the play tells that, three years after the events in *The Barber of Seville*, Figaro is due to be married (hence the title), but the count whom he helped to win the love of

Rosine in the first play, being fickle, is already looking elsewhere, and takes a liking to Figaro's fiancée, Suzanne. Soon, he is hoping to enact an ancient *primae noctis* law and take Suzanne for himself on her wedding night.

Louis felt that the work stirred up bad feelings between the classes and was particularly upset by a scene in the fifth act, wherein Figaro castigates the count for believing that he is so superior simply because he was born into rank and privilege:

> Just because you are a great nobleman, you think you are a great genius—Nobility, fortune, rank, position! How proud they make a man feel! What have you done to deserve such advantages? Put yourself to the trouble of being born—nothing more. For the rest—a very ordinary man! Whereas I, lost among the obscure crowd, have had to deploy more knowledge, more calculation and skill merely to survive than has sufficed to rule all the provinces of Spain for a century!

In the years leading up to the French Revolution, these were obviously not the words that a nervous king wanted to hear. Beaumarchais made a number of corrections and deletions, and Louis finally permitted the play to be performed in 1784.

With the advent of the French Revolution, things heated up for Beaumarchais. He was at one point accused of being a loyalist to the Old Regime, so he took refuge in Germany. He was finally able to return to Paris in 1796 and lived out his life without further trouble.

One of the more interesting—and sinister—theories about Beaumarchais pertains to his personal life. He was married three times, and his first two wives died under mysterious circumstances. The first, Madeleine-Catherine Franque, died ten months after they were married, while the second, Geneviève-Madeleine Lévêque, passed away about two years into the marriage. His third wife, Marie-Thérèse de Willer-Mawlaz, was his lover for about twelve years before they tied the knot, so perhaps she passed the test; she lived until 1816.

So what happened? Well, rumors circulated, then and now, that Beaumarchais poisoned his first two wives to inherit their wealth. He had lifted the title "de Beaumarchais" from his first wife's equally dead husband, which is a bit crass and opportunistic, and may have led some to suspect that he was ambitious enough to have planned their deaths. Both wives came from prosperous families, and Beaumarchais certainly enjoyed the financial benefits of legally joining with them, but was he cold-blooded enough to kill them merely for their money and titles? It would have been a terrible risk, but if so, he got away with it and prospered despite the many other dangers of the time. No charges were ever brought against him, so if he was guilty, he took his secrets with him to the grave.

The obnoxious Licensing Act of 1737

The butt of many jokes

We've seen that Collier and his cronies were none too happy about the lewdness and permissive behaviors that pervaded the Restoration stage. While the particularly bawdy comedies that held sway for three decades had begun to wane by 1700, other subversive topics did not, including social and political satire, even when critical of the government. And this was a bigger concern. Despite the fuming of offended theologians, the greater threat came in the form of support for restoring the Stuarts to the throne. You may recall that James II, the last Stuart king, was deposed, and while he was a Catholic, many still felt that he was the divinely ordained monarch.

In Scotland especially, there was support for bringing back the line of Scottish kings to rule, which tied in nicely with ideas about Scottish nationalism and pride. These sentiments were finding their way onto London stages and potentially filling people's heads with dangerous ideas.

Also, a lot of playwrights just enjoyed tweaking the noses of politicians, who were just as prone to corruption, laziness, and incompetence then as now. Henry Fielding (1707–1754) gleefully wrote plays that satirized the establishment, and his works are sometimes credited with bringing about the Licensing Act, though it was also said that a satirical play called *The Golden Rump* was the real cause. It turns out that both King George II (1683–1760) and his prime minister, Sir Robert Walpole, first Earl of Orford (1676–1745), had, shall we say, generous builds and a lack of height. Both were very wealthy and lived in a time when such well-off folks were expected to show off their wealth by eating copious amounts of expensive food and putting on weight. One unfortunate side effect of this expectation was that they left themselves open to ridicule about their shapes, and this mockery could be vicious and cruel. King George in particular was said to possess a large posterior and was suffering from hemorrhoids, which apparently was hilariously funny to his eighteenth-century enemies and those in the political opposition. They had no qualms at all about using physical problems to get a cheap laugh.

The scandalous play was said to be based on *A Vision of the Golden Rump*, a satirical allegory published in the political journal *Common Sense* (an opposition periodical), wherein the narrator has a vision of attending "The Festival of the Golden Rump." An idol in the shape of a satyr representing George is attended by figures obviously meant to be Walpole and Queen Caroline; she holds a bladder with an attachment and pumps liquid gold into the idol's anus from time to time to ease its bowels. An explicit engraving of the scene was soon printed and circulated. Rumors began to spread that a play based on the vision was being written (possibly by Fielding himself) and would soon be presented, with much mirth and merriment, no doubt.

Of course, this went over about as well as you might expect, and apparently for Walpole, it was the last straw. The result was the Licensing Act, which sought to censor political criticisms and force all plays to be approved by the government. Anyone found guilty of putting on an unapproved play would be punished as a common vagabond. The language of the Act is something of a tortuous tangle of legalese, but the intent is clear enough, if you can wade through the official-sounding word salad:

> Every person who shall, for hire, gain or reward, act, represent or perform, or cause to be acted, represented or performed any interlude, tragedy, comedy, opera, play, farce or other entertainment of the stage, or any part or parts therein, in case such person shall not have any legal settle-

ment in the place where the same shall be acted, represented, represented or performed without authority by virtue of letters patent from His Majesty, his heirs, successors or predecessors, or without licence from the Lord Chamberlain of His Majesty's household for the time being, shall be deemed to be a rogue and a vagabond within the intent and meaning of the said recited Act, and shall be liable and subject to all such penalties and punishments, and by such methods of conviction as are inflicted on or appointed by the said Act for the punishment of rogues and vagabonds who shall be found wandering, begging and misordering themselves, within the intent and meaning of the said recited Act.

In other words, any performer going about their profession without the express permission of the Lord Chamberlain (who acted for the Crown) would be deemed a rogue and a vagabond, and could be punished in the same way. In theory, this idea went back to Tudor times and even earlier, which is why traveling players had to work under the patronage of a noble or other wealthy person. In practice, the law often looked the other way or failed to enforce the statutes. With the growing Jacobite political threat, this lenience was no longer an option.

Almost immediately, some saw Walpole as the originator of the rumor of a *Golden Rump* play. It was never proven, but many accused him of making up the story as an excuse to ram the legislation through and silence his critics. No copy of the play has ever been found, either in print or in a handwritten scrawl. Maybe it has just been lost, but maybe Walpole invented it to get what he wanted. In any case, he had the support of the king and parliament.

What were the results of this new law? Walpole's new legislation basically said that anything the government disliked or considered inappropriate for whatever reason could be censored. Even worse, a tight control on public performances was enacted by the closure of every London theater except for two, those at Drury Lane and Covent Garden. This law had the effect of quashing a vibrant scene and removing the flourishing culture that allowed playhouses to compete by encouraging playwrights to pen as many new plays as they could. Essentially, it put the brakes on the entire theatrical movement and drove many authors and actors into other professions.

This paranoid censorship had a long shelf life, being upheld in the Theatres Act of 1843, which renewed the demand that the government approve all new plays. Incredibly, this law was only finally revoked by an updated Theatres Act in 1968.

Despite its heavy-handed tactics, the law only applied to new works from that year onward, so earlier plays could still be shown, but obviously not without some risk if they were controversial. There was a revival of Shakespeare's plays in the aftermath of the Act, probably because he was deemed to be "safe," so that was a small positive.

Further, there was something that Walpole, in his smug I've-shown-them arrogance, did not anticipate. Many playwrights began to embrace a new form of writing, the novel. With it, they could tell their subversive stories in a more private manner, and copies could circulate quietly all over the country, rather than having to be publicly declaimed in London to a limited audience. This allowed for the spread of new ideas in a much more efficient and dangerous manner, and authors could write anonymously to avoid persecution.

Also, the public began to realize that the plays given official sanction were probably going to be pretty dull, or even just plain bad. Soon there developed a distinction between "legitimate" and "illegitimate" theater, and you can guess which one was more interesting. New forms like pantomimes, puppet shows, popular operas, and music hall came about as a way of circumventing censorship and providing audiences with the entertainment they really wanted, even if polite society was supposed to turn up its collective nose at these lowbrow indulgences.

Philippe Fabre d'Églantine (1750–1794)

Getting ahead of himself

Fabre d'Églantine was an actor, playwright, and poet who was actively involved in politics during the tumultuous years leading up to the French

Revolution. An ardent enemy of the monarchy, he believed that the Old Regime's system was morally and ethically corrupt, and so was its drama. He held that new plays could break away from previous dramatic conventions and could help point the way to a more just society. His added surname "d'Églantine" ("wild rose") came from his claim that he had been awarded a silver or golden rose in a literary competition, but he may have just made this up to enhance his status.

He settled with his wife in Paris in the later 1780s, just as things were getting a bit hot and tense. His first few plays failed, but he produced *Philinte, ou La suite du Misanthrope* ("Philinte, or the Continuation of the Misanthrope") as a sequel to Molière's *Le Misanthrope*, but with a decidedly more political slant that favored republican ideas, written in his belief that the messages of such works could help remake society by spreading new ideas far and wide.

His zeal for change brought him favor from the revolutionary government. He sat in the new National Convention (the assembly created to form a new republic from the ashes of the deposed monarchy) and voted for the execution of King Louis XVI. This brought him into conflict with the Girondins, revolutionaries who felt that the whole thing had started with good intentions but was spiraling out of control; they were right. Their concerns ended up getting them guillotined and France saw the beginning of the Reign of Terror. Meanwhile, d'Églantine helped with the design of the new French Republican Calendar, which was intended to replace the religiously oriented Gregorian calendar, and proposed ten-day weeks and a year based on agricultural cycles and terminology.

During this dangerous time, d'Églantine got caught up in his own intrigues. In early 1794, he was accused of being involved in fraud with the French East India Company (a commercial venture set up in 1664 to compete with similar businesses from the English and Dutch). He was part of a group in the Convention that had issued a decree to drive up the company's stock price. Then, the company was forced to liquidate, a handy bit of insider trading. Evidence was uncovered that this group had falsified the liquidation decree and then blackmailed the directors so that money from the sale went back to the conspirators, including, presumably, d'Églantine. He and several others were accused of fraud.

D'Églantine maintained his innocence, but in the rampantly paranoid world of the revolutionaries, it didn't really matter. He was sentenced to die by the guillotine and was executed on April 5, 1794. It was said that as he was taken to meet his fate, he passed out handwritten copies of some of his poems to the people gathered to watch another of the endless gruesome spectacles of the time.

As he waited to die, he lamented his unjust fate. One of his accused coconspirators, Georges Danton, replied, "Des vers. . . . Avant huit jours, tu en feras plus que tu n'en voudras!" which means, "Within a week, you will make more of them than you want to!" It was a grim pun; "vers" can mean either "verses" or "worms."

7

The Nineteenth Century

This bold new century would see a strong reaction to the rationalism of the Enlightenment and the burgeoning Industrial Revolution, and yet also witness the ushering in of undreamed-of technologies that would completely transform the Western world by the century's end. A key artistic movement of the first half of the 1800s was Romanticism, which, as the name implies, was far less concerned about in-one's-head reason and much more devoted to deeply felt emotions, the individual's wishes and dreams, and the natural world. And whereas Enlightenment philosophy had looked back to the ancient Greeks and Romans as models for the perfect society (hence all of those neo-Classical buildings from the later eighteenth century), the Romantics found some of their main inspiration in medieval imagery: Celtic and Arthurian myth, neo-Gothic architecture, Robin Hood's tales, stories of magic and curses, and all of the decidedly-non-rational subjects that such legends contained.

The Romantic Movement wasn't confined to any one European country. It featured a set of beliefs with which writers, painters, and composers could express themselves fully, regardless of their national origin. The image of the young tortured artist of whatever type laboring away in squalid conditions by a dim candle, as alcohol and wasting sickness take their toll, is a popular take on the Romantic life, and honestly, it's not all that inaccurate. These guys and gals were living the rock-n-roll lifestyle long before there was such a thing, and stories of their rises and falls are legendary. Alcohol, drugs, scandals, social diseases, and early deaths were all part and parcel of the Romantic life, at least for its younger and more daring devotees.

The Gothic novel, which appeared in the mid-eighteenth century, was a perfect genre for writers to express themselves in, and figures such as Mary Shelley, Mary's husband Percy, and Lord Byron took to it with relish; Mary, of course, gave the world a classic character in Frankenstein's monster. Dramatists were also only too happy to draw from this Romantic well of inspiration, creating new types of works that challenged perceptions. An entire genre of vampire plays arose (as if from the dead?) to great popularity as the century progressed; the vampire was a perfect figure for horror, romance, and tragedy long before Bram Stoker gave the world his memorable Count Dracula in 1897.

Theater in general prospered and newer forms, like vaudeville and satirical puppet shows, flourished alongside Shakespeare and the "higher" arts of the more respectable theaters. However, trouble still brewed. Major riots erupted over theatrical disputes. Some actors gained fortune and fame, while others fell from grace horribly. Plays became more daring in what they chose to depict. This chapter will look at some of these theatrical goodies and show that despite becoming more "modern," the Western world still retained many of the terrors of its past.

August von Kotzebue (1761–1819)

Taking a stab at it

Born in Weimar, August von Kotzebue was a controversial German dramatist. He divided his time between Germany and Russia, not always willingly; in fact, the man did a crazy amount of traveling. Among his achievements were collaborations with Beethoven, who composed music for his plays *The Ruins of Athens* and *King Stephen*. Von Kotzebue wrote more than two hundred plays, including the scandalous *Doctor Bahrdt with the Iron Brow*, which was a harsh ad hominem attack on various thinkers and journals of the later Enlightenment. The police investigated and he denied writing it, but the suspicion ultimately alienated those friends that he had originally sought to defend.

Training as a lawyer, he obtained legal positions in Russia and then Estonia, before moving on to Paris, back to Germany, then back to Estonia, and finally to Vienna, where he worked as dramatist to the court's theater. But he didn't remain there long, and soon he returned to Weimar, where he had a falling out with fellow writer Goethe—von Kotzebue was not a big fan of the burgeoning Romantic movement in literature. So he decided to return once again to St. Petersburg, but on the journey, he was arrested on suspicion of supporting the French Revolution and shipped off to Siberia. This might have been the end, but it turns out that one of his comedies was flattering and appealed to Tsar Paul I of Russia, who then released him and presented him with an estate back in the Baltics; he was also given the directorship of the theater in St. Petersburg. At last, something permanent.

Um, no, not really. Paul was assassinated in 1801, so von Kotzebue felt compelled to return to Germany, this time settling in Berlin. That was all well and good until 1806, when Napoleon won a victory at the Battle of Jena–Auerstedt and gained control of Prussia. So, once again, von Kotzebue fled to Russia and Estonia and stayed put, at least for a while. There, he freely and safely wrote satires about Napoleon.

In 1816, he was sent back to Germany as consul general for Russia and found himself again in Weimar. Over the next couple of years, he made enemies of the German nationalists (those who wanted a united German state) when he denounced their demands for free and more open expression in the press and universities. Many saw him as a spy for Russia, though this was probably not true. In March 1819, one such nationalist, Karl Ludwig Sand, went to von Kotzebue's house and, meeting him at the door, produced a dagger and stabbed him several times in the chest. However, von Kotzebue's young son witnessed this and began to cry, whereupon Sand was overcome with guilt and stabbed himself, staggering away from the crime scene. His attempt at suicide failed, and he was nursed back to health, conveniently in time for his execution by beheading.

As a result of von Kotzebue's murder (and other civil unrest), the governing body issued the Carlsbad Decrees, which cracked down on nationalist sympathies and radical student organizations, and imposed strict censorship of new and dangerous ideas, particularly in the press, probably not what von Kotzebue would have wanted, but there you have it.

Heinrich von Kleist (1777–1811)

Blown away

Heinrich von Kleist is remembered these days as one of the great early Romantic German dramatists and writers, but he himself felt that he lived in the shadow of Goethe and other contemporaries and so never was able to achieve all that he wanted. Still, poets in the Romantic, Nationalist, and Existentialist schools drew inspiration from him and his internal conflicts. Born into a minor noble family, he served in the military for seven years, but resigned in 1799, feeling that he had wasted precious time. He attempted proper university education, but his studies of the philosophy of Kant (some of the most difficult and dense words ever put to paper) convinced him that reason was useless—many modern students of Kant would probably readily agree!

He resolved to wander Europe and devote himself to emotions like a true Romantic, though his work didn't focus on the usual longings for nature. His first tragedy, *The Schroffenstein Family*, explored the human mind's inability to comprehend truth by itself, through the story of two rival families and the star-crossed lovers from each of them, as in *Romeo and Juliet*. In Paris, he attempted another tragedy, *Robert Guiskard* (about the life of an eleventh-century Norman knight), but he was so dissatisfied with it that he burned the manuscript. The French didn't take to him, so he set out for Prussia, where he took a post in civil service in Königsberg. He didn't see it through and left for Dresden but was arrested by French forces and imprisoned for six months as a spy at the modern border between France and Switzerland. Yes, he was living the tragic Romantic lifestyle already, but it was only going to get worse.

Throughout it all, he was rather obsessed with his *Lebensplan*, or "life plan," which he had developed after leaving the army in 1799. This was a way of planning out how his life would unfold, so as to give a greater sense of security. It involved studying philosophy, theology, and mathematics in the university city of Göttingen; the problem was, little things like getting arrested and imprisoned tended to mess with that. He spent time in Dresden and Berlin, working on poetry and plays that explored realistic human emotional conflicts and fallibilities. His own life would soon encounter those same conflicts.

He became emotionally entangled with a young woman, Henriette Vogel, who was gifted with a fine mind and musical talent, but who was dying—yes, a romantic tragedy was brewing. Seeing her impending death and his own perceived failures, he agreed to a murder-suicide pact with her. On November 21, 1811, on the banks of a small lake outside of Berlin, he shot her and then himself. This seemed the only possible end to him, and in his last letter to his sister he wrote of meeting death with "inexpressible serenity." Because of the suicidal nature of their deaths, they were denied burial in consecrated ground and were instead buried at the site where they died. As you might expect, this little area soon became a place of Romantic pilgrimage. The gravesite fell into some disrepair over the next several decades, which probably only added to its reputation.

Today, von Kleist is regarded as one of the finest German writers of his era, at last receiving the acclaim that he felt was denied him during life. The wandering writer who feels unappreciated for his gifts and cannot accept the world, dying by his own hand with his beloved on the shores of a lake . . . It's almost too stereotyped to be true, but it all happened!

Alexander Griboyedov (1795–1829)

Getting ahead of himself II

Griboyedov's death qualifies as one of the more grisly among those of his fellow theatrical colleagues, akin to something out of a war movie or a horror story, or some combination of both. Born in Moscow, he supported himself by working for the civil service; in his free time, he wrote plays, poetry, and some music. His plays were entertaining if unmemorable, except for one, *Woe from Wit*, a satire of post-Napoleonic Moscow that portrayed stereotypes to a degree a little bit too uncomfortable for the censors, who made significant cuts before they allowed it to be printed. However, unofficial copies circulated, as such things are wont to do, so the Russian people did get to read what he intended, if not actually see it acted onstage. It is now considered a classic of Russian literature.

His work in diplomacy ultimately resulted in him being sent to Tehran as an ambassador in the aftermath of the Russo-Persian War (1826–1828). This conflict had ended with Persia defeated and forced to sign the humiliating Treaty of Turkmenchay, in which Persia agreed to cede control of several northern territories to Russia, along with various other concessions. Needless to say, Russians were not popular with Persians at this time, and it was dangerous for diplomats to even be in the country.

Indeed, not long after his arrival, an incident occurred that was to have tragic consequences. An Armenian eunuch escaped from the harem of the shah, as did two Armenian women from the harem of the shah's son-in-law; they sought refuge in the Russian mission. The furious shah wanted them returned, but Griboyedov refused.

This defiance caused an uprising among angry locals, and egged on by their local religious leaders, they stormed the building. The Cossacks that were assigned to protect the embassy did their best to hold back the mob, but they could only do it for so long. Eventually, Griboyedov and his assistants were caught out when the attackers broke through a ceiling and descended on them. Griboyedov was shot and killed and his body was thrown from the window to the masses below. It is said that the corpse was decapitated and that the head was put on display in the stall of a local food vendor. The rest of the uniformed body was paraded through the streets in celebration before being dumped on a garbage heap a few days later. It was eventually identified and taken back to Tbilisi in Georgia for burial.

The Persians claimed that there was more to the story, saying that Griboyedov and his cronies had insulted the locals and kidnapped some women who had converted to Islam, taking them against their will back to the embassy. This, they claimed, caused the riot. Actually, there is some evidence that British spies incited the mob, because they wanted to limit Russian influence in the area and possibly start another conflict. Poor Griboyedov was caught up in a situation that he had no part in making.

Meanwhile, the shah, realizing that this incident had potentially catastrophic consequences, sent his grandson to live in Moscow as a kind of goodwill hostage, and he offered the Shah Diamond, a priceless eighty-eight-carat diamond, as a gift to the Russian Tsar Nicholas I. It can still be seen in the collection known as the Kremlin Diamond Fund.

Alexander Pushkin (1799–1837)

He couldn't stomach it

Pushkin is often thought of as the father of modern Russian literature. A Romantic poet, playwright, and novelist, he left a number of excellent works in his short life. He was born into noble stock—his great-grandfather on his mother's side was the African Abram Gannibal, who was taken from Cameroon to Constantinople as a slave for the Ottoman sultan, but who shortly after ended up the Russian court, being presented to Peter the Great; the two became friends and Gannibal prospered.

As a young man, Pushkin was attracted to social reform and radical causes, despite his upper-class status. This obviously didn't sit too well with the ruling establishment, and in the spring of 1820, he was exiled to southern Russia, under the pretense of an "administrative transfer" from his work. He spent time in the Crimea and the Caucasus, then finally settled in Moldavia. During this time, he became a Freemason and also joined the Filiki Eteria, a secret society dedicated to the ousting of the Ottomans in Greece and to establishing an independent Greek republic.

He came into conflict with the Russian government again, which then confined him to his mother's estate in northwestern Russia in 1824.

The following year, he petitioned Tsar Nicholas I for release, and this request was granted, but soon after, his work was associated with the Decembrists revolt—wherein a group of officers protested Nicholas taking the throne. Pushkin's work was popular with them, so he was guilty by association. The uprising was suppressed, its leaders executed or exiled, and back to his mother's estate Pushkin went.

During this confinement, he wrote his most famous play, *Boris Godunov*, about the life of the tsar of that name (1551–1605). However, given Pushkin's trouble with the authorities, the censor would not permit it to be shown; the excuse given was that the play included depictions of the Orthodox Patriarch and monks, and it was forbidden to portray them onstage. The work was originally intended as a closet drama—a type of play that was not staged but rather read aloud by one person, or perhaps a small group, in private. In any case, the censorship was not lifted until 1866, and a full public performance was only staged in Saint Petersburg in 1870, based on an altered edition. Amazingly, the uncensored version was only first performed in 2007 at Princeton University in an English translation.

Despite these difficulties, Pushkin's works came to be viewed favorably and he was a great inspiration to the generation of Russian composers who followed him, such as Glinka, Tchaikovsky, and Mussorgsky, all of whom set his works to music as operas. Another of Pushkin's dramas, *Mozart and Salieri*, perpetuated the false story that Salieri murdered his younger rival out of jealously, thus keeping alive an urban legend that found its way into the twentieth century in Peter Shaffer's play, *Amadeus,* and its film version.

By the 1830s, he was allowed to travel freely again and had married a much younger woman, Natalya Goncharova, who was greatly admired by the court and the tsar himself. In fact, Pushkin suspected that he was permitted some of his freedoms simply because the tsar desired her company at court. He grew increasingly suspicious of her dealings and in 1837, accused her brother-in-law Georges d'Anthès of having an affair with her. They settled the dispute by a duel, in which d'Anthès got the first shot off and wounded Pushkin in the stomach, fatally, it turns out.

Pushkin managed a return shot that only grazed his opponent's arm. Pushkin pardoned his foe on his death bed and died two days later, while d'Anthès was eventually exiled from Russia, since dueling was illegal.

Fearful of a political demonstration and violence at Pushkin's funeral, the tsar had it moved from Saint Isaac's Cathedral in St. Petersburg to a much smaller church and restricted attendance to family, close friends, and court members. The body was then secreted away at midnight and buried at his mother's estate, a quiet ending for a would-be revolutionary.

The Old Price riots (1809)

Sometimes bad things happen for mundane reasons. When the Theatre Royal at Covent Garden burned down on September 20, 1808, it was a great tragedy, as the props, costumes, and play scripts were lost, along with original music by composers such as George Frideric Handel and Thomas Arne. Worse, at least twenty-two people were killed when the roof crashed down on them. The total damage was estimated at about £250,000, an absolutely enormous sum for the time. The fire was believed to be accidental, probably caused by some smoldering fabric set off by a spark from a theatrical gun that was not properly extinguished after a performance.

Work on a new theater began soon after, and it was completed and set to reopen almost exactly one year later, on September 18, 1809. There was a problem, though. The costs for building the replacement were so high that management was forced to raise prices, an age-old problem that brings age-old protests. Price hikes were introduced across the board, and some seats that had previously been open to the public were converted into private boxes for rent at expensive annual sums, which exposed some of the class divides that were already causing dissention in other areas of London life.

This gentrification of their entertainment did not sit well with the public, and on opening night, they were at the venue and mad as hell. While the manager, John Philip Kemble, attempted to give a rousing

speech from the stage about the restoration of the theater, filled with patriotic pride, the crowd grew increasingly restless. The *Times* reported:
"We believe not a single word . . . was heard by the most acute listener
in the house: hisses, groans, yells, screeches, barks, coughs, shouts, cries
of 'Off! lower the prices! six shillings! pickpockets! imposition! Cutpurse!'" It may or may not be significant that the intended play for
opening night was *Macbeth*, which has a long history of bad luck attached to it (see the chapter on superstitions in act II). Was this mishap
yet another example of "the Scottish Play" causing disruption?

In any case, thus began the Old Price riots, which, despite their name,
didn't do all that much rioting and caused little damage or injury. They
were intended as a form of loud civil disobedience to force the manager to
revert to the, well, old prices. Kemble mishandled some things in trying to
deal with the disorder, such as when he hired professional boxers Daniel
Mendoza and Samuel Elias to act as bouncers for some of the louder and
more unruly patrons. This, as you can imagine, didn't go over well, and the
disruptions escalated. These riots would carry on for the next two months,
and Kemble was ultimately forced to apologize and lower prices back to
what they had been previously—score one for the people! In the future,
theaters were more careful about how they raised prices in view of this
boisterous revolt, being fearful of another uprising.

Vampires onstage: a nineteenth-century obsession

Blood-sucking freaks

For modern readers, the word "vampire" conjures up Dracula, whether
in Bram Stoker's novel or the character's countless screen appearances.
Or perhaps it's the more recent vampire fandoms, from Lestat to *Buffy* to
Twilight. Somehow the concept of a blood-drinking monster (often
tragic and all too human) never loses its appeal, and new works about
these immortal creatures appear every year.

In the nineteenth century, there was a craze for such beings on the
theater stage, where they made the jump from literature. Beginning in
France in 1820, the vampire play soon found its way to London and

eventually to America, with at least thirty-five productions appearing over the course of the century. They originated as gothic dramas with themes of romanticism and the triumph of good over evil, but eventually, they reveled in implied perversions, moral ambiguities, violence, and demonic overtones. Playing on fears associated with death and sexuality, the vampire's actions allowed audiences to revel in the forbidden; the drinking of blood had erotic and religious overtones, and could even be an uncomfortable mixture of the two.

One of the most important vampires before Dracula was Lord Ruthven. He had many of the familiar vampire characteristics: he was a reanimated dead body (or sometimes a fallen angel), though a handsome and appealing one, he was wealthy, he wandered the world, and he was always looking for new victims—specifically, young women—desiring their blood. The first play to feature him was *Le Vampire*, a three-act melodrama that debuted in Paris in 1820. The setting of the play is, unusually, the Inner Hebrides islands off the coast of Scotland. In the story, Ruthven is a somewhat tragic figure, who genuinely loves one of the female characters, but he is also a murderer who delights in killing and mutilating his victims. He is eventually destroyed, not with a wooden stake, but a humble pistol; several of our more familiar tropes were not yet present. The play was a huge hit; not only did the performances sell out, but so did the copies of the script, though the critics naturally hated it. One review lamented: "Ruthven tried to [drink the blood of] the young bride who flees before him. Is this a moral situation? The whole play indirectly represents God as a weak or odious being who abandons the world to the demons of hell."

The play's success spawned imitations, of course, with another critic noting: "There is not a theatre in Paris without its Vampire!" Some of these plays were serious, some were well-done, and some were awful. A few were comedic parodies. The idea of the vampire became so popular that plays started including the word in their titles to help bring in audiences, even when there were no vampires in the story!

An English adaptation of the play was inevitable, and by August 1820, *The Vampire, or the Bride of the Isles* opened in London, spawning its own imitations, operas, ballets, comedies, and other such works. It offered up more spectacle than its French counterpart, with elaborate sets and the striking scene of Ruthven being dispatched by a lightning bolt and disappearing into the earth (through a type of trap door onstage). Perhaps surprisingly, it was a critical as well as a commercial success. The vampire craze had bitten England (though not as severely as it had France) and would continue on and off for decades. Several of the plays were set in Scotland, which seemed to be a curious blend of familiar and exotic for audiences, though probably less so for English audiences than for French ones. Since those audiences tended to be made up of the lower classes who were not thoroughly educated in the ways of geography, even a relatively nearby country such as Scotland contained some air of the unfamiliar.

Over the next few decades, the English would incorporate elements of German Romantic and supernatural themes into their vampire plays, including Faustian pacts and demonology, which added a darker feel to many stories. There were plays with wonderful names like *Thalaba the Destroyer* (which used Orientalist images of the "mysterious" East, a departure from the slightly less mysterious Scotland), *The Vampire Bride, or the Tenant of the Tomb*, several called simply *The Vampire* (originality was apparently not prized), and *Giovanni the Vampire!!! Or, How Shall We Get Rid of Him?* (okay, this one was a satire, based loosely on the character of Don Giovanni). Other plays brought in werewolves and even Frankenstein's creature to create onstage monster mashes that prefigured the classic horror B-movie film crossovers.

The craze faded as the century wore on, and vampires began to appear more often in burlesque productions and comedies. These vampires were mainly harmless, mostly objects of laughter and fun, but there was still enough of an appetite for them that they never completely vanished. And so it seemed the vampire had been tamed. Little did people know that Bram Stoker would soon unleash the most terrifying vampire of all on an unsuspecting literary world, restoring these creatures of the night to their proper place in the horror genre.

Oscar Wilde (1854–1900)

About those curtains . . .

The incomparable Oscar Wilde cannot possibly be covered here in any way that does him justice. Playwright, poet, humorist, and writer, Wilde shocked the prudish sensibilities of the Victorian Age and paid the ultimate price for daring to do so. He was imprisoned for homosexuality, and the ordeal took a permanent toll on his health; he died only shortly after being released. He is known for his dark novel *The Picture of Dorian Gray*, a splendid gothic horror that exposes the undercurrent of vice and sin in society, when a beautiful youthful man makes a Faustian deal to remain young forever, while only his portrait ages. It prompted one newspaper to declare that the work was "heavy with the mephitic odours of moral and spiritual putrefaction." They just don't write reviews like they used to!

Wilde's plays were, perhaps surprisingly, quite popular, though sometimes there was a definite disconnect between what the public liked and what the censors allowed. For example, his *Salomé* was written in French and tells the story of the eponymous dancer in the title, who ultimately demands the head of Jokanaan (John the Baptist) on a silver platter. It was not permitted to show in London because the Licensing Act forbade the depiction of biblical characters onstage; it played in Paris in 1896.

His society comedies, such as *Lady Windermere's Fan*, enjoyed enormous popularity, and while on the surface they were amusing to polite society, there is still subtle criticism of the strict social rules that governed everyday affairs. His final comedy, *The Importance of Being Earnest*, was very well received and established him as a major literary force. A farce about adopting fake identities in order to escape from social obligations, it has similar themes to Wilde's early works, but the humor was enough to win over audiences and its opening night was a triumph.

That triumph was short-lived, however. Wilde had a powerful enemy, the Marquess of Queensberry, who was enraged that his son Lord Alfred Douglas was having an affair with Wilde. On the play's opening night, the marquess had planned to attend and throw rotten vegetables at the stage to cause trouble and disruption, but Wilde had been tipped off to this little plot and had him barred from entering the theater. Queensberry, not to be deterred, formally accused Wilde of homosexuality, which resulted in his arrest for libel. Wilde wished to press the charge in response, against the advice of his friends. Queensberry hired private detectives to dig up the dirt on Wilde and found what he needed to have the libel charge dismissed. Wilde was brought to trial and ultimately sentenced to two years of hard labor from 1895 to 1897. Afterward, he went into exile in France and died there of cerebral meningitis in 1900, the years in prison having worn him down. A humorist to the last, he is said in his final days to have had some choice words about his hotel room's decorations. Depending on whom you believe, he may have said, "Either these curtains go, or I do," or perhaps, "This wallpaper will be the death of me—one of us will have to go." He may actually have said the second of these quotes sometime earlier in his life; there are several variations, and no one knows which, if any, are true. In any case, his wonderful wit survived even in the face of denunciation and poverty.

His remains were transferred to Père Lachaise Cemetery in 1909, and soon after, his grave became a site of literary pilgrimage. In 2011, the tomb was cleaned of the hundreds of lipstick kisses left on it over the years, and a glass barrier was erected to prevent further damage. The barrier itself is now also covered in kisses and love-note graffiti. Wilde would probably be amused.

Alfred Jarry (1873–1907)

Absinthe, ether, at least two bottles of any vintage, and merdre

Jarry was a diminutive French writer who explored symbolism—the idea, also found in Impressionism, that an artistic subject conveyed symbolic, rather than direct, meaning—and proto-absurdism in his works. At less than five feet tall, he managed to make quite an impression. His works shocked even liberal Paris by pushing the boundaries and reveling in satirical views of society.

Born in Laval (west of Paris, near Brittany), he had an early taste for the absurd and grotesque. When he was fifteen, he and a classmate wrote a play mocking one of their teachers through a caricature named Père Heb, a bloated figure with three teeth who would later become the main character of his infamous play *Ubu Roi*.

Moving to Paris as a teenager, Jarry was eventually drafted into the army, but he was so short that his uniforms did not fit, and his appearance was so comical that he was excused from marching in drills and parades. He was eventually discharged for "health reasons," though this could just as easily have been due to his diminutive size. Afterward, he gave himself over to writing provocative works and imbibing large amounts of alcohol, as you do.

In December 1896, Jarry's most infamous play, *Ubu Roi* ("King Ubu"), premiered—and failed—at the Théâtre de l'Œuvre. It is an absurd drama that lifts various ideas and motifs from Shakespeare's plays, including *Hamlet*, *King Lear*, *Macbeth*, and *The Winter's Tale*, along with Sophocles's *Oedipus Rex*. Parisians had never seen anything like it. It tells the tale of the repulsive Ubu, a misshapen monster drawn from his earlier Père Heb. Ubu represents greed and stupidity, people who are not worthy of what they have, and those who do terrible things in the name of questionable ideals. He leads a revolution in Poland and succeeds in killing the king and the royal family. When the king's ghost demands vengeance, Ubu begins killing the people for their money. One of Ubu's servants escapes to Poland and convinces the Russian tsar to declare war on the tyrant. Ubu marches out to fight them, while his wife attempts to steal his money, but is stopped by Bougrelas, the crown prince who is now trying to lead a new revolt against Ubu. Ubu defeats the Russians, but is attacked by a random bear; um, okay. His wife then comes to him, pretending to be the Angel Gabriel; um, right. Bougrelas enters the scene, but Ubu defeats him by hitting him with the body of the bear; um, whatever. The Ubu and his wife flee to France. The end. Huh?

This kind of bizarre narrative was a precursor to the Theater of the Absurd, which used slang, vulgar words, and odd patterns of speech to explore existentialist and even nihilist subjects and characters who can see no purpose in life or in the situations they find themselves in. The play was meant as a satire and commentary on the dark side of society, inspired by a hapless teacher from Jarry's youth. Before the performance, Jarry spoke to the audience and said, "You are free to see in M. Ubu however many allusions you care to, or else a simple puppet—a school boy's caricature of one of his professors who personified for him all the ugliness in the world." This caveat didn't help matters, though. As the play opened, Ubu walked out onstage and addressed the crowd with his opening word, "Merdre!" ("shit" with an extra "r" added in). Well, *that* got the audience's attention! For the next fifteen minutes or so, the play could not continue, as there was so much commotion. Jeers, booing, cheering, and whistling filled the theater from those offended and those delighted. Eventually things settled down enough for the play to continue, but its absurdity and increasing outrages were proving to be too unsettling. A riot broke out at its conclusion and the play was subsequently banned from the stage.

Jarry responded by adapting it to a puppet theater and delving ever further into shocking, avant-garde works that mocked society and religion. He adopted some of Ubu's traits, including referring to himself in the royal "we." He moved into a small flat—the roof was so low that only he could fit in it without crouching—and began carrying a revolver when he went out. When one of his neighbors complained that the gun could kill her children, he replied that if that happened, "we should ourselves be happy to get new ones with you." Well, that's one way to build community spirit! Picasso, incidentally, acquired and wore Jarry's gun after his death; he also collected several of his manuscripts.

Beyond his writings, Jarry was entirely devoted to alcoholic drinks, referring to absinthe as the "green goddess" and to alcohol in general as a "sacred herb." He was said to have once painted his face green and ridden through Paris on his bicycle in honor of his love for absinthe. If he could not obtain alcohol, he drank ether, which was a popular alternative for some poor or destitute addicts. His friend Rachilde (the pen name of writer Marguerite Vallette-Eymery) wrote, maybe with some exaggeration:

> Jarry began the day by consuming two litres of white wine, then three absinthes between ten o'clock and midday, at lunch he washed down his fish, or his steak, with red or white wine alternating with further absinthes. In the afternoon, a few cups of coffee laced with brandy or other spirits whose names I've forgotten, then, with dinner—after, of course, more aperitifs—he would still be able to take at least two bottles of any vintage, good or bad. Now I never saw him really drunk.

Drunk or not, in the end, a combination of poverty, alcoholism, drug use, and tuberculosis did him in at the age of thirty-four, an almost perfect embodiment of the Romantic ideal for how a writer should exit this life.

8

The Modern Age

The term "modern" is always a bit perplexing and, honestly, not very helpful. In art and music, it has been used to describe works created after 1900 as a way of distinguishing them from the Romantic era, but obviously, this classification only works to a certain point. A painting or piece of music created in 1905 likely has more in common with the nineteenth century than it does with art or music created in 2005, unless the latter piece is deliberately retro. So it's not really all that useful to apply the "modern" label, but it has become a convenient way to categorize works, even if it's not particularly accurate these days.

After all, if something made in the first decade of the twentieth century is "modern," then what must the same thing be a hundred years later? Well, there is a category called "post-modern," which tries to define those works of art and literature that came "after" the modern era. The big problem with this naming strategy, of course, is that new definitions are always racing against time, and like all of us, they inevitably lose (yes, that's depressing). At what point does "post-modern" no longer apply because something even newer has replaced it? It starts getting a bit silly after a while. So, in the interest of cutting down on confusion and maybe even (regrettably) reducing the potential silliness a bit, we will refer to all dramatic creations and productions from the twentieth century as "modern" and be done with it.

Here are some examples of modern dramatic bizarreness that prove that our recent and technological innovations in no way hindered the gruesome and the strange from permeating the theatrical world. Odd deaths continued, stupid accidents happened, and if anything, drama got even weirder than ever before.

Pedro Muñoz Seca (1879–1936)

Laughing until the end

Muñoz Seca was a noted Spanish writer of comedies who enjoyed great success in his lifetime, but whose life ended in tragedy. He wrote about three hundred plays, both long and short, and was known for his cultivation of a new theatrical from, the *astracanada*. This genre made great use of puns and wordplay, slang and slapstick comedy, and his best-known example, *La venganza de Don Mendo* ("The Revenge of Don Mendo"), is a parody set during the Middle Ages about a knight who loses everything in a bet and is then betrayed by his lover. He assumes a new identity as a minstrel and seeks to restore himself.

Muñoz Seca was highly educated, having studied philosophy and law in Seville, and after relocating to Madrid at the beginning of the twentieth century, he taught Greek, Latin, and Hebrew and also worked as a lawyer and civil servant. Somehow, he found the time to turn out an astonishing number of comic plays over the next few decades, most of which were well received.

However, the real world all too often interferes with the best intentions of artists. Spain experienced considerable amounts of political turmoil in the 1920s and '30s, first being ruled by the inept dictator Miguel Primo de Rivera (with the king's support) and then going through the declaration of the Second Spanish Republic in 1931, during a time when the world was in the grips of the Depression. Civil unrest, strikes, and even assassinations became more common as the decade progressed, ultimately leading to the Spanish Civil War and the rise of Franco's fascist dictatorship.

Muñoz Seca's works became more political in the 1930s—he started writing plays that satirized the republic and its failings. His play, *La oca* ("The Goose"), for example, looked at the effects of antimonarchist laws and the seizure and redistribution of lands, which left peasants increasingly unhappy. Leftist papers denounced the play as "stupid." This provocative writing was not the best idea, and with the increased turmoil of the time, he ended up putting himself in danger. Various revolutionaries accused him of being sympathetic to the old monarchy, a serious offense. He and his wife were arrested in 1936, though she was later released. He was accused of sedition, or whatever trumped-up charge they could come up with to silence him. It was enough for him to be sentenced to death, and he was shot by a Republican Army firing squad in November 1936. Knowing he had no chance of escape or reprieve, he remained a humorist to the end. In his last words, he indulged in some black comedy, telling his captors that they could take his land, home, money, and his life, "but there is one thing that you cannot take from me—the fear that I have!"

John Barrymore (1882–1942)

An acid tongue, to say the least

Barrymore was an American actor whose talents were showcased onstage, in films, and on radio, though he preferred to think of himself as primarily as a stage actor, being called the greatest living tragedian for his performance as Hamlet. However, he left the theater in the 1920s to concentrate on silent and then talking films, weary of the endless repetition of live performance. A part of the legendary Barrymore acting family, he was the grandfather of actress Drew Barrymore.

Barrymore struggled with alcoholism throughout his life, and though this would be tragic in itself, he is listed here because of his remarkably sharp tongue and for the semi-urban legend about his final send-off (more on that below). Barrymore was highly opinionated about art, other people, and just about everything, it seems. A number of amusing stories about him have circulated over the years. He was already drinking fairly heavily in his twenties, and one account relates that he slept through the 1906 San Francisco earthquake after a night of considerable imbibing. The army apparently pressed him into service to help clean up the post-earthquake mess, to which his uncle quipped, "It took a calamity of nature to get him out of bed and the US army to make him go to work."

Fortunately for theater lovers, his work ethic was rather stronger when it came to his roles; he was quite hard on himself, actually. After his first performance as Hamlet, he sat in his dressing room feeling that he had failed. A sycophantic well-to-do fan came in to congratulate him, kissing his hand and saying, "O master! I enjoyed your performance so much!" To which Barrymore replied, "Not half so much as I am enjoying yours."

Despite his many years as a screen actor, he stubbornly refused to memorize lines for films, requiring stagehands to hold up cards with his parts written on them so he could see them and read them while he acted. Because he was John Barrymore, this was tolerated. Occasionally, directors and others would castigate him for this behavior, to which he would reply that his memory was full of beautiful words from *Hamlet*, *A Midsummer Night's Dream*, the sonnets, and other such works. He once added, "Do you expect me to clutter up all that with this horseshit?"

While performing in the play *Redemption* at the Plymouth Theater in New York in 1918, Barrymore was especially annoyed by the fact that several people in the front rows were coughing. During intermission, he sent someone out to buy a large fish, which he then concealed under his coat as the second act began. When the inevitable coughing once again commenced, he produced the fish, flung it at the offenders, and announced, "Chew on that, you walruses, while the rest of us get on with the play!"

He died in May 1942 of cirrhosis, complicated by kidney failure and pneumonia. Fellow actor Errol Flynn made the rather astonishing and grotesque claim that Barrymore's body was "borrowed" by film director Raoul Walsh and some others (under the pretense of taking it for Barrymore's disabled aunt to view) and was brought to his (Flynn's) home. Flynn wrote:

They got into the house and brought the corpse inside. They moved my favorite chair . . . so that I would see [it] as I entered. They sat Jack [Barrymore] in the chair, propping him up. I was drunk—sad drunk—when I reached home. . . . As I opened the door I pressed the button. The lights went on and my God—I stared into the face of Barrymore! His eyes were closed. He looked puffed, white, bloodless. They hadn't embalmed him let. I let out a delirious scream!

Flynn ran out of the house, where he was stopped by the very amused pranksters and informed that it was "only a gag." Those crazy Hollywood directors! Flynn said that he immediately sobered up but was so shaken that he couldn't sleep for the rest of the night. One of Barrymore's good friends denied this whole incident, saying that he was with the body all evening, but Flynn's seemingly sincere account and the general jerkish nature of the whole prank give it some credibility. Perhaps Barrymore left the world with one last dramatic performance?

Michel de Ghelderode (1898–1962)

A vision of the end

Michel de Ghelderode was a Belgian playwright whose works explored the avant-garde and reveled in the dark and grotesque. He was less interested in realism, preferring to portray the freakish onstage by use of puppets, mime, masks, and elaborate stage sets. He wrote some sixty plays and about a hundred stories, and his influences included the Commedia dell'Arte, puppet theaters, the bizarre paintings of Bosch and Breughel, and religious imagery.

In his play *The Bizarre Horseman*, for example, he includes a scene of a rider approaching some Breughel-like individuals, who mistake him for Death and strike up a cacophonous song of welcome. One of them proclaims, "Let's dance to Death!" while another declares, "I'll dance till I drop!" Such scenes recall the somewhat-grotesque depictions of musicians and dancers found in the works of those Renaissance masters.

A common theme in many of his works was the use of religious figures and biblical scenes without the beliefs that usually accompany them.
Such themes are often instead wrapped up with vulgarity in the form of
sexual, gluttonous, and scatological humor. The religious aspects of his
works came partially from the influence of his mother, Jeanne-Marie
Rans, who before giving birth to four children had been a candidate for
admission to holy orders and retained her faith throughout her life.

Ghelderode wanted to enrich his fantastical dramas with the concept of "total theater"—the idea that a production should appeal to the
senses in a grand way and enrich the emotions and the mind. A play
could include not only dialogue, but also music, art, sonorities in language, and sounds and lighting designed to induce an almost
hallucinatory sensation in viewers. He advocated for lavish and complex
theatrical special effects and many of his plays are set in a grotesque and
distorted medieval Flanders, which evokes the landscapes and twisted
figures of those Bosch and Breughel paintings. He wrote specifically for
a puppet theater in some instances (Les Marionnettes de la Renaissance
d'Occident), and many of his plays for human actors call for those performers to behave more like marionettes than human beings. They strike
static poses and make odd facial expressions, giving their performances
an unreal and unsettling quality.

Ghelderode suffered from poor health for most of his life. When he
was sixteen, he was afflicted with typhus and claimed that at one point,
he saw a mysterious lady by his bedside. She told him, "Not now, sixty-
three." He interpreted this to mean that he would recover (which he did)
and that he would live until the age of sixty-three. In fact, he died only
two days before his sixty-fourth birthday.

The Derby disaster at the London Coliseum (1905)
Stop horsing around

Sir Oswald Stoll (1866–1942) had a fantastic idea, or so he thought. He
was the manager of the newly opened London Coliseum, sometimes

called the Coliseum Theatre; in fact, he managed several of these popular theaters around Britain. Mere weeks after the Coliseum's opening on December 24, 1904, Stoll planned to stage a spectacle that would be a sure crowd-pleaser: producing a version of the Derby horse race, live onstage! With real horses and jockeys! King Edward VII loved horse racing, the public loved horse racing, and here it was being combined with an exciting theatrical production; what could possibly go wrong? Well, quite a bit, in fact.

The plan was to place said horses and riders onto a carousel-like revolving construction. This would allow the horses to be brought up to a full run (in the opposite direction) while essentially remaining in place on the stage, and would be a magnificent way to simulate the thrill of an actual race in a small, enclosed area. These kinds of crazy spectacles weren't all that unusual at the time, when every theater was trying to outdo every other one to bring in crowds. The use of live animals was also fairly common. Since there weren't a lot of health and safety regulations inconveniencing everyone's fun, the producers basically said, "Hell yeah, let's do it!"

And of course, it all went horribly wrong. At some point during the onstage race, one of the horses stumbled and was thrown into the orchestra pit. The jockey, Fred Dent, was killed, and several musicians were injured. The *Medical Press and Circular*, a weekly London journal, was not at all amused and objected to future performances:

> Real jockeys on real racers ride an imitation Derby on a rapidly revolving platform. It is needless to point out that the planting of a horse's foot on the non-revolving centre of the platform would lead to instantaneous somersaults. The fatal accident a few days ago resulted from some such mishap. The whole performance is so absolutely dangerous to life and limb that in our opinion it should be stopped at once. . . . Should one of the racers fall on the revolving platform, the deadly havoc that might instantly be wrought is terrible to contemplate. The fall of a leading horse would rake the field as if a volley of shrapnel were fired into the ranks of the racers. The management of the Coliseum,

having now had due warning, will have to be held responsible for any subsequent accident in this part of their performance.

Stoll managed to survive the incident with his career intact and learned his lesson about bigger not always being better; he eventually went into filmmaking, probably a safer option.

Ödön von Horváth (1901–1938)

Going out on a limb

An Austro-Hungarian playwright who fell afoul of the Nazis, von Horváth wrote a good number of novels and plays. He received literary prizes and much acclaim. His play *Tales from the Vienna Woods* (1930), a farcical attack on fascism, won him the prestigious Kleist Prize (a German literary award) in 1931. It told the story of a group of people in a town who remain complacent while fascist forces come to power. When the Nazis seized control, this story obviously didn't go over so well; his works were banned, and he feared for his safety. In 1933, he fled Germany for Vienna, where he continued to write plays, including the amusingly titled *Figaro Gets a Divorce* in 1937. After the annexation of Austria in 1938, he escaped to Paris, where he continued to write against Nazi aggression.

He was not safe for long, however, and it had nothing to do with political turmoil. Poor von Horváth was out on the Champs-Élysées near the Théâtre Marigny during a thunderstorm. He was visiting a friend to discuss the possibility of filming his play *Youth Without God*, a tale of the struggle of an individual against a totalitarian state. A branch fell from a nearby tree and struck him, delivering a killing blow. Coincidentally, he had told a friend only a short time before, "I am afraid of streets. Roads can be hostile to one, can destroy one. Streets scare me." His plays would not be revived in Germany until the 1960s, and an attempt to stage *Tales from the Vienna Woods* in Vienna shortly after the war incited a riot. Apparently, even after the fall of the Nazis, the subject matter was too sensitive and recent.

Von Horváth seems to have had an odd or humorous outlook on life. Once while he was hiking in Bavaria, he found the corpse of a man long dead. You would think this discovery would induce concern or outright panic, but not in our young man. Next to the body was a knapsack and inside was a never-sent postcard saying, "Having a wonderful time." When asked how he reacted, he answered, "I posted it."

Tennessee Williams (1911–1983)
All bottled up

Williams was a celebrated American author of plays, novels, screenplays, poetry, and other works. It was his plays that brought him the most recognition, earning him a Tony award and two Pulitzer Prizes (among other accolades) by the late 1950s. Among his most famous plays are *The Glass Menagerie* (1944), *A Streetcar Named Desire* (1947), and *Cat on a Hot Tin Roof* (1955), all of which were later made into films. Williams achieved fame and recognition, but his personal life was dogged by problems, controversies, and issues with addiction.

The son of an abusive and alcoholic father (whose temper led to his having a portion of one ear bit off in a fight over a poker game), Williams would eventually succumb to alcohol problems of his own. A homosexual in a world still deeply disapproving of it, he nevertheless maintained an ongoing, if stormy, relationship with actor Frank Merlo. They traveled frequently because Williams seemed to need a constant change of scene to stimulate his artistic work. He visited and lived in New Orleans, New York, Rome, London, and Barcelona, among other locales, noting that doing this prevented a downward spiral into depression: "Only some radical change can divert the downward course of my spirit, some startling new place or people to arrest the drift, the drag."

With Merlo's death from lung cancer in 1963, Williams began a seemingly irreversible slide into depression. He wrote a good number of plays over the next two decades, but the shine seemed to have worn off and they were not the critical darlings that his earlier work had been. Several were outright failures. His health began to be affected—he suffered from a number of medical conditions, including arthritis and heart problems, and once commented, "I've had every disorder known to man." His brother committed him to a hospital for a time in 1969.

Williams agreed to being prescribed amphetamines for his depression and sedatives for his insomnia, and he became addicted to both. He died in the Elysée Hotel in New York on February 25, 1983. That he was the victim of an overdose is not particularly surprising, but it was the nature of his death that was quite strange. He was found lying next to the bed with a plastic cap lodged in his throat; the cap had come from a bottle of eyedrops that he frequently used (he also had cataracts). It seems that he had ingested so much in the way of alcohol and drugs that his gag reflex was suppressed (an empty bottle of wine and barbiturates were found in the room). So he may have been attempting to put drops in an eye and dropped the cap into his mouth, but was unable to cough it back up. It's possible that the sedative he was using, Seconal, was also in part responsible for killing him. The death was ruled an accident.

Albert Camus (1913–1960)

Can't see the forest for the trees

Camus was a French-Algerian writer, playwright, philosopher, journalist, and essayist who embraced absurdism. This existentialism-like philosophy maintains that humanity's attempts to find meaning in existence will ultimately fail. We want to feel significant and have purpose, but in the face of a cold, uncaring universe, that objective is thwarted. Camus nevertheless held that we should continue the struggle to find meaning, for in recognizing that the universe is not comprised of absolutes, we are thus freed and so can create our own meanings simply by searching for them. Despite similarities between this view and those of existentialism, Camus denied that he subscribed to existentialist beliefs, once remarking, "Sartre and I are always surprised to see our names linked."

He was also devoted to communism (but later associated with French anarchists) and football—a logical combination, or not. He played professionally for an Algerian team in the later 1920s. When once asked whether he preferred theater or football, he confidently answered "football." As far as communism was concerned, he was later very critical of Soviet actions, and some think that this may have come back to haunt him, as we will see.

He began his literary endeavors as a playwright and a theater director, and while he drifted into other genres over time, he was always interested in the medium and considered his theatrical work to be very good. He wrote four original plays and adapted preexisting stories for the stage, though none of these were as popular as his other writings. At the time of his death, he was planning more dramas for live performance, as well as for television and film. The events of a cold winter day put an end to those plans.

On January 4, 1960, Camus was traveling with Michel Gallimard (his friend and publisher) in Gallimard's car, returning to Provence from Paris. Camus had originally intended to take the train with his family back home, but his friend had convinced him to go by car instead. The roads were icy and dangerous. Just south and east of Paris, near Sens, Gallimard lost control of the car and slammed into a tree; Camus died instantly. Investigators found the train ticket for the return journey and an unfinished novel with his body. Gallimard also died a few days later. The French nation mourned the loss of their Nobel Prize–winning writer, and tributes poured in.

But was the crash a tragic accident? Not everyone thinks so. The Czech poet and translator Jan Zábrana noted in his book, *Celý život*:

> I heard something very strange from the mouth of a man who knew lots of things and had very informed sources. According to him, the accident that had cost Albert Camus his life in 1960 was organised by Soviet spies. They damaged a tyre on the car using a sophisticated piece of equipment that cut or made a hole in the wheel at speed.

> The order was given personally by [Soviet foreign minister Dmitri] Shepilov as a reaction to an article published in *Franc-tireur* [a French

magazine] in March 1957, in which Camus attacked [Shepilov], naming him explicitly in the events in Hungary.

Camus had blasted Shepilov for his role in sending Soviet troops to crush the uprising in Hungary in 1956. Not long after, Camus also very publicly supported the work of Boris Pasternak, whose *Doctor Zhivago* had been banned by Stalin. Did Shepilov retaliate with a very fatal payback? It's an intriguing theory, but many don't believe it is true. Camus's biographer Olivier Todd spent time researching old Soviet archives but could find no evidence that Moscow had ordered the assassination, noting, "While I wouldn't put it past the KGB to do such a thing, I don't believe the story is true." Further, Gallimard's offer seems to have been rather spur-of-the-moment, so when would the KGB have had the opportunity to sabotage the tires? Unless Gallimard was also in on it—he *did* die later, so maybe he didn't intend to perish at all. But now we're getting into the realm of conspiracy theory, best left to those in tinfoil hats with the luxury of abundant time to write lengthy blogs.

Intermission

And so, for a moment, the curtain drops, and the house lights come up. While you're getting a drink or waiting in line for the facilities, you may be thinking about a few things. Obviously, many important playwrights and actors didn't appear in the previous scenes; the omission of several good stories and people is inevitable, unless we want an encyclopedia, which we don't.

The thing is, many of said omitted playwrights lived surprisingly calm and "normal" lives—except for the Elizabethans and Jacobeans, who seemed to wallow in a never-ending parade of scandal and violence—and so wouldn't have been good candidates for inclusion, anyway. Who wants to read about something boring like living a long, happy, productive life?

The lack of women is a notable and unfortunate stand-out feature that is representative of the sidelining that such creative souls have faced throughout so much history. However, English actresses and female playwrights were finally getting some credit by the seventeenth century, and women have played important roles in continental theater for a very long time.

Musicals, vaudeville, pantomime, and Broadway in general are missing from these accounts, simply because they represent whole other genres of entertainment, involving music as much as acting. It seemed like a bit of a task to try to cram them all in, when there were so many purely theatrical grotesque goodies to survey. Perhaps another book for another time . . .

So, now the show moves away from chronological history and treats you to a buffet of the bizarre, from fascinating facts and questions about Shakespeare (of course he had to have a whole chapter devoted to him!) to violent (yet hilarious) Italian comedy, to appalling amounts of blood and guts onstage, haunted theaters, and the endless superstitions that plague actors. Return to your seat; the curtain rises, the house lights dim, and the players take their positions to continue with the show—merde!

Act II

A Dark and Weird
Theatrical Miscellany

1

The Shakespeare You May Not Know

William Shakespeare, a name known to almost everyone, beloved by drama enthusiasts, and feared by high school students everywhere. We native speakers are told that we need to love his works because they are among the greatest things ever written in the English language. Indeed, some consider his ability to express emotion and human turmoil to be unsurpassed, though others find him boring and don't care. So, why is he so important?

Well, he created some of the most memorable characters in all of literature, and the list of phrases that he invented that are still in use is astonishing:

- All that glitters is not gold (*The Merchant of Venice*)
- It's Greek to me (*Julius Caesar*)
- Wear one's heart on one's sleeve (*Othello*)
- Break the ice (*The Taming of the Shrew*)
- A laughing stock (*The Merry Wives of Windsor*)
- Jealousy is the green-eyed monster (*Othello*)
- Heart of gold (*Henry V*)
- Knock knock! Who's there? (*Macbeth*)
- Love is blind (*The Merchant of Venice*)
- Wild-goose chase (*Romeo and Juliet*)

- For goodness' sake (*Henry VIII*)
- In my heart of hearts (*Hamlet*)
- One fell swoop (*Macbeth*)
- Set my teeth on edge (*Henry IV, Part I*)
- What's done is done (*Macbeth*)
- Play fast and loose (*King John*)

This brief selection isn't even close to being exhaustive. The number of words that Shakespeare seems to have invented—or are at least recorded for the first time—is equally impressive. His poetry and plays thrive and never seem to go out of fashion, being endlessly reinterpreted for the modern stage. His plays have been imagined in virtually every setting possible, from the distant past to the twenty-first century to the far future (the movie *Forbidden Planet* is an adaptation of *The Tempest*, for example). He is truly a writer for all times.

Given Shakespeare's popularity, it may come as a surprise to many that we know very little about the man and his life; years at a time are missing from his biography, leaving scholars to hypothesize and attempt to reconstruct what may have happened. This distinct lack of written records has led some to believe that Shakespeare didn't write the plays attributed to him at all. Since the late eighteenth century, some conspiracy theorists have believed that Shakespeare the man was just a hack writer and mediocre actor, and that the true author of the plays hid behind his name and wrote them anonymously, because in those days, playwriting was not considered a particularly respectable profession or exercise of one's literary talents; poetry was the true art. This belief was especially prevalent among the upper classes, where the "real" Shakespeare is often supposed to have dwelled. We'll delve into the authorship controversy later in the chapter.

Other questions about the man also abound. For example, what were his religious beliefs? The answer may surprise you. What exactly was his relationship to his wife, whom he married in haste after she became pregnant and to whom he left his "second best bed" in his will? He lived away from her for months, even years at a time, so they probably weren't all that close, despite having three children.

In this chapter, we'll delve into some of those mysteries and in keeping with the spirit of this book, we'll also examine the bloodier side of his works. You may just walk away with a greater understanding and respect for the man, even if you're still not quite sure what he's talking about sometimes.

Was Shakespeare a secret Catholic?

One of the more intriguing theories circulated in recent decades (through proposed much earlier) is that Will's family had strong Catholic sympathies, always a dangerous set of beliefs to hold, particularly in the paranoid, spy-filled Protestant England of the 1580s. This was the time when Mary Queen of Scots was implicated in a plot to assassinate Queen Elizabeth I. This led to Mary's execution in 1587 and the subsequent showdown with Spain's Armada in 1588.

Shakespeare's mother, Mary Arden, came from a prominent Catholic family. She was second cousin to William Arden, a wealthy gentleman. William Arden's son, Edward, shared his father's faith and employed his own secret priest, disguised as a gardener. Edward and his son-in-law, John Somerville, devised a plan to assassinate Queen Elizabeth, for which they were executed by decapitation in 1583. As with all traitors, their heads were placed on pikes at the entrance to London in Southwark, on the bridge across the Thames (near the playhouses). It's possible that Edward at least was innocent, having been accused by the Earl of Leicester, who despised him. The fact that other Arden family members were released from arrest and suspicion after Edward's execution may prove that the accusation was a vendetta.

Shakespeare's father, John, may well have been Catholic as well, as we will see. Several scholars have shown that Stratford-upon-Avon was still strongly in favor of the older faith, and only presented the outward appearance of conforming to the new religion for safety's sake. Indeed, the town's vicar was expelled for supposed "popery." Simon Hunt, who was probably young Will's teacher when the future poet was aged seven to eleven, eventually left England for Douai in northern France and became ordained as a Jesuit priest. Speaking of priests, John Frith, the minister who married Will and Anne Hathaway, was an ex-Catholic priest who came under suspicion by the Protestant authorities as being "unsound" and possibly having slipped back into his old beliefs.

The "secret Catholic" theory also suggests that Shakespeare lived some of his "lost years" (there is little record of his activities during the 1580s) in Lancashire in northern England, which became something of a hotspot for recusant Catholic activity, since it was far to the north and away from London politics. There, the story goes, he worked as a player and possibly as a musician and tutor for various Catholic employers. Another of Will's possible schoolmasters, John Cottom, was a proud Catholic who was associated with missionary work to convert or reconvert the English on the sly. Because of his beliefs and the fallout from his brother's efforts to restore the old faith, he was forced to leave Stratford in a hurry and relocate to, yes, Lancashire. Some theorize that Will might have gone with him, or been invited at a later time.

The accounts of Alexander Hoghton, a noted Catholic who lived near the Cottom family estate in Lancashire, record that he employed one "William Shakeshafte" who seems to have been a player, a musician, or both. He is mentioned more than once as someone of talent. Soon after, Shakeshafte seems to have been in the employ of another wealthy Catholic, Thomas Hesketh. In his apparent time at Hesketh's home in Rufford, this young man would likely have encountered traveling groups of actors, who, as we have seen, had to leave London whenever there was an outbreak of plague. One of Shakespeare's later business partners, Thomas Savage, was also from Rufford and was related by marriage to the Hesketh family. That connection may or may not mean anything, but it's a curious coincidence and would explain how Will was later able to make an entry into the London theater scene. He would have made many contacts with players and companies formerly patronized by Catholic drama enthusiasts in the north.

All of this is interesting and could be evidence that Will was harboring some potentially dangerous beliefs. There are problems with the theory, of course. One of the biggest is that "Shakeshafte" was a genuine surname, common enough in northern parts, so the idea that there was an entertainer named William Shakeshafte who had nothing to do with our bard is completely plausible. Further, if Shakespeare were attempting to lay low in the north, it would make little sense that he would adopt a name so similar to his own and use his given first name openly. Why not go for a completely different pseudonym, like Marmaduke Malemayns, Mathusela Cockayne, or Valentine Plymmyswoode? (Note: these are authentic possible Elizabethan name combinations for boys—make of that what you will.)

However, speaking of names: Shakespeare's twins, Hamnet and Judith, were named after his neighbors, Hamnet and Judith Sadler, known to be Catholic. Further, these neighbors seem to have taken on the role of being the children's godparents, an intimate association that in those days meant at least some spiritual instruction and guidance as part of their duties. This is hardly something that a committed Protestant would want for his offspring.

Scholars who support the Catholic theory have combed Shakespeare's works for evidence that he might have been communicating Catholic allegiances, and believe that they have found many, especially in those plays that have to do with authority and rebellion, such as *Julius Caesar, Hamlet, Titus Andronicus, Romeo and Juliet*, and others. In *Julius Caesar*, for example, Caesar represents Roman authority, and his murder is a rebellion against that authority that throws the Republic into chaos, pitting friends and family against one another, like the Protestant Reformation had done. This could easily be seen as a not-so-subtle endorsement of a return to Catholic rule, and thus, a return to the established order of things. *Hamlet* features the very important ghost of Hamlet's father, a figure who has returned to speak from a purgatory-like place; purgatory is not part of Protestant doctrine. The question of whether Shakespeare made use of autobiographical details in the plays is tricky, however (see the section on the authorship controversy below).

Shortly before his death, Shakespeare purchased a large London tenement, the Blackfriars Gatehouse, which had long been used as a hideout for secret Catholics and priests. He paid a good deal of money for it, which may show that he had a real interest in what was (presumably) still going on there.

There is one final bit of evidence, or not. In the mid-eighteenth century, some workers were puttering around in the Shakespeare family home in Stratford and found a curious document in the rafters, a "Last Will of the Soul" apparently written by (or for) John Shakespeare (Will's dad), in which he declared his adherence to the Catholic faith. It resembled similar declarations known to have been clandestinely used in Elizabethan England. If true, it would be the smoking gun (flintlock pistol?), proving that the family had such religious sympathies, and it would make a good case for Will sharing these beliefs. The problem, of course, is that not everyone believes that this testament is genuine, given how long it took to be found. But if it isn't, who put it there and why? What would be the point of hiding a forgery in the house, unless someone were trying to frame John and his family? But if that were the case, why stow it away somewhere so obscure that it took more than a century to be discovered? As always with Shakespeare, there are many questions, and the answers sometimes lead to even more questions.

Does any of it even matter? Not really these days, but historically, defining Shakespeare as a Protestant would have been a matter of English national pride and identity, which is perhaps why the theory of his possible Catholicism was for so long resisted—it was considered revolting, almost blasphemous in Victorian times. For centuries, the twin pillars of Anglo-Saxon cultural and linguistic self-respect have been the complete works of Shakespeare and the (very Protestant) King James version of the Bible. To suggest that the source of one of these pillars may have had a stronger allegiance to a spiritual authority in another country would certainly have undermined some of England's nationalism and Protestantism. Such beliefs became increasingly intertwined after Drake and the elements checked Catholic Spain's naval power in 1588 and

England began to "rule the waves" and set the stage for building an empire. But *that* is another whole discussion!

The utterly awful *Titus Andronicus*

Titus Andronicus is one of the bard's earliest plays, and it is so thoroughly awful, bloody, and disgusting that it deserves its own entry. Really, he wrote nothing like it again, and that's probably just as well. Its violence and horror scenes are so over the top that it almost comes close to comedy; almost, but not quite. Think of it as sixteenth-century torture porn. It contains (at least) fourteen murders, six dismemberments, one live burial, rape, and cannibalism, all wrapped up in one five-act play. Undoubtedly, it drew inspiration from Kyd's outrageous and popular *Spanish Tragedie*, and audiences were certainly thrilled by the blood and gore—seriously, baking people's heads into a pie? Imagining how some of these scenes might have been portrayed on an Elizabethan stage is actually amusing, so maybe we're back to comedy after all.

Set in ancient Rome, the play begins with Titus Andronicus returning from a successful ten-year military campaign, but almost immediately, things start to go to hell. He has lost most of his sons but acquired some prisoners: Tamora, the Queen of the Goths, her three sons, and Aaron the Moor, her lover. Titus sacrifices her eldest son, Alarbus, which earns him her unending hatred, and she plots revenge. Improbably, she becomes the new empress to the new emperor, Saturninus, and then she schemes to have two of Titus's sons framed for murder, after which they are sentenced to death.

She then tells her own sons, Chiron and Demetrius, to rape Titus's daughter, Lavinia, who endures one of the most appalling fates of any of Shakespeare's characters. The sons do as their mother asks and then cut off Lavinia's tongue and hands so that she cannot tell anyone who did it. Aaron then convinces Titus to have his own hand cut off to spare the lives of his sons; Titus agrees, but is later presented with their heads anyway. Titus tells his remaining son, Lucius, to flee from Rome, so Lucius leaves and makes an alliance with the Goths to return and besiege the city. All of this seems to drive Titus mad, and who can blame him? Tamora goes to him in disguise and, pretending to be the spirit of Revenge, offers him vengeance if he will convince Lucius to postpone his attack.

But Titus was only pretending to be insane and succeeds in capturing her sons, killing them by slitting their throats and draining their blood, and then baking their body parts into a pie. In the play's bloody climax, Titus kills Lavinia, because her shame is too much for him to bear; how thoughtful of him. He then triumphantly reveals to Tamora that she has just eaten her sons in the pie and stabs her with a butcher's knife. Titus himself is killed by Saturninus in revenge, Lucius kills Saturninus to avenge Titus, and a wholesale bloodbath erupts. Among the survivors are Lucius and Aaron. Lucius becomes the new emperor and has Tamora's corpse thrown to the wild animals. He then orders Aaron to be buried up to his neck and left to starve to death.

This crazy play may have been Shakespeare's attempt to cash in on the revenge tragedies that were popular at the time, trying to outdo even the excesses of Kyd's *Spanish Tragedie*. Or perhaps he wrote it as a kind of parody and made it as repulsive as possible in a gesture of black humor. The play has been a source of embarrassment for some Shakespeare scholars and advocates over the centuries, hardly being his best work. Some have tried to prove that he didn't write it at all. It's also possible that he wasn't the sole author—he may have collaborated with George Peele (1558–*ca.* 1598), who was well known for his own bloody dramas; many now agree that Peele wrote parts of act I and act IV. Of the play's many detractors, T.S. Eliot was one of the most direct when he declared it to be "one of the stupidest and most uninspired plays ever written."

Shakespeare wouldn't have been bothered. The play was a hit and its lowbrow nature was very appealing to theatergoers who were always eager for blood, whether real or imaginary. But thankfully, he left behind the revenge tragedy as a genre and moved on to far better things.

The bloodiest moments in Shakespeare's plays

Even outside of *Titus Andronicus*, there is no shortage of blood, gore, violence, and other foul deeds in Shakespeare's plays. In fact, a comprehensive discussion of such violence might make for a book (or at least chapter) in itself. What follows is a list of some of the best (worst?) examples from his plays of the kinds of onstage violence that Elizabethans and Jacobeans reveled in. Brace yourself.

Murders and executions

Claudius (*Hamlet*, act V, scene 2): Hamlet, realizing that Claudius is behind the treachery that will lead to his own death, stabs Claudius with the poisoned blade he wields, and then forces him to drink from a poisoned goblet.

Gertrude (*Hamlet*, act V, scene 2): Hamlet's mother, Queen Gertrude, accidentally drinks from the poisoned wine cup meant for Hamlet. Oops.

Polonius (*Hamlet*, act III, scene 4): Polonius, while spying for Claudius, hides himself behind a curtain in Gertrude's room in order to eavesdrop on her conversation with her son, Hamlet. Hamlet hears him make a sound and stabs his sword through the curtain as an act of precaution against a possible assassin. Sure enough, he kills the sneaky Polonius.

Julius Caesar (*Julius Caesar*, act III, scene 1): A group of conspirators believe that Julius Caesar is leading them into tyranny. They surround him and stab him multiple times. As he dies, he utters his famous phrase, "Et tu, Brute!" for even his friend Brutus was among the betrayers.

Duncan (*Macbeth*, act II, scene 2): Duncan is the rightful king of Scotland and is visiting Macbeth at his castle, Dunsinane, when he is killed. Macbeth, being told that he will be king, murders Duncan with daggers as he sleeps, though the action takes place offstage.

Desdemona (*Othello*, act V, scene 2): Desdemona has been erroneously accused of adultery by Iago, and Othello, in a jealous rage, smothers her, before realizing his mistake.

Duke of Clarence (*Richard III*, act I, scene 4): Clarence is arrested on false charges of treason and imprisoned in the Tower of London by his brother, King Richard III. Awakening from a dream in which he drowned, he finds that two of Richard's henchmen have arrived to kill him. They stab him to death and then thrust him into a cask of sweet wine (which also contains two hogs' heads) just to be sure that he's dead. So in a way, he "drowns" after all.

Suicides

Cleopatra and Mark Antony (*Antony and Cleopatra*, act IV, scene 15, and act V, scene 2): Antony's naval forces have lost to Caesar's, and he blames Cleopatra's treachery for the defeat. He threatens to kill her, so she has word sent to him that she has killed herself. Overcome with guilt, he draws his sword and falls on it, but learns before he dies that she hasn't killed herself. The two reconcile, he dies, and she decides to take her own life by letting venomous asps bite her, thus robbing Caesar of the prize of humiliating her in Rome. When Caesar learns of their deaths, he orders that both be buried with honor.

Ophelia (*Hamlet*, act IV, scene 7): Ophelia has gone insane from Hamlet's apparent cruel behaviors and because he killed her father, Polonius. Queen Gertrude relays the information that she climbed a willow tree, the branch broke, and that she plunged to her death in the river below. She was so far gone that she did not even attempt to save herself, which makes her death a kind of suicide.

Portia (*Julius Caesar*, act IV, scene 3): Portia is Brutus's wife and when she realizes that he will not be able to defeat the forces of Antony, she kills herself by swallowing fire. Well, that's one way to do it.

Othello (*Othello*, act V, scene 2): Othello has spent much of the play being riled up by Iago, who intended to drive him mad with jealousy and rage over his wife's supposed infidelities. When he learns that Desdemona, whom he has just murdered, is completely innocent, he stabs himself with a dagger in his chest, and so dies beside Desdemona.

Romeo (*Romeo and Juliet*, act V, scene 3): Everyone knows this classic case of a tragic mix-up. Romeo discovers Juliet in her tomb and thinking her to be dead, he drinks the poison he bought from an apothecary, speaking his famous last words: "Thus with a kiss I die."

Juliet (*Romeo and Juliet*, act V, scene 3): Things go from bad to worse, as Juliet awakens from her deathlike slumber and sees the dead body of Romeo beside her. Her plan has failed, and she cannot bear to be without him. She kisses him and stabs herself with his dagger, dying and falling on his body.

Deaths in battle

Hamlet (*Hamlet*, act V, scene 2): Possibly the most famous of all of Shakespearian deaths, Hamlet is stabbed by Laertes's blade, whose weapon is poisoned.

Henry Percy, "Hotspur" (*Henry IV, Part I*, act V, scene 4): Prince Hal (the future Henry V) fights with and mortally wounds Hotspur. During the fight, that old chubby knight, Falstaff, wanders into the scene and cheers on Hal, because a good fight to the death needs some comic relief. Falstaff pretends to be dead after a scuffle with another knight, and Hal eulogizes him. The prince leaves, and Falstaff springs back to life, stabs the dead Hotspur, and then claims to Hal (when he reenters the scene) that Hotspur was not dead, but that he bravely finished him off. Always a con man, that Falstaff!

Macbeth (*Macbeth*, act V, scene 8): Macduff fights against Macbeth, desperate to kill him and rid Scotland of his tyranny. Macbeth is confident that he will win, because the witches have prophesized that no man born of woman can kill him. But what Macbeth does not know is that Macduff was not "born," but rather "from his mother's womb | Untimely ripp'd" (i.e., emerged through a Caesarian or some other violent method of delivery). This unnerves Macbeth after he learns of it and, sure enough, he loses, with Macduff reentering the scene holding Macbeth's head and taking the kingship for himself.

Richard III (*Richard III*, act V, scene 5): Richard III, the notorious hunchbacked villain, meets his end at the hands of Henry Tudor (later Henry VII), who slays him during the battle of Bosworth Field. The portrayal of Richard as a hideous villain was no doubt written to please the Tudor queen, Elizabeth, since Henry VII was her grandfather.

Mercutio (*Romeo and Juliet*, act III, scene 1): Mercutio is Romeo's best friend and is neither Capulet nor Montague. When Romeo will not fight Tybalt (Juliet's cousin), Mercutio challenges Tybalt to a duel instead, to defend his friend's honor. Romeo tries to stop the fight, but Tybalt kills Mercutio. As he dies, Mercutio utters his famous phrase, "A plague o' both your houses! They have made worms' meat of me."

The authorship controversy—did Shakespeare write Shakespeare?

Surprisingly, many don't know much about this not-so-little controversy, but it has circulated in (or plagued) the dramatic community for well over a century. The basic premise is fairly simple: someone from a humble country background, as William Shakespeare was, could not possibly have had the education and worldliness to write the vast array of plays attributed to him, works that brought in all sorts of topics, from philosophy to history to geography to political commentary. Therefore, the plays must have been written secretly by someone else with the appropriate education and/or social status and ascribed to the actor, theater manager, and mediocre playwright named Shakespeare. But why would anyone do this? If one had written some of the greatest literature in the English language, wouldn't that person want to proclaim it to the world and grab all of the glory?

Well, therein lies the problem. What *would* motivate someone to remain anonymous and give their greatest work to an actor and hack writer who didn't deserve such praise? Possible answers to that question raise even more questions. The usual reason given is that plays for the public were seen as being too "common," too lowbrow for anyone of noble ranking to indulge in writing; poetry was the proper literary outlet. So perhaps the noble (or even royal) author of these works had to hide his (or her) identity to avoid public shame, and chose instead to have these masterpieces published under the name of a commoner to avoid the scandal. Further, if an author did not give his real name, he could be freer with political commentary, especially if it were critical of the government, not always an option for a courtier to do openly.

A word of warning: if you doubt Shakespeare's authorship, you're probably not going to like this entry. But if you're already furrowing your brow a little in skepticism about this secret author business, you're not alone. This theory seems intriguing at first, but the problem is that to date, something like seventy possible alternative authors have been suggested (including Queen Elizabeth herself!), and the "evidence" offered for some of them blatantly contradicts the evidence offered up with equal sincerity for others. We'll briefly look here at a few of the more popular choices: Sir Francis Bacon, fellow playwright Christopher Marlowe, and the perpetual darling of conspiracy theorists, Edward de Vere, the Earl of Oxford.

Statesman, philosopher, and scientist Francis Bacon (1561–1626) was proposed in the mid-nineteenth century by one Delia Bacon (she hinted at being a distant relation), who became obsessed with the idea of his secret authorship and spent considerable time at places in England where he had resided, doing no actual research, but attempting to "absorb" impressions about his hand in writing the plays. Her resulting work, *The Philosophy of the Plays of Shakspere Unfolded*, published in 1857, is nearly seven hundred pages of unreadable nonsense that doesn't actually name Bacon as the author but instead just implies it.

This inauspicious beginning to anti-Stratfordian studies led to some more grounded work a few decades later, when various researchers claimed to have found anagrams in the texts and in the First Folio (the first edition of Shakespeare's plays from 1623) which, when rearranged, made simple Latin phrases stating that Bacon had written the plays. The problem is that the phrases were often clunky and forced. One writer claimed that a line from *Hamlet* yielded the Latin *Fr. Baconi Nati*, which would translate as "of the birth of Fr. Bacon," a rather odd way of claiming authorship. The problem with looking for secret codes is that you can find almost anything you want—see the works of Nostradamus or the "Bible code." One researcher tried applying a code method (extracting key letters at various points in the text) to the First Folio and came up with "Gertrude Stein writ this Great Work of Literature," which would be quite an impressive feat, considering that she lived from 1874 to 1946!

Nevertheless, the idea that Bacon was behind Shakespeare's plays had some prominent early supporters, including Mark Twain (who also believed that Queen Elizabeth was secretly a man) and Helen Keller, but later enthusiasts went a bit overboard and started crediting Bacon with pretty much every other work of literature from the time: the plays of Marlowe, Kyd, and Greene; Edmund Spenser's *Faerie Queene*; the *Essays* of Montaigne; and even the King James Bible. You can see that it was getting rather ridiculous, considering how much Bacon wrote under his own name. When would he have had time to write all of these works secretly? Further, he disliked the theater, considering it to be frivolous, so he hardly would have devoted so much time to writing nearly forty plays in secret.

Nevertheless, Bacon's advocates, who saw him as a champion of early republicanism against the tyranny of the monarchs, Elizabeth I and James I, interpreted the plays to find evidence of his authorship and political sentiments. According to one fringe theory, Bacon was Queen Elizabeth's secret son, but before she could name him as heir to the throne, her secretary of state, Robert Cecil, had her strangled.

So, if not Bacon, what about Marlowe? He was nearly the same age as Shakespeare, had a Cambridge education, was an excellent playwright, an undoubted genius, and in acting as a spy, he was certainly worldly and well-traveled. Yes indeed, he might be the perfect candidate! There is one little problem, however, as you may recall. From May 30, 1593, onward, Marlowe spent all of his time being dead. *Ah*, say the conspiracy theorists, *but he wasn't really dead at all!* They propose two possible theories for how Marlowe could have written the plays: the first is that he was needed as a spy on the continent, and so his death was faked to whisk him away to new adventures, but because he didn't want to forsake writing, he arranged with Shakespeare to send him new plays that Will could publish under his own name. Will would make money from them and gain fame, while Marlowe could continue to do what he loved while still serving queen and country in secret.

The second theory is that Marlowe's death was faked because he needed to hide his homosexual affair with Thomas Walsingham, who, like his relative Francis Walsingham, was involved in the queen's espionage. In this version, Walsingham arranged for Marlowe to fake his death and then hid him away in southern England, where the two continued their love affair and Marlowe cranked out his plays and let Shakespeare take the credit. One proponent of this fake-death theory actually obtained permission to open Walsingham's grave in 1956; he was absolutely sure the tomb would include letters and maybe even manuscripts of lost plays that would prove his theory. But he found nothing. In fact, the grave did not even contain Walsingham's body, which probably only led to more speculation.

And then there is Edward de Vere, the seventeenth Earl of Oxford. He has become the favorite alternate author, with a group of "Oxfordians" giving him their wholehearted support. They believe that he had the necessary education, literary gifts, and travel experience to make him the perfect hidden author of the works attributed to Shakespeare. He had a decent enough reputation as a poet in his own time, and was a patron to other poets and playwrights. Oxfordians have been very successful over the past few decades in getting their candidate to the front of the line, such that they have managed to sideline most other contenders. So what's the deal with Eddie? Could he be our candidate at last? Well, it's not looking all that good.

De Vere may be all the rage now, but no one had ever considered him a possible "man behind the man" until the early twentieth century. In 1918, a schoolmaster with the splendid name of J. Thomas Looney (which he insisted was pronounced "loney") published a book titled *Shakespeare Identified*. Looney asserted that the Earl of Oxford had the education, had traveled, knew foreign languages, and was immersed in courtly life—in other words, he had the requisite cultural background. He had written poetry and allegedly plays (though these have not survived). But he was also arrogant, irresponsible, greedy, and given to anger and violence—he once murdered a servant and was let off when the jury determined that said servant must have impaled himself on the sword. He frequently quarreled with fellow courtiers, and never failed to remind others of his high status.

Looney, like the Oxfordians that came after him, was convinced that the plays were autobiographical, and that there were enough correspondences between Oxford's life and plots in the plays to prove that he was the true author—Oxford's father died young, for example, like Hamlet's, and he had three children, like King Lear. The problem with this theory was that autobiographical writing was rare at the time, while it was all the rage during Looney's. It is quite likely, therefore, that Looney was projecting the contemporary conventions onto the playwright. His interpretations, incidentally, alleged that the plays' author was entirely pro-monarchist and anti-democratic—the polar opposite of Bacon's more modernist views and a useful illustration of how one's reading of the works might vary based on the authorship theory the reader is trying to defend.

The theory of autobiographical plays brings up other problems— how much correspondence should there be between the author's life and the details of the plays? For example, one of Oxford's interests was tin mining, a venture that he was sure would make him richer. And yet, no mention of it occurs in the plays. By contrast, at various times these works contain references to leather, tanning, and uses for animal hides; since Shakespeare was the son of a glover, these references seem logical enough. Would the Earl of Oxford have even cared where his super-soft gloves came from? So the autobiographical approach is tricky in support of either argument. In the end, casual references to leather don't prove that a glover's son wrote the plays any more than having three children proves that Oxford wrote *King Lear*.

And another question: Why would Oxford want to hide his identity? Even if the writing of plays was considered beneath those of his rank, he was very vain, and if he had produced such magnificent works, he most certainly would have wanted to proclaim them to the world. It could have been to hide political opinions that were unpopular with his queen. But he could just as easily have released the plays anonymously, rather than hiding behind a figurehead, which would only increase suspicions and force William into some uncomfortable situations. If Shakespeare had no real literary talent but was only an actor pretending to be a playwright, how would he get around being asked to make up a verse or a scene on the spot, as could well have happened (it was not uncommon for corrections and additions to be made during rehearsals, for example)? Would he have stammered and deflected? How often could he have done that before the truth came out? This problem is equally true for any other candidates that some believe were "hiding" behind Shakespeare.

Further, given that Oxford was one of the highest-ranking earls in England, he could conceivably have published his work under his own name. This brings up problems for the sonnets and the long poems (often also attributed to Oxford), which were dedicated to the young Earl of Southampton. The dedications of these works, which border on sycophancy, are hardly what one would see from a senior earl to one of lesser rank, especially in those days when precedence and knowing one's place was of absolutely crucial importance in courtly politics. It's very unlikely that a powerful and arrogant man like Oxford would have fawned over a youth who was new to court and several stations beneath him.

Some Oxfordians have posited that Southampton (like Bacon) was actually Oxford's secret son by Queen Elizabeth I, who hid herself away during her pregnancy, a conspiracy idea known as the Prince Tudor theory. Some have gone even further and suggested that Oxford was also Elizabeth's son, who then later fathered Southampton with her; ew. You can see how silly this is getting. So perhaps these dedications and the poems themselves were the work of an affectionate father to his child. That just might make some sense, until you learn that Oxford's daughter, Elizabeth, was engaged to Southampton at one point, which would have made her his half sister. So yeah, probably not so much, but given that he was apparently Southampton's brother *and* father, I suppose anything is possible!

Once again, the biggest stumbling block is the whole lifespan issue. From 1604 onward, Oxford was taking a perpetual nap underground, while Shakespeare continued to write plays for many years. *Not a problem*, claim the Oxfordians. The earl simply had a stack of plays that were released at various intervals under Shakespeare's name over the next decade or so. But even if we are prepared to buy into this conspiracy theory, we still have to account for the evolution of Shakespeare's works. The later plays are more Jacobean in flavor: the language of these works reflects the changing tastes at the Stuart court (many plays became less direct and more "wordy"), and they contain references to masques (which were the rage during James's reign) and indoor performances (the Blackfriars Theater was a popular indoor venue by 1610).

They also clearly mention political and world events that happened after Oxford died: *Macbeth* drew on the conspiracy of the Gunpowder Plot of 1605 and James's fascination with witches, while *The Tempest* was partially inspired by an eyewitness account of the sinking of the ship called the *Sea Venture* in 1609. Writer William Strachey was aboard the ship when it floundered and ran aground off the coast of Bermuda. The following year he wrote his recollection of the disaster, and Shakespeare subsequently wrote a similar shipwreck description in *The Tempest*, having clearly borrowed from Strachey's account. In response, Looney and others have conveniently rejected *The Tempest* from the canon.

So, unless de Vere was being contacted by séance (actually, more on that below), it seems unlikely that he had anything to do with Shakespeare's later plays. *Ah*, counter the Oxfordians, *but perhaps the plays were mostly finished, but then spiced up with additional material to make them more topical.* The problem is that five of the late plays were definitely co-authored—*Pericles, Timon of Athens, Henry the Eighth, The Two Noble Kinsmen*, and the sadly lost *Cardenio*—and show clear signs of equal partnership and simultaneous authorship, such as small continuity errors in sequential scenes, which would have happened when two authors wrote at the same time.

Finally, as with the other contenders, the Oxfordian case requires a pretty grand conspiracy of silence that no one ever bothered to reveal or accidentally let slip, not even after Shakespeare's death. Actors and their ilk were not especially known for sobriety, and after a few drinks, if any of them knew that Shakespeare was a fake, in all likelihood it would have been all over the tavern and then the city. But somehow, no one else discovered this plot until Looney revealed the truth to the world in 1918, thus at last opening the floodgates of Oxfordian scholarship.

One Oxfordian, Percy Allen, was convinced that the matter could be settled by séance; the spirits of Shakespeare and Oxford would reveal the truth! He worked with the medium Hester Dowden, but there was a slight snag: Dowden had already determined with an earlier client that Bacon had authored the plays. This was remedied when she revealed to Allen that actually Oxford was the author, Shakespeare prepped them for performance (and added comedy), and Bacon oversaw the whole endeavor. Marvelous! Obviously, this didn't convince many people.

Ghostly explanations aside, none of the proposed alternative authors seem compelling. Moreover, the contemporary evidence from Shakespeare's times does not raise any qualms about the authorship. For instance, Ben Jonson—who also didn't have a university education but curiously doesn't seem to have his reputation as a genuine playwright questioned—wrote of Shakespeare in his private papers and spoke of him as a writer of plays, joking that Shakespeare should have blotted out far more of his own lines than he did. But Ben confessed that he loved the man to the point of idolatry and honored his memory. Would he have really said such words of a fake? And in a journal that was never intended to be made public?

In the accounts for the Master of Revels (the official in charge of courtly theatrical entertainment) from 1604–1605, Shakespeare is listed seven times as the author of various plays performed for the king. Would the inner circle of royalty *really* have been conspirators in keeping a dead earl's secret? Or Bacon's? And would such a secret have been kept for so long?

Some people seem to have a difficult time believing that genius can manifest itself in unlikely places; they want a reason or a logical explanation for everything. The vehemence of some anti-Stratfordians (whose long-winded blogs and websites can be quite a slog) recalls the hyper detail of other conspiracy sites that turn over every little fact to prove a point, but sometimes simply ignore common sense and the bigger picture. Occam's razor still applies; the simplest solution is most often the correct one, and there are more than enough reasons to believe that a country man from a glover's family created some of the greatest works in the English language.

Shakespeare's ear and the golden earring

There are several paintings and images claiming to be of Shakespeare; a much larger number based on these early examples appeared in subsequent centuries. They have helped to create the popular image of the man that we know today: balding, but with hair to his shoulders, a beard or goatee, and middle-class clothing. The so-called Chandos portrait of Will is possibly a painting of him from life (the famous Martin Droeshout engraving from the First Folio of Shakespeare's plays didn't appear until seven years after Shakespeare's death), and recently, another painting, the Cobbe portrait, has also been suggested as being genuine. Many now believe that an artist named John Taylor (*ca.* 1585–1651) painted the Chandos portrait, though tradition has held that it was painted by Richard Burbage, Shakespeare's friend and a principal actor in the company. Burbage had some skill in painting and portraiture, among his many other talents. The picture may later have been owned by William Davenant (the actor with the missing nose who implied that he was Shakespeare's illegitimate son). It was the first painting to be acquired by the National Portrait Gallery in London, in 1856. The Gallery's experts consider it to be an authentic representation of Shakespeare, made during his lifetime.

The painting is unusual, in that it shows a man who does indeed resemble the later Droeshout engraving, with a bit more hair (which may have been added at a later date) and a darker, almost Mediterranean, complexion. Some theorize that Shakespeare actually had Jewish or Arabic blood, or maybe was part Italian or Spanish, which might explain his love for Italy and its prominence in so many plays. That Shakespeare was English (and as we have seen, Protestant) has long been an almost sacred belief for his legions of admirers. So ensconced was this belief about his national identity that Victorians fairly recoiled at the idea that Shakespeare could be anything other than a red-blooded Anglo-Saxon. They tended to dismiss the Chandos portrait's authenticity on the grounds that the subject simply did not look "English" enough to be Shakespeare.

Later, Sigmund Freud (a great admirer of Shakespeare's works and an advocate of Oxford as the author of the plays) thought that the portrait was genuine and believed that it showed clear French features. He proposed that "Shakespeare" was a corruption of the French name "Jacques Pierre." More recently, Iraqi historian and journalist Safa Khulusi (1917–1995) argued that the family name was originally "Shaykh Zubayr" and was Anglicized, which could explain why it has so many different spellings (more than eighty at last count). He proposed that words of Arabic origin appear more commonly than might be expected in the plays, and that the Chandos portrait clearly shows a man with Middle Eastern features and a beard in a style that Arab and Turkish men wore at the time. Ultimately, it's difficult to confirm or deny any of these theories, which are fun but unprovable; it may just be that this depiction was the style in which the painter chose to represent Shakespeare, assuming that it *is* him.

But let's say, for the sake of argument, that the painting does portray Shakespeare, as the National Gallery maintains. One feature stands out, and that's the gold ring worn in his ear. Is it significant? Well, men's earrings were not uncommon among the upper classes; often a pearl or some other jewel was worn in the left ear. The Puritan and satirist Philip Stubbes (*ca*. 1555–*ca*. 1610) wrote in 1583 in his wonderfully titled pamphlet, "The Anatomie of Abuses," about all of the vanities in which the upper classes indulged, and he had pointed things to say about the fashion of earrings:

> Another sorte of dissolute minions & wanton Sempronians (for I can term them no better) are so far bewitched, as they are not ashamed to make holes in their eares, wherat they hang rings, and other Jewels of gold and precious stones. But what this signifieth in them I will houlde my peace, for the thing it selfe speaketh sufficiently. But because this is

not so much frequented amongest Women as Men, I will say noe more
thereof, until I further occasion be offred.

Clearly, he wasn't impressed with the look.

For those of lower ranks, it seems that the earring could indicate a devotion to a more bohemian lifestyle: artists, poets, painters, musicians,
players, dramatists, and a dozen other such creative and unconventional
types. This was the crowd that Shakespeare ran with and the portrait, in
showing the earring and the open collar, may have been a conscious choice
to portray him among them, in sharp contrast to the fact that he had a
wife and children back in Stratford and so was reasonably "respectable."

One other group associated with gold earrings at the time was, of
course, pirates! Though we might more often associate the word with
Long John Silver, peg legs, parrots on shoulders, and *Arrrr*s, piracy goes
back much further. It's relationship with authority has been varied. In
Elizabethan times, there was a group known as the Sea Dogs, who were
authorized by the queen to raid and loot Spanish ships and bring their
treasures back to England for the crown. The most famous of these oce-
anic canines included: Sir Francis Drake, Sir Walter Raleigh, and Sir
John Hawkins. Notice something? Yeah, they're all knights. Or rather,
they were all knighted for their, ahem, "services" to the queen, which included piracy among other nautical feats. This activity wore down the
Spanish fleet over time and made these "privateers" (as they were also
known) extremely rich. They differed sharply from outlaw pirates, of
course, but the risks they took were no less dangerous.

One fashion of less-wealthy pirates at the time was to wear a gold
loop in the ear. This was to ensure that they always had a ready supply of
money at hand, to pay for things such as their funeral expenses, should
the need arise. Does this mean that Shakespeare might have been a pirate? Some have suggested so, but it's doubtful, even knowing that many
of his prime years are lost to us. It makes for a wonderful story, though:
the young man leaving a small country town, seeking adventure in London, boarding a ship and witnessing privateering firsthand, and later

wearing an earring to remind himself of those days while he wrote his masterpieces. A fun idea, but almost certainly a fiction. Shakespeare's ear was adorned with a golden ring for the same reason as those of his buddies and colleagues: he was a part of a group of artists indulging in the fashion of the time to identify themselves with a scene, rather like tattoos or hipster beards, and for a lot of people, they were probably just as obnoxiously trendy and annoying.

Where is Shakespeare's head?

What is it with famous people whose heads go missing after their deaths? Mozart, Haydn, Beethoven, and now apparently Shakespeare too? Well, a lot of it has to do with the macabre practice of treasure and relic hunters, looking for unusual keepsakes. However, there was also a popular pseudoscience in the nineteenth century known as phrenology, which held that you could determine the level of someone's intelligence and abilities by measuring the size and shape of their skull. It was believed that certain talents resided in specific parts of the brain, and so looking at the indents and shape of a given skull could provide clues about that person's abilities. Shakespeare would have been an obvious target for such curious quacks, so it's probably not at all surprising that his head was removed in the dead of night at some point.

But the question of Shakespeare's potential missing skull has been the subject of legend even before the emergence of phrenology, since the late eighteenth century, in fact, when rumors circulated that the bard's head had been removed from his grave. You may recall the rather grim warning placed at his tomb, presumably to prevent this very thing from happening:

> Good friend, for Jesus' sake forbear,
> To dig the dust enclosed here.
> Blessed be the man that spares these stones,
> And cursed be he that moves my bones.

Apparently, the threat of a curse may not have been enough to scare off some determined grave robbers. *Argosy* magazine reported in 1879 that Shakespeare's skull had been stolen from Holy Trinity in Stratford-upon-Avon in 1794, but it seemed like little more than sensationalist nonsense. The thing about nonsense, though, is that it sometimes turns out to be true.

Recently, a team of archeologists was doing a survey of the grave, using ground-penetrating radar (GPR) to scan the area. This was done for a TV documentary as part of the bard's four-hundredth birthday year celebrations and studies in 2016, because nothing says "happy birthday" like poking around in a grave. The researchers were able to disprove that he had been buried standing up (another legend) and that he had been buried very deeply as a further precaution against having his bones moved; in fact, he is only interred about three feet underground and wrapped in a simple shroud, rather than resting in a coffin.

But they did discover something quite odd. The radar scan showed clear signs of disturbance at the head end of the remains, as if something has been dug up and then refilled. Further, they found "a very strange brick structure" cutting across the head, indicating that someone may have filled in the empty space. They couldn't conclusively prove that no skull is in there, but it seems likely.

There is another local legend that states that his head actually resides in the crypt of St. Leonard's Church in Beoley, Worcestershire, a few miles away. The team diligently tested the skull, but found it to be that of a woman in her seventies, putting the nail in the coffin (so to speak) of another legend.

So, Shakespeare's skull probably *was* stolen at some point, no doubt to assist in someone's "research" in a dark, dusty Regency or Victorian laboratory somewhere. Remember Victor Frankenstein and his work? Look how that turned out! The skull was probably lost forever a long time ago, but we can only hope that if it did see the light of day, it was at least used a few times as a stand-in for poor Yorick in Hamlet's famous speech (more on Yorick skulls below). Even Will might have approved of that.

William Henry Ireland: the great Shakespeare forger

The significant lack of surviving documents featuring Shakespeare's own writing is irritating and is one bit of fuel for conspiracies about him not writing his own plays. Collectors and antiquarians over the centuries have searched in vain for some scraps: fragments of the plays in his own hand, letters to friends and family, legal documents, and other such things. So it was for Samuel Ireland (1744–1800), a noted English writer, scholar, and publisher of contemporary travelogues. He was also an enthusiastic collector of all things Shakespeare and once traveled to Stratford in the hopes of uncovering some precious lost manuscripts (one legend says that he was informed to his horror that several authentic documents had been destroyed only a week before he arrived, though this is unlikely), but it was not to be.

So, you can imagine his delight when his son, William Henry Ireland (1775–1835), announced to his father in December 1794 that an undisclosed contact had provided him with several documents from the bard's life, written in Shakespeare's own hand! The collection included a deed signed by Shakespeare, a letter from him thanking his patron, the Earl of Southampton, for support, a letter from Queen Elizabeth I, a love poem to Anne Hathaway, "original" manuscripts for *King Lear* and *Hamlet*, and other treasures, which had all been conveniently awaiting discovery in a chest and were now seeing the light of day again nearly two centuries later.

The elder Ireland was beside himself with joy and immediately began to study them in depth. Convinced of their authenticity, he showed them to other experts, who mostly also proclaimed them as genuine. In 1795/96, Samuel Ireland published a lavish book about the findings, titled *Miscellaneous Papers and Legal Instruments under the Hand and Seal of William Shakespeare*. This brought the documents national attention and greater scrutiny, but nothing immediately negative happened.

Then in 1796, an even more amazing discovery was announced. William claimed to have found a lost play, *Vortigern and Rowena*, written in the bard's own hand and long forgotten. He presented it to his over-joyed father. Almost immediately, however, there was skepticism. But while some experts and actors declared the work to be a fraud based on its inferior style, others, including Samuel, were convinced of its authenticity; as much as anything, he probably just really wanted to believe it. He eventually arranged for it to be performed at Drury Lane on April 2, 1796. Some had suggested that it be shown on April 1, thinking the whole thing was a spoof.

One scholar in particular, Edmond Malone, had published only two days before his *An Enquiry into the Authenticity of Certain Papers and Legal Instruments*, an exhaustive (and boringly named) four-hundred-page tome that refuted the documents and declared them to be contemporary forgeries. His supporters packed the house for the play's first, and ultimately last, showing. One of the lead actors, John Philip Kemble (1757–1823), who also managed the theater, was likewise deeply skeptical. During the performance, he made sure to add extra emphasis to one line: "And when this solemn mockery is o'er." Malone's supporters knew he was on their side and began catcalls and other disruptions. The play failed and was not shown again until a 2008 revival.

Things unraveled quickly after the disastrous opening, as more scholars came forward to denounce the entire collection. William, realizing the game was up, was prompted to write *An Authentic Account of the Shaksperian Manuscripts*, wherein he confessed to the forgeries and tried to clear his father's name, which was now being sullied by its association with the whole thing. Indeed, Samuel's next travelogue failed and his reputation never recovered. He remained defiant, however, and to his dying day, the poor man was convinced that all of these manuscripts were the real deal.

One problem was that many who read William's confession were equally unimpressed with his claims. The papers were forgeries, yes, but could a young man who was only eighteen at the time really have created work that was good enough to fool even top scholars, at least for a little while? His father, being far more knowledgeable on all things Shakespeare and frustrated by the lack of original documents, they charged, was far more likely to be the actual forger, and was now letting his son take the fall for it. However, William continued to insist that he was indeed the man behind the manuscripts, and Samuel's defiant insistence in the face of ridicule that they were genuine would seem to point to the younger Ireland being the culprit. William's own budding career as a writer suffered greatly from the affair; he could have improved his standing by blaming his father, but he didn't. His later attempt to publish *Vortigern and Rowena* as a play that he had written also met with no success; he was known mostly as a hack writer throughout his life and died in poverty.

In the end, it seems that an enthusiastic young man wanted to give his father something he had always dreamed of finding, regardless of the consequences. But after the whole thing blew up, it broke the old man's heart, and he could never let go of the idea that he had stumbled onto one of the greatest Shakespearean finds of all time.

Yorick's skull, like, for real

It's one of the most iconic scenes in Hamlet, and even non-aficionados recognize it—that moment when the doomed Dane holds up a skull, saying, "Alas, poor Yorick!" Poor Yorick indeed; Hamlet may have known him, but we don't. He's a court jester who is already dead by the time of the story. The image of Hamlet holding the skull and musing on the fleeting nature of life—"Where be your gibes now? Your gambols? Your songs?"—is a striking one, but surprisingly, it may not date back to the bard's own time. The first artistic representation of Hamlet holding the dead fool's skull dates only from the eighteenth century, though actual players may well have been using skull props for much longer.

What kind of prop would it have been? A fake sculpted skull certainly would have been used, but why not go for that extra bit of realism and use the actual thing? Let's bone up on the facts: there are stories (some quite recent) of theater companies using real human skulls for the "role" of Yorick. It naturally brings up some tricky legal and ethical issues, but in most cases, it involves someone (often some kind of entertainer) leaving their body/skull to a given theater company for just that purpose, and if that's their last wish, who are we to deny them?

Most famously, acclaimed actor David Tennant made use of the skull of pianist André Tchaikowsky (no relation to the composer), who died in 1982 and willed his skull to the Royal Shakespeare Company so that he could take on the famous posthumous role. While the company was glad of his generosity, it seems that his anatomical donation was used only in rehearsals for many years, until Tennant decided in 2008 that it would bring more drama and impact to hold the actual skull during live performances in Stratford and later in London. Actor Jude Law also made use of a real human skull for his London portrayal of the tragic prince, which was purchased from a bone dealer in Salt Lake City. Comedian Del Close also wished for his skull to be used as Yorick's, or in any other way the company should see fit, after his death in 1999. But despite claims that his skull was used by the Goodman Theatre in Chicago, it was not; the skull actually came from a medical supply company.

If these kinds of stories are strangely common in modern times, you can imagine what might have been going on in the eighteenth and nineteenth centuries, when ideas like phrenology were all the rage; the skulls of the famous became collector's items, and more than a little graverobbing happened to supply said "researchers" with appropriate items. Yes, many theater companies seemed only too happy to acquire an actual skull or two for that added bit of realism. The Walnut Street Theatre in Philadelphia, for example, was said to have owned a donated skull in the later nineteenth century; it was autographed by a succession of actors who performed as Hamlet. That's quite a bone-chilling heirloom! Undoubtedly, many other companies wanted that extra bit of realism, and engaged in similar—wait for it—skullduggery.

2

The Commedia dell'Arte

The Italian Commedia dell'Arte is an utterly splendid exercise in comic anarchy, with roots possibly going back to ancient Roman times—the Atellan farces featured masked buffoons and stock characters, for example—though its first appearance in a more-or-less recognizable form seems to be during the Renaissance, shortly after 1550. Its heyday was between the sixteenth and the eighteenth centuries, but it has survived into modern times and undergone a new renaissance of enthusiasm and popularity. Commedia plays are often decidedly lowbrow and emphasize physical comedy, showing off the best of slapstick humor—in fact, the very word "slapstick" comes from a specific prop used as a paddle to make loud spanking and smacking noises against unsuspecting characters; more on that below. Different characters had different *lazzi*, which were stock jokes and physical gags that could be inserted wherever a player thought they would be funniest. They were also useful if the play was stalling or someone forgot their lines.

A typical show relied heavily on improvisation around set sketches and plots and used stock characters that parodied various social classes in Renaissance and Baroque Italian culture. This allowed a troupe to insert contemporary jokes and social commentary relevant to the time and place; no two shows were ever quite the same. The characters most often would wear masks exaggerating their personality traits; this practice may stem from the tradition of masking at Carnival (the time between Epiphany and Ash Wednesday). Indeed, the Commedia masks often resemble grotesque parodies of Carnival masks. Despite being composed of traveling players and frequently entertaining (and appealing to) the lower classes, some Commedia troupes obtained very wealthy patrons and even played before nobility and royalty. They were somewhat atypical of the time (certainly in England) in that female roles were played by women, who indulged in the silliness with the same gusto as their male counterparts.

The Commedia's influence over the centuries has been immense. Its themes, gags, and physical comedy have found their way into the works of Shakespeare, Molière, Punch and Judy shows, vaudeville, and more recently, the creations of Charlie Chaplin, the Marx Brothers, Mel Brooks, and even the skits on the television show *Seinfeld*.

The cast of characters

The Commedia is filled with a host of wonderful, weird, and improbable characters that poke fun at all sorts of professions and stations in life. Arlecchino, or Harlequin, is the best known, but the others each have their own comic foibles and idiosyncrasies that have endeared them to audiences since the Renaissance. Here is a listing of some of the most memorable:

That old devil, Arlecchino (Harlequin): The most famous of the Commedia cast, he is the classic servant, often beholden to older and richer men such as Pantalone, Capitano, or the Doctor. His name possibly derives from the Old French *Hellequin*, a black-faced devil of legend who roamed the countryside at night chasing damned souls. This name could in turn come from the Old English *Herla cyning*, or *Erlking*, a figure from Germanic paganism, who was said to be the king of the fairies and was labeled a devil during the Middle Ages. Dante includes a demon named Alichino in *Inferno* from the *Divine Comedy*. Indeed, Arlecchino's mask is black, and a bit catlike (the black cat was long a symbol of evil in medieval and Renaissance Europe), and his costume is frequently a patchwork of diamonds or other patterns in black and red or multiple colors.

By the time of the Commedia, he had lost these diabolical associations, but was still not exactly a reputable character. He constantly schemes to relieve his masters of their money, but most often fails. Though he is a servant, he is smarter than some other characters (but certainly no genius), as can be seen by his mask's short nose—generally, the longer the nose, the stupider the character. At his belt he carries the infamous slapstick (see below), a classic prop and source of much comic violence. His movements are actually rather graceful and agile, a bit more so than his mental capabilities, involving a triple-time walk on tiptoes. Most often he is responsible for botching the deliveries of messages or forgetting his orders and getting distracted by something more interesting, such as food or the opportunity for sex. Much chaotic hilarity usually ensues as he attempts to put things right, and they most often go even more wrong.

Arlecchino's *lazzi* include: accidentally losing a limb (such as a hand), which flies into the audience; flailing around madly with all his arms and legs; somersaulting or sliding to get from one location onstage to another; misuse of props; and screwing up messages and orders by inserting his own ideas.

The deceitful and cruel Brighella: Sometimes called the most disturbing of the Commedia cast, Brighella (Italian *briga*: "intrigue," "trouble") is considered a fellow zanni (more on them in the next entry) and often paired with Arlecchino (sometimes as his older brother), though he is just as likely to be a tavern owner or some other middle-class character and the boss of the other zanni. He dresses in white with green trim, and sometimes carries a knife. His green mask often features a hooked nose and exaggerated eyebrows to emphasize his villainy. Brighella has many talents and is always quick to point them out and demonstrate them to others. He will also pretend to be whatever someone wants him to be in order to impress them or ingratiate himself to others and so achieve his plans. He thrives on criminal activity, such as deceit, false offers of assistance, theft, and occasionally even murder, if it suits him. He loves money only insofar as it buys the things that he wants, namely food and drink, but he is sometimes a skilled musician. A drunkard and a lout, his crimes are always over-the-top and humorous, and his lies are played for laughs. Brighella slinks about rather like a cat, almost tiptoeing, but ever-ready should the need to pounce arise. He keeps his head in place as his hips sway back and forth when he walks, with his legs far apart. The whole movement is rather ridiculous and adds to his overall buffoonish countenance.

Brighella's *lazzi* include: offering food to Arlecchino, as if to a dog, tossing it across the stage and whistling (Arlecchino chases after it and devours it); visiting the Doctor and being prescribed leeches for his ailments.

The zany zanni: This term can refer to the lower-class servants and schemers like Arlecchino and Brighella, or it can actually be a separate character with those same qualities. The name is a diminutive of Giovanni; our word "zany" comes from it and describes the nature of the character perfectly. When appearing as a separate character, he wears white clothing (originally made from flour sacks to indicate his poverty) and has a mask with an exceptionally long nose and a furrowed brow, marking him as notably stupid. He lives for food, drink, sex, and slacking off; maybe he's not so stupid after all? He moves in an exaggerated way and goes to sleep by standing on one leg, with the other leg crossed over his knee, like a stork. His sleep is accompanied by belching, farting, and snoring. His main comic plot purpose is, like Arlecchino's, to mess up things such as messages and plans and then try to make amends. He is indispensable to the comedy of the show.

The zanni's *lazzi* include: poor sight and/or hearing played up for comic effect; wandering accidentally into the audience or the stage area, only to reappear somewhere else in a later scene with little or no explanation of how he got there.

The foolish and miserly Pantalone: Pantalone is possibly named for a Venetian saint, San Pantalone, but as his name suggests, he wears distinctive red trousers or stockings. Indeed, the words "pantaloons" and "pants" derive from the stockings stretched over his skinny legs. He also wears a long black cloak with big sleeves and a red cap. Most importantly, he wears a prominent purse on his belt, to flaunt his wealth. An elderly man, he is portrayed as a widower or bachelor who nevertheless makes romantic overtures to all of the females in the show; he always fails. His mask features a long pointy nose and squinty eyes to accent his greed. Indeed, his greatest fear is losing his money, which pretty much guarantees that his servants (usually Brighella and sometimes Arlecchino) are constantly scheming up ways to liberate his coins from him. He is the butt of many jokes and schemes, often made to look like the fool, to the amusement of audiences. Pantalone is often the father of one of the Lovers, and plots ways to keep them apart—a villainous, if comical, role. He walks with a hunch in his back, bent over as if protecting his money, but he almost always loses it to the schemes of the zanni.

Pantalone's *lazzi* include: gags about medical procedures (urine tests, tooth extraction, etc.); farting; being impotent; hopelessly trying to woo a much younger woman.

The quack Doctor: *Il Dottore* is probably not a medical doctor, he simply has a university degree, or so he says. Sometimes known as Dr. Baloardo ("Dr. Stupid"), he might claim to have more than one qualification, from Bologna, or Padua, or some such impressive-sounding place. He is happy to blather in fake Latin, which sounds very impressive to the uneducated. Like Pantalone, he is an elder, and a cranky one who often conspires to keep the young lovers apart. He dresses all in black, appropriate to his supposed scholarly background, and is gene...us in his girth, requiring his costume to have extra padding. His mask... small but with a bulbous nose and exposed cheeks that are painted ...o show his over-fondness for alcohol. He walks on his heels and m... rs in figure-eight patterns, always moving when speaking and p... cating, led by his belly. And boy, does he like to ramble on; in fa... never shuts up and frequently cracks vulgar jokes alongside his... academic spiel, which includes many made-up, multisyllabic... He often has to be forcibly removed from the stage to shut him... diagnoses for all man-

The Doctor's *lazzi* include: offering u... assistance to perform ner of illness to the rest of the cast; ... drinking his own quack experiments and untested surgeries; ? ...ements; a *lazzi* involving potions; using ridiculously large r... · · ·). an enema (the less said about th

The bombastic Capitano (Captain): The Captain is a boisterous braggart who loves to tell you all about his military exploits, heroism, and romantic conquests. He is a descendant of similar characters in ancient Roman plays by Plautus and Terence. He is arrogant and pretends to be brave, but is actually a coward when confronted with anything threatening, which on a Commedia stage means most things; he is especially afraid of mice. That doesn't mean that he doesn't try to intimidate others, of course, but even this is usually silly and played up for comic effect. His real name is often some absurd list of titles, drawn from every source imaginable, and is improvised or invented by the actor playing him. Examples include Capitano Spavento di Vall'Inferna ("Captain Fright of Hell's Valley") and Il' Capitano Salvador de los Virgenes Burraches ("Captain, Savior of the Drunken Virgins"). His costume can feature silly exaggerations of military outfits, such as huge boots, a large hat, and some kind of military coat. He always carries a sword, but if ever forced to draw it, he will become terrified. His mask is more subdued than those of some of the other characters, and occasionally, he can be without one, though he can also sport the traditional long nose. He moves about with chest out in a proper swagger and walks in a ridiculous parody of a military march. He will very generously take time out to address the audience directly, only too happy to regale listeners (eager and otherwise) with accounts of his phony heroism.

The Captain's *lazzi* include: making excuses about why he cannot fight, even though he could if he *really* wanted to, of course; he beats Arlecchino a specific number of times (usually ten), but keeps losing count and has to start over; various gags about getting in fights and getting beaten up, or proving himself to be cowardly.

The innocent *innamorati* (the Lovers): The lovers are not comic characters, but their love is an important plot point. They are the young son and daughter of older characters such as Pantalone and the Doctor, and they are forbidden to see each other, like Romeo and Juliet. This, of course, offers all sorts of comic possibilities as they seek the help of the zanni against their fathers' respective plans. They wear no masks, but are heavily made up, and their clothes represent the latest fashions, since they are supposed to be very rich and trendy. Unlike the more grotesque figures of the Commedia, they are elegant and frequently very attractive; they represent the idealism of youth in the face of the stubbornness of old age. Their whole purpose is to be in love with each other. In fact, they are in love with the idea of being in love with each other, and as such, often have a hard time actually speaking to each other. They prefer to let servants do it for them, which leads to all sorts of funny disasters, such as miscommunications, missed meetings, messages delivered to the wrong recipient, and various other misunderstandings. If they quarrel, the young man will often go to great lengths to make it up to the young lady, again employing the help of the zanni; things go terribly wrong but somehow always work out in the end. Ah, young love.

The Lovers don't have *lazzi*, as the jokes happen around them. Some might argue that love is the best joke of all.

The coarse and volatile Pulcinella: Pulcinella's name may derive from *pulcino*, "chick," and he does indeed sometimes speak with squawks and chirps in an obnoxious French accent; he is associated with southern Italy and Naples. Usually portrayed as a hunchback, he is dressed in white and frequently wears an absurdly tall curved hat, while sporting a black mask with a beaked nose and wrinkles on the forehead, further calling out his birdlike nature. His function is something of an interlude character, often not interacting at all with the rest of the cast, but taking time out to address and insult the audience. He is violent and often pretends to be dumb if he is smart, or clever if he is stupid. He crouches and walks with small steps, but can be acrobatic on occasion. He is sometimes married to a servant named Rosetta, and his mistreatment of her became the model for the later Punch and Judy puppet shows (see below).

Pulcinella's *lazzi* include: picking fights but refusing to actually fight; trying to bargain down prostitutes to the least amount of money possible; pretending to be deaf, blind, and mute while begging for money; jumping around and making chicken noises.

The youthful servant Pedrolino: Pedrolino (or Piero) is a role often assigned to the youngest member of the troupe. He is a youthful servant, a valet, who wears hand-me-downs that don't fit him. The common gag was to see him clothed in a large smock (white or blue) with the sleeves being far too long and his hands thus invisible. He can then wave them around for comic effect, resembling a marionette. His shirt also frequently has a too-large collar and absurdly oversized buttons. He usually doesn't wear a mask, but instead sports a face painted white, allowing him more facial expressions than some of the other characters; he resembles a contemporary mime. He is young and full of nervous energy, but also bashful and often doesn't address the audience directly. If he expresses love for another character and she mistreats him, he will blame himself. He could technically be seen as another of the zanni, but one with a heart, and his actions are more like those of the Lovers.

Pedrolino's *lazzi* include: comical imitations of Capitano; being (or pretending to be) mute—another association with modern mimes—thus causing comic confusion as the others try to understand what he is communicating; sleeve comedy, such as having them tied together, flailing them around in the air, and so on.

The scenarios

Commedia plays were not always written out as plays, especially in the earlier centuries. Rather, they made use of *scenari* ("scenarios"), outlines of stories that were meant to be improvised by a given troupe. So, while there might be a basic story, the actors would have to improvise dialogue, insert their *lazzi* at given points, and keep the whole thing going along to bring it to a logical (or illogical) conclusion. By the eighteenth century, these outlines might be posted backstage for the benefit of the actors who could read.

In 1611, Flaminio Scala (1552–1624), a playwright, director, and actor who portrayed the male lover in his troupe, published a large collection of his *scenari*, *Il Teatro della Favole Rappresentative* ("The Theater of Tales for Performance"). The collection contained fifty scenarios, forty of which were comedies. Commedia groups did occasionally perform serious works and tragedies, usually for wealthy patrons on more permanent stages.

The thing is, when reading through them, they seem a bit dry and even dull. This is because so much of the magic of a Commedia show relies on its physical comedy and improvised humor. It was up to the actors to take these simple outlines and turn them into something hilarious, using all of their considerable talents. Here is example of a *scenario* by Italian playwright, Carlo Gozzi (1720–1806):

> Brighella enters, looks about the stage, and, seeing no one, calls.
> Pantaloon, frightened, comes in
> Brighella wishes to leave his service, etc.
> Pantaloon recommends himself to him
> Brighella relents and promises to aid him
> Pantaloon says (in a stage whisper) that his creditors, especially Truffaldino, insist on being paid; that the extension of credit expires that day, etc.
> **At this moment:**
> Truffaldino (scene of demanding payment)
> Brighella finds a way of getting rid of him
> Pantaloon and Brighella remain

At this point, additional characters enter, and the scene continues. None of this seems very funny, but imagine how it could be interpreted, with exaggerated movements, grotesque masks, wide eyes, funny voices, pleading for more time to pay off the debt, making funny faces behind the villain's back, doing asides to the audience, bringing up topical or dirty jokes—the possibilities are endless. Each time the actors took the stage, the scenario would be different and could be tailored to the audience and to current events.

There were also "mixed plays," which were a combination of written-out dialogue with improvisations and *scenari*, as well as actual plays that still allowed room for the actor's own ideas and talents. Taken as a whole, Commedia productions were a unique form of theater, combining satire, physical comedy, vulgarity, and comic violence in equal measure, all to get audiences laughing.

The slapstick and physical comedy

The very term "slapstick" has come to mean physical comedy, usually involving people having mishaps, falling over, crashing into things, and other such actions that are unpleasant for those experiencing them, but completely hilarious for the rest of us. Why do we laugh at the misfortunes of others? That's a very good question with lots of deep psychological answers that may have to do with unconscious drives relating to aggression, projection, the feeling of safety in knowing that the action is happening to another, and the projection of our worst fears onto the experiences of others, allowing for a cathartic release. Or, it may just be because it's damned funny.

In any case, the slapstick was originally an actual object, a prop used in the Commedia, most often wielded by the zanni and intended for loud, painful, and comic effect. As used in skits, it was called the batacchio (or bataccio) and was a paddle-like wooden club with two slats, one on a hinge. When it was swung, preferably when the actor simulated whacking another character on the butt or any other part of the anatomy, one slat would slap against the other, creating a loud smacking sound that made spankings and beatings seem much worse and much funnier. The stick could be used again and again, producing these repeated loud cracks, while the actor on the receiving end wouldn't be hurt at all. It became an essential prop, crucial to the physical comedy at the heart of Commedia scenes.

It seems to have originated in the sixteenth century, and it quickly became a staple of Commedia humor. It was still in use in vaudeville and other comedies in the nineteenth century, but seems to have gone out of fashion after that. The idea of physical comedy was kept alive, though, and the silent films were a great age of Commedia-like laughs. Charlie Chaplin, the Keystone Cops, Buster Keaton, and the Marx Brothers were all heirs to the legacy of these zany masked clowns and their pain-for-laughs brand of humor. Their weapon of choice gave its name to a whole genre of violence and accidents for amusement.

Punch and Judy—violent and comical Commedia puppet shows

You may remember the scene from the film *This Is Spinal Tap* where the band, their fortunes ever waning as their ill-fated tour wears on, finally ends up at a county fair playing as the opening act for a puppet show. We tend to think of such shows as silly little whimsies for children's birthday parties, but the art of puppetry has a long and noble (or sometimes ignoble) history that can be anything but childlike in its theatrical content. And so it is with Punch and Judy.

Long a staple of English seaside entertainment, the original shows grew out of Commedia themes. Punch derives, as we have seen, from Pulcinella ("Punchinello" in English, hence the name) and brings that character's violent tendencies into the realm of puppetry. Indeed, so savage can his behavior be that it can result more in nervous laughter and shock rather than genuine hilarity. Traditionally, a single puppeteer would operate both Punch and his companions, sometimes assisted by a musician who would play fiddle or other instruments and draw in an audience, collecting their money and sometimes repeating dialogue that was difficult to hear.

Punch seems to have made his English debut on May 9, 1662, as recorded by the diarist Samuel Pepys, who was in Covent Garden in London near St. Paul's Church, when he wrote that he went: "into Covent Garden to an alehouse . . . Thence to see an Italian puppet play that is within the rayles there, which is very pretty, the best that ever I saw, and great resort of gallants." A modern plaque in Covent Garden marks the place where Pepys saw the soon-to-be-famous character. Rather than being a hand puppet—as he was most commonly depicted in the nineteenth and twentieth centuries—Punch and his comrades would originally have been marionettes, operated by one Pietro Gimonde.

A legend records that King Charles II and his mistress Nell Gwyn saw one of these early versions of the show, and the king was so impressed that he issued a royal decree permitting the performers to call themselves "professors." Well, this was the story they liked to tell about themselves, anyway, and they adopted the title without any further academic qualifications.

From the later seventeenth century onward, this grotesque character became something of a British institution, which is a little bizarre considering his Italian origin and violent nature. He wears a kind of jester's outfit and sports a sugarloaf hat (a pointed cap that curves forward at the top). He has a long crooked nose, a hunchback, and carries a slapstick that he is prepared to use on everyone. Indeed, there is little that Mr. Punch won't do: wife beating, child beating, child murder, attacking the police, even taking on the devil himself. The plotline varies and is less of a cohesive narrative than a series of encounters and skits between the characters. In some versions, Punch's wife, Judy, tasks him with babysitting and things soon go horribly wrong: he drops the infant, sits on it, or accidentally puts it in a sausage machine. When she returns, she is outraged and beats him. Police arrive and more violence occurs. During these skits, there are certain stock characters and actions that audiences expect to see at every performance. Punch and Judy are the ultimate dysfunctional family, and the violence that ensues has long been used to get laughs; traditionally Judy has been just as horrible and violent toward Punch, which plays on old Commedia jokes about a henpecked husband. What could be horrific and in very bad taste is mitigated by the fact that the puppets are wooden and their facial features are frozen, so no expressions of pain can be made; it causes the scenes to be more funny than offensive.

Further, Punch's voice is deliberately comic. It's produced by the swazzle, a device made of two strips of metal and a reed of cotton that the puppeteer voicing Punch holds in his mouth. It distorts his voice, making it sound like a high-pitched kazoo, and the character immediately becomes ridiculous, no matter how awful his actions. The problem with this little device, of course, is that it is small, and the operator risks swallowing it mid-performance. Sometimes professors would attach a bit of string to the swazzle; it dangled out of their mouths and could be pulled forward if it crept too far back toward their throats, but this plan didn't always work. Indeed, there grew up a tradition that no operator of

a Punch puppet could truly call himself a professor until he had accidentally swallowed a swazzle at least twice.

Irish puppeteer Martin Powell (*fl.* 1709–1720, *d.* 1729) is most
often credited with establishing the format and stock plot of Punch and
Judy shows, which spread from London to other English cities and Ireland. In the later eighteenth century, marionettes began to be replaced
with much lighter hand puppets, and the show evolved into a form that
is more familiar to modern audiences; it also gained a following in Paris
and the American colonies, where even George Washington was said to
be a fan. But the productions didn't lose their outrageous acts of violence
and slapstick comedy as the nineteenth century dawned. Indeed, they
thrived in Victorian England, when one would think that society's prud-
ishness would have called for them to be banned, especially if children
were in the audience. But the shows had no less respectable a defender
than Charles Dickens, who wrote in 1849:

> In my opinion the street Punch is one of those extravagant reliefs from
> the realities of life which would lose its hold upon the people if it were
> made moral and instructive. I regard it as quite harmless in its influ-
> ence, and as an outrageous joke which no one in existence would think
> of regarding as an incentive to any kind of action or as a model for any
> kind of conduct.

Actually, Punch and Judy's antics were originally intended for adults,
but over the course of the nineteenth century, they evolved into more of
a children's entertainment, possibly as a result of those Victorian societal
pressures. Certain characters, such as Punch's mistress, Pretty Polly, and
the devil, were eventually cut because they were deemed inappropriate
for young minds, but much of the comic violence remained. This is an
interesting commentary on societal values: the implication of infidelity
and images of Satan must be removed, but have all the violence you
want, that will make the kids laugh!

The show was always topical, and despite its stock plots and characters, it managed to poke fun at the establishment and sometimes used its

chaos to satirize those in power, introducing puppets into the skits that caricatured public figures, from Napoleon in the nineteenth century to Margaret Thatcher in the twentieth. In the wake of the restrictive Licensing Act, this kind of show, which was technically not a "play," could say the things that theatrical productions could not, and did so with relish. The ridiculous puppet and his big stick could hold up those in power to ridicule, with his silly voice and stupid appearance. It was a perfect way to mock politicians and others who thought too highly of themselves. Punch lives on. There was even a famous British humor and satire magazine called, appropriately enough, *Punch*, that began in 1841 and survived in various forms until 2002. The original Commedia actors would be pleased.

3

The Bloody Theater

It seems that theater audiences have always enjoyed a good bloodbath, from the appalling mass murders of the ancient Greek dramas, to the equally violent tragedies of the Elizabethans, to the horrors of twentieth-century Paris (see below). Where would Oedipus be without his self-blinding? How interesting would *Titus Andronicus* be without the mutilations and enemies baked into pies? There is probably something cathartic about witnessing such horrors in a controlled environment, safe in the knowledge that the gore is false (and maybe even over-the-top and comical), it's just a fictional story, and it can be left behind when one returns to the safety of the real world—well, as "safe" as the real world can be. Players and companies have employed a number of techniques over the centuries to represent such stomach-churning scenes, some more effective than others. From animal bladders filled with fake blood to hoses representing the intestines of the disemboweled, here is a messy tour through some of the yuckier aspects of depicting horrid deaths onstage.

Also, sometimes the deaths weren't that fake after all; the Romans apparently actually murdered some of their cast, who weren't exactly willing participants, it must be said. We'll also have a glance at some actors who got so into their roles that they took the drama too far and expired onstage or soon after, thus taking suffering for their art to a whole new level.

Fake carnage for the stage: animal-blood bladders, red rags, and many body parts

Blood and guts on the stage have a long, if not-so-illustrious, history, going back to ancient Egypt and its live hippo sacrifices. Things moved on from there, thankfully, but the audience's lust for graphic death scenes never waned. Here, we'll take a look at some of the highlights and low-lights of theatrical splatter, and the creative ways that it was brought to life, or death.

Ancient Greece: Surprisingly, given the gruesomeness of many Greek tragedies, there was a convention, at least in those tragedies, that violence and killing were not be shown. It was perfectly okay to depict the *results* of violence, or even to have piles of fake dead bodies lying about, but one could not show a stabbing, a hanging, or even a poison-ing (which would have been easy to simulate). In a tragedy, one could not even show a violent act, such as hitting another actor. Even violence against animals, such as a ritual sacrifice, could not be portrayed. Even more strangely, comedies had no such prohibitions, at least when it came to throwing punches, and it was perfectly fine to smack someone for laughs, a tradition that survived and flourished in Rome and probably into the Middle Ages and Renaissance, when the Commedia became so popular.

But why was there a ban on showing violent acts in the one genre where they would be most appropriate? Several explanations have been offered. One that seems likely has to do with Greek drama originating in religious rituals and devotion to Dionysus, and the sense that the god might be watching the play and thus be offended if people were to be shown being killed. Killing was forbidden in temples, of course, so even a fake killing wouldn't go over well. This would certainly explain the lack of simulated deadly blows and actual animal sacrifice, since plays re-tained a sacred element. But as far as plain old hitting was concerned, comedy had no such prohibitions; so why would Dionysus be offended by such violence in a tragic story but amused by it in a funny one? Tra-gedians were likely trying to create a certain atmosphere in their works and this prohibition over time became an artistic convention. We don't know exactly where or when this practice began, but it was likely less about some religious or moral authority using the no-fun police to force tragedies not to show actual blows, and more about aesthetic considerations and the belief that violence could be even more horrible if you only showed its effects.

Ancient Rome: The naughty Romans changed things considerably, and not for the better. While initially they modeled their plays on those of the Greeks, with Bacchus (the Roman Dionysus) being the great dramatic patron, in time Roman audiences wanted much more spectacle and grandiosity in their entertainments. This was the society that thrilled to gladiators fighting each other to the death and animals mauling hapless victims in the great arenas, after all, and those shows were not for the squeamish.

While following Greek models, Rome's comedies went ever more over the top, with painful physical hilarity akin to the later Commedia and even actual sexual activity eventually taking place in front of crowds. Tragedies, of course, demanded blood and death, and why bother talking about these events that had occurred offstage, when you could simply show them actually happening? If the plot called for, say, someone to be stabbed to death, there was no need to worry about faking it, you just killed someone for real. Wait, what?

Well, the Romans apparently devised a rather ingenious solution for how to convincingly portray onstage death (though how true this is remains unclear): just as some condemned prisoners were sent to the arenas for the amusement of the masses and their executions turned into entertainment, in plays, the condemned were sometimes brought to theaters and dressed as characters from the story. When a given character was due to die, the actor playing the part would simply step aside (or vanish backstage) momentarily, and the condemned, wearing the same outfit, would be pushed forward to take the thrust of the dagger or the swipe of the sword for real. Since they were most often wearing masks, the illusion of the actor dying was preserved, and the death was horrifically authentic. This might be taking method acting a little too far.

The Middle Ages: The medieval world did away with the excesses of Roman theater (probably a good thing), but the need to depict certain grisly scenes from Christian history became important, not for titillation, but for strict spiritual instruction. As a result, players started getting creative with faking horrific killings. Some plays detailed the lives and deaths of martyrs and saints, and what better way to scare an audience into good behavior than by showing them exactly how such pious people met their gruesome ends? Here is an example: A later twelfth-century French play, *Le Mystère d'Adam* ("The Mystery [Play] of Adam"), was a dramatization of Genesis, and for the murder of Abel at the hands of Cain, instructions were given that the actor playing the victim have a small pot of blood concealed on him, so that when the moment came, he could go out in a blaze of messy glory.

Later, in the fourteenth and fifteenth centuries, the producers of mystery plays got even more creative, pre-coating Christ's whips and the crown of thorns with animal blood so that it would trickle down all over the actor's face and body at the appropriate moment. They also used small animal bladders filled with blood that could be pierced by the nails during the crucifixion, giving the impression of Christ's blood pouring out.

Even better, there were dummy substitutes for actors playing martyrs, so that when their grisly time came, said dummies could be abused appallingly, and would burst forth with animal blood, animal intestines, etc., to give a hideously realistic slant to their torturous deaths. These dummies could be burned (as many good martyrs were), and the odor of charred animal flesh would do a pretty good job of representing what human remains would smell like in similar circumstances. So medieval parents: take the kids to see a mystery play—it'll be a great family day out!

The Renaissance: The use of gory special effects only increased with the rebirth of all things Classical. Humanism, scientific inquiry, and beautiful art, music, and sculpture abounded, so why not new ways of depicting terrible suffering? Well, that's what the Elizabethans thought, anyway.

We have already discussed Kyd's remarkably violent *Spanish Tragedie* from the 1580s, with its multiple onstage deaths, suicides, and other unpleasant activities. Remember Hieronimo, the fellow who bites off his own tongue to save Bel-Imperia's reputation? You just *know* that the players were itching to show that one off! So how did they do it? It was pretty easy, really, and pretty gross. The actor playing Hieronimo hid a lamb's tongue in his mouth, and possibly a small bit of bladder holding some fake blood. So when the appropriate moment came, he could bite down, spit out the tongue—which would flop and splat on stage—and drool a little blood for added emphasis. The effect would have been striking and revolting.

Elizabethan stage directions could be equally graphic. A prop list for Christopher Marlowe's *Tamburlaine* of 1587 specifically includes a pile of severed limbs. These could be made out of cloth and easily sewn together. They would not have looked terribly realistic, but the effect would have been enough to be shocking in displaying Tamburlaine's cruelty. Shakespeare's *Titus Andronicus* included such directions as "Enter a messenger, with two heads and a hand," thrown out as casually as if he were instructed to carry a basket or a jug of wine.

Some scholars now doubt that these kinds of productions had gallons of blood onstage, animal, fake, or otherwise. It simply would not have been feasible to use real liquid, which would have stained clothing and been almost impossible to wash away, especially after every performance. Theatrical costumes were expensive and could not be discarded after only a few uses. Gushing wounds might instead have been simulated with red strips of cloth, while certain swords and knives might have been painted red and swapped out when killing scenes happened. Of course, none of this would have been as shocking as seeing red liquid spray everywhere, but it would have made certain tricks, such as the spitting out of a lamb's tongue, all the more awful when they did happen.

One area where there seems to have been a real danger was in the use of guns and gunpowder. One English account from 1587 describes a play being given by the Admiral's Men, and notes that an actor fired his musket at another, missed, and accidentally killed a child and a pregnant woman instead, and injured a man in the head. Aside from the tragedy itself, one has to wonder just what the hell they were thinking in firing live ammunition in an enclosed space, and even more, what were they expecting to happen if the musket's shot had actually hit the intended actor? Maybe he was wearing some kind of breastplate under his costume, but it seems like an awful risk to take. Apparently, there were repercussions, and the Admiral's Men were not invited to perform at court during the Christmas season that year. Well, I hope they learned their lesson!

The seventeenth and eighteenth centuries: After these bloodbaths, stage violence seemed to die down for a while, especially in France during the seventeenth century. Seriously, France fought in at least seven wars in less than eighty years: the Thirty Years' War (1618–1648), the Fronde (civil wars, 1648–1653), the Franco-Spanish War (1635–1659), the War of Devolution (1667–1668), the Franco-Dutch war (1672–1678), the War of the Reunions (1683–1684), and the Nine Years' War (1688–1697). Good lord! No wonder they had gone off watching people get hacked up in the theater; there was enough of that going on in real life. They turned instead to the silliness of the Commedia and Molière's farces, among other diversions.

For its part, England had to contend with its own bloody civil war that ended with a king's head being lopped off for real. As we saw, an entire religious and political movement, the Puritans, banned stage plays altogether in the 1640s and 1650s. After the restoration of Charles II, it was only natural that bawdy comedies would take some precedence. Interest in these began to wane with the arrival of the new century, and plays that were overtly political eventually ended up being the subject of a crackdown with the boring Licensing Act of 1737. English theater turned to tamer subjects for the next half century or so, and it was only with the arrival of the new "gothic" genre that darker themes began to be explored in literature and drama.

The Gothic Era: The first gothic novel is usually held to be Horace Walpole's *The Castle of Otranto*, published in 1764. Amusingly, Horace was the son of Sir Robert Walpole, the same chap who introduced the Licensing Act to censor plays . . . *Let me explain, Dad!* Subjects like a deep mystery, an old house with hidden secrets, a family beset by some generational curse, and other such themes would become staples of the genre. At the time, the Enlightenment was all the rage, with its emphasis on reason and science, so these new stories about superstitions, ghosts, and hidden dangers didn't go over so well with some critics. But the style persisted and eventually found its way to the theaters, where it opened up new possibilities for onstage shocks.

One fine example was George Colman the Younger's *Blue Beard, or Female Curiosity!: A Dramatic Romance*, which premiered in January 1798. It is a retelling of an existing story of a wealthy nobleman with a striking blue beard. He tells his new young wife that she may go anywhere in his castle except for one room. While he is away on business, he reminds her not to unlock the door. Of course, curiosity gets the better of her and she enters the forbidden passageway, only to discover that it leads to a chamber of horrors, containing the mutilated bodies of his former wives, who presumably also disobeyed him by coming down to satisfy their curiosity. When Bluebeard returns and discovers her disobedience, he tells her that she will suffer the same fate. Before he can kill her, however, her brothers arrive and kill him instead.

The play takes a different angle and adds a supernatural element—the ghosts of his former wives inhabit the room of death, called the Blue Chamber. One of the more striking scenes recalls some of the stage horrors of the Tudor period, while foreshadowing the imagery of the Grand Guignol (as we'll see):

> The door instantly sinks with a tremendous crash, and the Blue Chamber appears streaked with vivid streams of blood. The figures in the picture over the door change their position, and Abomelique [Bluebeard] is represented in the action of beheading the beauty he was before supplicating. The picture and devices of love change to subjects of horror and death. The interior apartment (which the sinking of the door discovers) exhibits various tombs in a sepulchral building, in the midst of which ghostly and supernatural forms are seen—some in motion, some fixed. In the centre is a large skeleton seated on a tomb (with a dart in his hand), and over his head in characters of blood is written "The Punishment of Curiosity."

In the play's climax, it is the skeleton of one of his victims who rises and stabs Bluebeard to death and drags him below the stage, while a chorus celebrates his defeat. This kind of ghoulish entertainment was devoured by audiences eager for the theater to push boundaries.

The nineteenth century: Such early Victorian potboiler plays were soon to have another source of inspiration. By the 1840s, popular newspapers called "penny dreadfuls" circulated in London, with serialized stories of crime and lurid goings-on. One such publication, rather strangely called *The People's Periodical and Family Library*, published a story in 1846 titled "The String of Pearls: A Romance," in which one of the supporting characters was a barber who disposed of his customers with a sharp razor and turned them into tasty meat pies as a way of bringing in extra income. Manager, actor, and mostly-hack playwright George Dibdin Pitt (1795–1855) saw great potential in this freakish fellow and, in 1847, he brought out "The String of Pearls; or, The Fiend of Fleet Street," a play performed at the Britannia Theatre in London. Set in the eighteenth century, it portrayed the crimes of one Sweeney Todd in lurid detail, and claimed in 1850 that they were based on a true story. This claim is debatable, and researchers have failed to come up with any records of a murderous barber being hanged for his cannibalistic crimes, but given the cesspool of criminal activity that certain parts of London were from the mid-eighteenth century until the end of the nineteenth, the idea is not that far-fetched. Indeed, Dickens, in *Martin Chuzzlewit* (published only a few years before the penny dreadful tale), wrote of "dens of any of those preparers of cannibalic pastry, who are represented in many country legends as doing a lively retail business in the metropolis," so the idea was already circulating in urban myth, if not in fact. *The People's Periodical* often published fictionalized stories derived from true crimes, and the public had a seemingly insatiable appetite for reading about them, so the tale could easily have gotten around that Sweeney Todd was a real person.

Pitt was famous for this kind of violent melodrama, given the charming name of "bloodtubs" in the eighteenth century. Indeed, the Lord Chamberlain's Office, citing the Licensing Act, would not permit some of his plays to be performed. Still, he wrote about two hundred and fifty such potboilers, which were rather like the pulp stories and dime novels of the early twentieth century. They included gothic themes such as symbolic dreams and nightmares, atmospheric settings, and family conflicts, as well as military and nautical adventures. Sweeney Todd's exploits somehow passed the censors, and other adaptations of the tale followed over the rest of the century. Pitt's production used a special tilting barber's chair that disposed of the victim by dumping him below the stage. This allowed the actor (presumably falling into some padding) to make a hasty exit while also representing Todd's method of transferring the corpses to the cellar where they were prepared for their special culinary future. The idea of using a prop razor to simulate the cutting of throats, allowing fake blood to spurt all over the stage (no doubt to gasps and screams), must have been irresistible to the various producers who kept bringing versions of the tale to Victorian audiences.

All of these examples provide some fascinating glimpses into the mindset of playwrights, theater owners, and producers, what they thought their audiences wanted, and how they could best go about showing it to them. The lure of gory drama has been with us for a long time, it seems. Companies did the best they could with the effects and technologies that they had, but even in the later nineteenth century, their efforts were *nothing* compared to what was about to follow, the infamous Grand Guignol!

The horrors of the Grand Guignol in Paris and London

Le Théâtre du Grand-Guignol ("The Theatre of the Great Puppet," named for a French puppet, Guignol, who was used to make social commentary) was a fascinating experiment in horror and gore on the live stage, perhaps even more so because of the time in which it originated, the Belle Époque, which was characterized by its optimism, prosperity, and relative peace before the very real horrors of the first World War set in. The Grand Guignol ran from 1897 until 1962, and though situated in a small venue in Paris, it maintained its popularity for decades, only waning after World War II; it seems that two devastating conflicts in only twenty years brought enough of their own terror, violence, and evil, so Parisians no longer craved the fictional variety.

Set in a former neo-gothic church (appropriately enough), the show was the brainchild of novelist and playwright Oscar Méténier (1859–1913), whose work embraced realism, the idea of creating stories about everyday people and situations using straightforward storytelling. Initially the theater showed plays about classes of people that were considered "beneath" serious artistic attention or inappropriate for the stage: prostitutes, criminals of all kinds, beggars, and others that polite society preferred to pretend didn't exist.

Playwright Max Maurey (1866–1947) took over as director in 1898 and began to shift the content of the plays to one more focused on horror and gothic themes. Fellow playwright André de Latour, Comte de Lorde (1869–1942), was brought in to create new dramas, and he reveled in the idea of telling stories of horror and mental illness, penning some one hundred and fifty plays. He was later dubbed "the Prince of Terror" by his colleagues.

De Lorde's naturalistic focus was an important distinction from other genres of horror; the plays of the Grand Guignol were mostly not of the supernatural variety (i.e., involving ghosts, demons, or vampires). Rather, they looked at the terrible consequences of very human actions, which could include murder, torture, revenge, surgeries gone wrong, and other awful fates that could conceivably happen in the real world. Modern slasher and torture porn films are the latest version of this unsettling genre, and the plays certainly did not shy away from fake stage gore when necessary. The Grand Guignol exploited these stomach-churning visuals to maximum effect: fake severed heads that dropped to the stage, simulated crucifixions, animal eyeballs (bought from taxidermists) stuffed with fake blood for eye-gouging scenes, hoses filled with stage blood for entrails . . . the appalling list goes on and on. The blood was ascribed to a "secret recipe" and could apparently coagulate and form scabs.

Many of the theater's ghoulish special effects came from the efforts of Camille Choisy, who was director from 1914 to 1930. During his time, the Grand Guignol reached its heights (or depths) and attracted its largest crowds, including royalty. Choisy hired the young actress Paula Maxa (1898–1970) in 1917, and she became a headlining star in the theater's productions, later amusingly being referred to as "the most assassinated woman in the world." The range of her appalling, simulated onstage deaths is staggering and includes: being shot, strangled, scalped, disemboweled, hanged, quartered, guillotined, poisoned, cut into multiple pieces, eaten by a puma, burned alive, squished by a steamroller, and any number of other awful fates. After her death in any given play, lighting and other effects were used to rapidly transform her appearance into that of a corpse, adding to the horror. She took her work very seriously and was noted for her professionalism. She once remarked, "Before I go to bed, I look under my bed with fear. I fear the dark, the storms, the sea, the unknown and my own darkness."

Many in the audience had no idea what they were truly in for, despite the inevitable pre-show warnings. There are plenty of tales of people gasping, screaming, fainting, and even vomiting in reaction to the shows. The theater employed a house doctor to assist should anyone be too seriously affected, but apparently, one show was so intense that he also fainted during the performance! Still, Parisians and tourists came in droves, seeking the lure of the forbidden, a chance to confront uncomfortable fears, and maybe even a cathartic release. A grotesque escapism was on offer, and audiences could take comfort in the fact that it was all illusion.

The plays could definitely be quite shocking. A particular favorite—if you can call it that—was de Lorde's *Le Laboratoire des Hallucinations* ("The Laboratory of Hallucinations"). In the story, a doctor discovers that his patient in the operating room is having an affair with his wife, so he proceeds to perform graphic brain surgery on the unfortunate fellow, rendering him insane from hallucinations and brain damage. But the terror does not stop there; the victim has enough sense remaining to rise up, grab a chisel, and drive it into the doctor's head. The end.

Other plays include *L'Horrible Passion* ("The Horrible Passion"), about a young nanny who strangles the children that are in her care and

L'Homme de la Nuit ("The Man of the Night"), the story of a necrophiliac that may have been based on the atrocities of an actual person from mid-nineteenth-century France. Clearly, these were not tales for the faint of heart. In an effort not to send crowds away feeling too unsettled, the shows also offered comedies as a palate-cleanser, a tradition that went right back to ancient Greece and its satyr plays.

An attempt was briefly made to bring a version of the show to London, and between the years 1920 and 1922, it did relatively well, enticing the same kinds of morbid curiosity in Londoners as it did in Parisians. But the shows fell afoul of the Lord Chamberlain's Department and faced serious censorship under the ever-present Licensing Act. Ultimately, the production could not sustain itself and folded.

The show came to New York in October 1923, and ran for several weeks, but was not especially well-received. One critic humorously summed up a later American performance from 1927: "A noisy, violent sketch of a night in a French Consulate during the Boxer uprising. . . . Machine gun firing, shrieks, maniacal laughter are heard with terrible descriptions of torture—eyes gouged out, breasts torn off, nails plucked from fingers. One even saw one mutilated fellow run in with his hands cut off. Thereafter the play began to be disagreeable." Many audiences and critics found the whole thing laughable rather than horrifying.

The French theater faced scrutiny and censorship more than once even in relatively tolerant Paris. By 1930, a new director, Jack Jouvin, decided to change the focus away from brutal gore and emphasize instead psychological thrillers and dramas. He fired Paula Maxa, which seems a ridiculously stupid thing to do, given her popularity. Jouvin had control issues and basically changed the Grand Guignol's whole nature, but this proved to be unpopular and the theater started to decline. Later, the gore was brought back, but in the aftermath of World War II, the shocking displays of violence undoubtedly seemed distasteful to many, in view of the death and devastation that so many had suffered.

Time magazine noted, in an article from January 16, 1950: "The war made horror trite and started emptying the Grand Guignol's seats. Another blow: the theater's chief playwright, Andre ('Prince of Terror') de

Lorde, died (in bed) at the age of 90. No new twists in torture or tricks of realism—e.g., 'blood' that coagulates as it cools—could lure the crowds back. Even worse, the sounds of skulls being crushed and bodies plopping into acid vats began drawing guffaws instead of gasps."

Indeed, author Anaïs Nin noted that she went to a performance in 1958 and the theater was empty, so the signs of its imminent death were clear. Still, the shows continued to try to shock; one play from 1960 had the wonderfully explicit title *Les Coupeurs de Têtes* ("The Choppers of Heads"). But such lurid dramas were not enough to sustain enthusiasm. Facing the inevitable, the Grand Guignol closed its doors forever in 1962. Charles Nonon, the theater's last director, observed, "We could never compete with Buchenwald [the concentration camp]. Before the war, everyone believed that what happened on stage was purely imaginary; now we know that these things—and worse—are possible." Another *Time* magazine article noted with eloquent humor on November 30 of that year, concerning the theater's closure: "The last clotted eyeball has plopped onto the stage. The last entrail has been pulled like an earthworm from a conscious victim."

Actors who gave their all for their final performances

The history of theater is filled with stories of actors who, whether in ill health or just overexertion, taxed themselves so heavily that they expired from their craft and gave their audiences more memorable performances than they had planned. Here are a handful of notable examples:

Edmund Kean (1787–1833) was a British Shakespearean actor, whose talents took him on many travels, including two trips to the United States, which may seem surprising given the testy relationship between the two nations in the early nineteenth century (the War of 1812 and all that). He was also successful in Canada, which makes more sense, since they never rebelled. His performance in Quebec so impressed some Huron natives in the audience that they wanted to meet with him after the show. He told them that he desired to become a member of their tribe, and they granted his wish, even giving him a new name, Alanienouidet. Kean was quite ready to stay indefinitely in their village, but some of his friends compelled him to leave, and then kindly sent him to an asylum to recuperate and think things over.

Among his accomplishments, Kean is credited with restoring the tragic ending to *King Lear*, which, believe it or not, had usually been performed with a happy ending for the previous century and a half. This new (yet old) depressing ending didn't go down well with everyone; they must have missed the whole part about it being a "tragedy."

His final—and quite tragic—bow came during a performance of *Othello*. Taking the title role purely out of financial need, he arrived at the theater knowing full well that he was in no condition to go on, but he persevered. During act III, scene 3, he collapsed, telling his son (playing Iago) that he was dying. Indeed, he never recovered and died some weeks later.

Irish actress Margaret "Peg" Woffington (1720–1760) enjoyed a brief but illustrious career in London, during which time she had affairs with the Earl of Darnley, an MP, and noted actor and dramatist David Garrick (1717–1779). Her status was such that she was able to become a member and then the president of a previously all-male dining club, the wonderfully titled Sublime Society of Steaks (now *there's* a restaurant chain waiting to happen). Woffington's life was a mixture of successes and not-so-great times, and her career came to a sudden end in 1757. In a Covent Garden production, she was portraying Rosalind from Shakespeare's *As You Like It*. Everything seemed to go well enough, but by the fifth act, she felt unwell. In the middle of speaking a line, she trembled, yelled "O God! O God!" and collapsed, apparently from a paralytic stroke; she was quickly removed from the stage. She never acted again and spent her final years convalescing. A portrait was painted of her in 1758, in bed and gazing at the viewer with a sense of resignation.

The French actor and dramatist Zacharie Jacob (late sixteenth century–1667/68), known by his stage name, Montfleury, was famous for his dramatic roles, and his dramatic girth, so much so that Molière mocked him for his size. He in turn fired back at Molière, but his temper was not satisfied with a mere trading of insults. He also accused his rival of having committed incest, and denounced him before King Louis XIV. When Molière married the young actress Armande Béjart in 1662—a woman half his age—it was viewed as scandalous. As we have seen, some thought that Armande was in fact the daughter of Madeleine Béjart, rather than her younger sister, as was claimed. If so, this could very well have meant that Molière was her father, since he and Madeleine had been lovers at the time that she was born. It would bring Molière down to Earl-of-Oxford levels of "ick," if the conspiracy theorists are to be believed.

In any case, Montfleury played this allegation up as much as he could to make himself look better, but the king apparently did nothing about it. Alas, Montfleury only had a few years to live and his poor health caught up with him in 1667. While playing the role of Orestes in the neo-Greek play *Andromaque* by the playwright Jean Racine (1639–1699), he overexerted himself and ruptured a blood vessel, possibly due to a metal belt that he wore to support his enormous belly being cinched up too tightly. He collapsed onstage and died shortly thereafter.

Henry Irving (1838–1905) was a well-respected Victorian actor and, in 1895, he became the first actor to be awarded a knighthood. Novelist Bram Stoker worked for Irving as the manager of the Lyceum Theatre in London, and most scholars agree that Irving provided a model for the character of Dracula (while the historical Vlad the Impaler provided the name and the setting). Indeed, Stoker had originally wanted to write the story as a play, with Irving taking the role of the infamous count, but the actor had no interest in it. He called the story "dreadful" and rejected the idea completely.

Irving was renowned for his Shakespearean roles and traveled widely, and his end came about in a suitably dramatic way. He was touring and giving a performance in Bradford in 1905. On October 13, while acting the title role in Alfred Tennyson's play *Becket*, Irving reached the point in the play where Thomas Becket is murdered by Henry II's knights. As he spoke Becket's dying words, "Into thy hands, O Lord, into thy hands," he suffered a stroke and collapsed. He was taken to a nearby hotel, where he died shortly afterward. It was an appropriate way to go for one who was seen by many as the most important actor of the age.

Finally, beginning in about 1823, one encounters a number of accounts of rather spectacular deaths on stages; these descriptions were published and reprinted in various magazines and collections of anecdotes. They are worth quoting at length because of the splendidly formal and verbose way that they are retold:

> Mr. John Palmer, well known as an actor on the London boards . . . terminated his dramatic career and his life on the Liverpool stage, in 1798. [Palmer received news of his son's death, causing him great distress. He still attempted to perform and] he fell a sacrifice to the poignancy of his own feelings, and in which the audience were doomed to witness a catastrophe which was truly melancholy. In the fourth act, Baron Steinfort obtains an interview with the Stranger [Palmer's role], whom he discovers to be his old friend. He prevails on him to relate the cause of his seclusion from the world: in this relation the feelings of Mr. Palmer were visibly much agitated; and at the moment he mentioned his wife and children, having uttered (as in the character) "O God! God! there is another and a better world!" he fell lifeless on the stage. The audience supposed for the moment that his fall was nothing more than as studied addition to the part; but on seeing him carried off in deadly stiffness, the utmost astonishment and terror became depicted in every countenance. Hammerton, Callan, and Mara, were the persons who conveyed the lifeless corpse from the stage into the scene room. Medical assistance was immediately procured; his veins were opened, but they yielded not a single drop of blood; and every other means of resuscitation were had recourse to, without effect.

Clearly, getting overly emotional onstage could lead to tragic consequences. Sometimes, actors could get so absorbed in their characters that it apparently did them in:

In the history of the stage, there are several instances . . . of performers who in favourite characters, have given way to such an intensity of feeling, as to occasion instant death. In October, 1758, Mr. Paterson, an actor long attached to the Norwich company, was performing the Duke, in "Measure for Measure," which he played in a masterly style. Mr. Moody was the Claudio; and in the third act, where the Duke (as the Friar) was preparing Claudio for execution next morning, Paterson had no sooner spoken these words,—

—Reason thus with life:
If I do lose thee, I do loose a thing
That none but fools would keep; a breath thou art;

than he dropped in Mr. Moody's arms, and died instantly. He was interred at Bury St. Edmunds, and on his tombstone his last words, as above, are engraved.

Another actor kept an audience applauding for far longer than they should have, though he paid the ultimate price for it:

A gentleman of the name of Bond, collecting a party of friends, got up Voltaire's play of "Zara" (which a friend had translated for him), at the music room in Villiersstreet, York Buildings, and chose the part of Lusignan for himself. His acting was considered as a prodigy; and he so far yielded himself up to the force and impetuosity of his imagination that on the discovery of his daughter he fainted away. The house rung with applause; but finding that he continued a long time in that situation, the audience began to be uneasy and apprehensive. The representatives of Chatillon and Nerestan placed him in his chair; he then faintly spoke, extending his arms to receive his children, raised his eyes to heaven, and then closed them forever.

Such wonderful eloquence in the face of certain doom!

4

An Abundance of Superstitions, Curses, and Bad Luck

There is probably no other field in the arts that is as plagued with superstitious beliefs as the theatrical world. The sheer number of superstitions is staggering, mystifying, and often comical. Some of you may be familiar with a few of them, such as never saying Mac—er, "the Scottish Play," the fear of unlucky colors, the unlucky peacock, and other such prohibitions and anxieties. But there are many more, and in this chapter we'll delve into some of the best (worst?) of them, as well as how and why some of them came about.

What motivates otherwise rational people to throw out said rationality and instead decide to cling to these strange and often inhibiting practices? Well, our conscious, thinking minds are only a part of our mental makeup, and it could well be that superstitious beliefs reside in a deeper, older part of our brains, one where we want to make order of the seemingly random chaos around us and try to find connections to help us do that.

Many of these beliefs probably have origins in old folk practices that themselves came about by accidental discovery. Someone did something and saw a certain outcome for good or bad, and so decided that their actions must have influenced that result. It's the old correlation/causation conundrum. So, while we may scoff at what we see as silly fears and self-imposed limits, most of us have engaged in them at one time or another.

Don't deny it, or otherwise be prepared to break a mirror or walk under that ladder on Friday the 13th to prove your point. Are these superstitions all much ado about nothing? Read on and decide for yourself . . .

Never whistle backstage

Beware! If someone whistles backstage, the play will fail, the actor in question will fail, or die, or have bits fall off, or whatever! Actually this particular prohibition, which is believed to bring about bad luck for a production, has a practical purpose and a logical origin. In earlier times, the rigging in theaters resembled that of a ship, and sailors were often hired to operate ropes and pulleys to change scenes and sets. In the days before electricity, cues for scene changes and other directions were communicated by various whistles, which were a kind of code language, borrowed from similar practices used by the sailors on their boats. If an actor absentmindedly whistled backstage, there was a danger that this could be misinterpreted as a scene change, resulting in a disaster for the production, and possibly even injury or death if, say, a heavy backdrop was moved before everyone was clear of it.

Now, obviously, such changes are all communicated by intercoms, video, cue lights, and other such wonders of technology, but the prohibition remains due to tradition, and it's probably best if no one challenges it.

Never wish anyone "good luck"

Instead, one should always say "Break a leg," or perhaps "Merde!" which is simply French for, well, you know. We're not quite sure when this practice began; it may have been as recently as the 1930s. Bernard Sobel wrote *The Theatre Handbook and Digest of Plays* in 1948, and he noted that "before a performance actors never wish each other good luck, but say 'I hope you break a leg.'" This is one of the earliest references, which may mean that this particular superstition hasn't been around for too long. There are many explanations for this odd tradition, some plausible, some pretty ridiculous. Here are just a few:

Wishing everyone "good luck" is tempting fate, or malevolent spirits, which are only too happy to come in, disrupt things, and make a mess of the production.

In Shakespeare's time, "break" often meant "bend," so if one was "bending a leg," they were bowing, or making a "Reverence," a type of greeting, especially to one's social superior: placing one foot behind the other and bending the knee. The phrase thus might have originated as a wish that the actor receive many curtain calls and take many bows (i.e., that he would give a splendid performance).

Another theory claims that those who were seated at theaters would stomp their feet rather than applaud a fine performance. If they stomped hard enough, they might break the legs of the chairs they were sitting in; yes, this one seems like a bit of a stretch. An even less plausible theory asserts that in ancient Greece, audiences did the same foot-stomping, but in the hard stone amphitheatres, they risked breaking foot or leg bones if they stomped too hard. So, a "broken leg" was a sign that one had given an excellent performance.

An American legend says that the phrase refers to John Wilkes Booth, the actor who assassinated Abraham Lincoln. When fleeing from the scene, he broke his leg, either from jumping down to the stage as he fled, or perhaps falling off of a horse. Why anyone would want to give a performance in memory of a notorious murder is unclear, but these kinds of things aren't exactly logical.

One more theory is that the phrase originated with vaudeville shows, when producers overbooked the number of acts that a show could contain. Each act had a chance to prove that they were worthy, but if they were rejected, they could be pulled before reaching the stage proper. "Breaking a leg" meant that an act was able to move past the visual plane of the curtains lining each side of the stage, which were known as "legs," and actually be on the stage, at which point they would be paid. So wishing that someone would "break a leg" may have originally been a wish that they were worthy enough to be paid for their performance.

The mysterious ghost light

According to theater lore, a "ghost light" must be left on after the theater closes and everyone has gone home for the night. This light is a single source of illumination that must never be turned off, electric bills be damned. From a practical point of view, it allows the first person to enter the theater and the last person to leave to move about without falling and breaking something, a leg or otherwise. But of course, it's not just a practical tradition.

As the name implies, the light remains on to ward off evil and/or angry spirits from descending into the theater and causing trouble. If the light is turned off and the spirits are inadvertently summoned, they could cause all manner of problems for the future of the production. Alternatively, the light may provide just enough illumination so that if any such ghosts want to perform, they will be able to do so, and so leave the plays of the living undisturbed. Some say that this is also the origin of the practice of leaving the theater "dark" one day a week (i.e., closed); it gives aspiring spectral thespians a chance to hone their skills. Incidentally, one should never actually say that the show is "closed" on that day off, because that invites the possibility that it will actually close for good.

And what about the days before electricity? Well, some believe that gas lamps or even candles were used for the same purpose, but flames obviously could be exceedingly dangerous. Having your theater burn down would be much worse luck than annoying the occasional spirit visitor.

Speaking of open flame, it was long considered unlucky to have exactly three candles burning onstage as a part of the set during a performance. If this were to happen, the actor positioned nearest to the shortest candle would either be the next person to die or the next to get married; an interesting commentary on one's potential fate?

Peacock feathers are forbidden

One fairly widespread belief is that no one must ever bring even a single peacock feather to a theater, much less take it onstage, whether as part of a set or a costume. Such a reckless action will almost certainly result in disaster befalling the production, including everything from set damage to injuries to a failed show. The unique shape and designs of the feather top are believed to represent an evil eye that will curse the production.

These beliefs may have ancient Greek origins in the myth of Argus Panoptes, a giant who was covered with a hundred eyes. He served Hera as a guardian of the nymph Io, whom Zeus desired. Zeus schemed and had Hermes kill Argus. In Argus's memory, Hera had his eyes preserved by transferring them to the feathers of the peacock's tail. But exactly how that relates to theater is uncertain.

Another theory suggests that the bird and its feathers were prized by the Mongols, who terrorized Eastern Europe in the thirteenth century and would likely have overrun the West if not for being called back to Asia in 1242 to elect the successor to their leader, Ögedei, who died in 1241. Some suggest that the fear of the bird may recall an older fear of Mongol attacks. This one is quite a stretch, though, since peacocks were valued as garden curiosities and also eaten at fancy banquets in Europe during the Middle Ages, complete with their colorful plumage stuffed back into the roasted bird carcass for effect.

More recently, when the television network NBC adopted a peacock logo and used the catchphrase "proud as a peacock," there were murmurings about tempting fate. Though a TV network is quite different from a theatrical house, some worried that the bad luck could carry over, since what is television if not a modern-day version of the theater? The logo doesn't seem to have caused much harm, however, or the network probably would have already discarded it. Of course, NBC did proceed to bring out shows like *Misfits of Science*, *We've Got it Made*, and *Manimal*, so maybe there's something to the curse after all.

Unlucky colors

It's no surprise that in the complex history of drama, some colors are considered unlucky. One color, blue, has a rather practical reason for being condemned. According to belief, blue should not be worn onstage unless it is also accompanied by or trimmed with silver.

In earlier times, certain types of blue dyes were difficult to manufacture and therefore expensive. If a company could afford to use them it meant that they were well-off financially. However, failing companies would sometimes go into debt to obtain such colors anyway, in order to present themselves as being successful. This, of course, could quickly lead to bankruptcy and ruin, and so blue-colored costumes came to be viewed with some suspicion. In order to counter claims that a company was hiding its failings and to calm fears, such companies might place themselves even further at risk by investing in real silver to adorn the blue, to show that they had genuine money or backing by a wealthy patron. From this, a superstition arose that blue must always be accompanied by silver, to prove that the company and the show would not fail.

Yellow is another unlucky color for the stage. This probably dates back to the Middle Ages, when yellow was a favored color worn by the devil in medieval mystery plays. So obviously, if an actor is wearing yellow, it could bring bad luck, make an actor forget lines, or at the very least invite some unwanted diabolical attention. Green is viewed with some suspicion as well, especially in France. It is thought that in medieval plays, the character of Judas often wore a green costume, thus tainting the color for all time. Also, legend says that Molière died while wearing the color, further marring its reputation.

Deadly flowers

We normally give flowers as tokens of affection and appreciation. Think about that for a minute—we hand someone we love or admire a bundle of plant sexual organs and expect them to be flattered by it. Anyway, the giving of flowers after successful performances is a long-standing tradition, whether as bouquets or even just individual flowers tossed by audience members onto a stage.

In the weird world of the theater, there was a tradition of giving flowers to the director or the lead on closing night from a rather special source. Since it was the end of the run, it was considered good luck to offer a bundle of flowers stolen from a grave. Apparently, this gift symbolized the closing ("death") of the show, which could then be laid to rest after a successful run. Obviously, one would never want to do this before closing night, because it could affect the show badly and perhaps make it close early.

Okay, so pilfering from the dead is completely unethical, disrespectful, and illegal. This strange practice probably came about simply because acting companies didn't have a lot of spare money, and beautiful flower arrangements could be expensive. Therefore, the local graveyard would be an ideal place to obtain such bouquets at the right price. The idea of a couple of actors sneaking into a cemetery late at night to retrieve various bundles of flowers is either a setup for a hilarious comedy skit or a horror film. You would think that with so many other theatrical superstitions about not wanting to tempt fate, upset ghosts, or disturb unseen evil forces, the last thing a company would want to do is indulge in a bit of grave robbing just to save a few coins. The bigger question is: What if someone accidentally says "Macbeth" in a cemetery? On that note . . .

The curse of "the Scottish Play"

This is probably the most famous of all theatrical superstitions, one that raises many questions and inspires even more ridicule. Essentially, no one should ever say the word "Macbeth" in a theater, or quote lines from it if one is anywhere but onstage. To do so will invite all kinds of disaster and probably some horrified reactions from those within earshot. If anyone is foolish (or foolhardy) enough to tempt fate, they will often be forced to perform a ritual to counter the evils they have unleashed. First the others will say, "Angels and ministers of grace defend us!" In a scene reminiscent of a Monty Python skit, said offender must then leave the building, spin themselves around three time counterclockwise (wonderfully known as "widdershins" in older English), curse (or actually say "Macbeth"), and then knock or request to be let back into the theater; the British comedy *Blackadder* has a particularly funny version of this ritual, with the title character causing havoc for two very superstitious Regency actors. Other ways of defusing the supernatural tension include reciting Puck's speech from the end of *A Midsummer Night's Dream* ("If we shadows have offended . . ."), or perhaps quoting from *The Merchant of Venice* ("Fair thoughts and happy hours attend on you"). Apparently, the spirits will then be appeased.

Clearly, this fear is something that many actors and directors still take very seriously. So what is the origin for what many would think is just nonsense? There are actually several theories, and a number of incidents that do seem to indicate that something strange can happen when the dreaded play is performed or mentioned. There is an unverified account that a young actor, Hal Berridge, who portrayed Lady Macbeth during the play's first performance in 1606, died, forcing Shakespeare to take on the role. This makes a great story but has never been proven. Berridge's ghost was said to have haunted the production and probably other productions after that.

The dark themes of the play left it open to accusations of sorcery behind the scenes and curses working against it. At the time, there were fears that the reciting of occult-like rituals and spells during a theater performance risked summoning actual demons (remember Marlowe and Faust?), which would most definitely ruin the production. Some even thought that Shakespeare had received the curses and dialogue from actual practitioners of black magic, and that they may have cursed the play after being displeased with how he had portrayed them. The general dark mood and tone of the story, coming as it did after the infamous foiled Gunpowder Plot (when Catholics planned to blow up Parliament and with it King James), most definitely cast a long shadow over the whole production. James himself was highly superstitious and believed that witches were plotting against him and his reign, using black magic and diabolical schemes.

Practical explanations for the belief that there is a curse associated with the play include the fact that *Macbeth* features a lot of stage combat and often has dark sets, so injuries are naturally going to be more likely; tripping or accidentally hitting someone too hard would be all too easy to do. Further, the play is fairly short and has long been a crowd-pleaser despite (or probably because of) its dark themes. So companies often added it at short notice, hoping to use it to draw in bigger crowds, especially if their other productions were disappointing or failing. As such, the play could end up being under-rehearsed, which would lead to all sorts of disasters, on the stage and off. If such a company was on the verge of going out of business anyway, it may well have seemed like a production of *Macbeth* had finished it off.

All of this may well be true, but there have been some strange occurrences over the centuries that do make one wonder if something evil is going on behind the scenes. The play is known for being connected with unrest and riots in the audience. In the seventeenth century, a performance of *Macbeth* was staged at the indoor Blackfriars Theater in London. At the time, those who were wealthy enough could actually pay to sit *on the stage* and show off their finery while the actors carried on nearby; whose stupid idea was that? During the play, one such nobleman did the equivalent of talking on his cell phone—he got up and walked in front of an actor delivering his lines to greet a friend on the other side of the stage. The actor protested to him and the noble, not used to being addressed in such a way by a lowly player, slapped him. This caused chaos and soon a riot broke out. We can only hope that someone gave said noble a good smacking.

Perhaps the most notorious example of a riot was at a performance of the play at Astor Place in 1849 in New York. The chaos originated over a dispute between two actors of the time, the American Edwin Forrest and the English William Charles Macready, over who was the actor best able to perform the leading roles in Shakespeare's plays. This dispute went well beyond the two of them—the rivalry found its way into newspaper stories and popular opinion. At the time, there was a strong anti-British sentiment among some Americans (the War of 1812 was still recent enough), and British actors or other entertainers who toured the US frequently met with hostility, derision, and heckling. These two actors came to represent that Anglo-American rivalry, especially in regards to class distinction. Forrest was strongly supported by the working class, who were emphatically pro-American, while Macready had the support of the upper classes, and those who still looked favourably on British high society.

On May 7, 1849, anti-Macready forces had bought up a number of tickets and deliberately disrupted the Astor Place show, causing it to close early. They tore up seats and threw everything at the stage from rotten eggs and fruits to shoes and bottles—in an earlier performance, someone tossed a half carcass of a sheep at him while he performed! Macready was determined to leave then and there, but was persuaded to attempt one more show. He shouldn't have bothered. On the ill-fated night of May 10, Forrest's supporters gathered *en masse* outside the theatre to protest Macready's performance as Macbeth. It's estimated that as many as ten thousand people came looking for trouble. Forrest was connected to some of the notorious New York gangs of the time, who probably lent a helping hand in the form of criminals eager to cause disruption. Knowing that there would be unrest, the police and then troops were sent in to quell the growing disorder. After warnings were issued, shots were fired, and rioting commenced.

In the end, between twenty-five and thirty people were killed and as many as two hundred were injured. One consequence of this disturbance may have been the further separation between "high" and "low" art, such that Shakespeare and other such "respectable" art forms increasingly became the province of the upper classes, while the lower classes gravitated to vaudeville and music hall shows that often lampooned high society. Perhaps the violence of this incident convinced the working classes that they were not welcome in more fashionable circles? Since Shakespeare's plays were a British tradition, they may have decided to favor more homegrown American arts instead. Did the curse of *Macbeth* damage the popularity of "high art" in America?

A few decades later, the play raised its ugly head again, when it was rumoured that Abraham Lincoln read it the night before he was assassinated. He wasn't viewing it at the theater when he died, so this is probably just an urban legend.

Another *Macbeth*-misfortune-related story is told of Russian actor Konstantin Stanislavsky. During the dress rehearsal of the play, he apparently forgot his lines, but for whatever reason, the prompter who was supposed to provide cues (i.e., to help actors remember their lines) failed to do so. That prompter was soon found dead while still in his stage box, and his death was seen as a bad omen that ended up closing the production.

More recently, the curse definitely seemed to befall one of the twentieth century's greatest actors and those around him. Laurence Olivier was rehearsing for the opening night of *Macbeth* at the Old Vic in London in 1937. He lost his voice, which delayed the opening by four days. During the run, he narrowly escaped injury from a falling sandbag located in the wings. Lillian Baylis, the theater's founder and manager, died of a heart attack only two days before the opening of the show (later, in 1954, a painting of Baylis at the Old Vic fell from the wall and crashed into a bar on the opening night of another production of *Macbeth*; this was obviously not a good omen). The play's director and one of the actresses were injured in a taxi accident. During a preview performance, Olivier's sword broke during a fight and a part of the blade flew into the audience, striking a man. It was a prop sword and so not sharp, but the man was so startled that he had a heart attack and died.

Ever worse was the onstage accident in 1947 at the Oldham Coliseum Theatre in Manchester. The climactic scene was, of course, the battle between Macduff (played by Antony Oakley) and Macbeth (played by Harold Norman) for the future of Scotland. Though in the play much of this conflict happens offstage and we learn later that Macbeth has been killed, it's always thrilling to have some of the fight shown for audiences. However, the swords being used were a little too sharp and Oakley accidentally stabbed Norman right in the chest. As the curtain fell on the scene, the curtain also fell on Norman, who died shortly afterward.

In 1967 (one wonders if there's something about years ending in 7?), director Peter Hall was producing the play at Stratford and had no time for such silly fears, telling everyone involved in the production to pay no attention to superstitions and focus on the show instead. Mr. Hall's arrogance was tamed when he contracted a serious case of the shingles, which caused the play to be delayed. After it finally opened, the critical reception was lukewarm, and it was not a success.

As recently as 2013, an actor performing the play in Manchester, England, with Kenneth Branagh was struck by Branagh's sword during a performance, and had to receive medical treatment onsite. He was able to finish the performance, but went to a hospital afterward, just to be sure.

So what does all of this mean? Go to any Internet forum about the Macbeth superstition and you'll find dozens, if not hundreds, of anecdotal accounts in the comments from people who claim that they or someone they know tempted fate by uttering the forbidden word or even simply acting in the play, and then later suffered the consequences. Stories of injuries (a broken bone, a bad cut needing stitches), disappearing or damaged props, a collapsed theater roof, a car accident the following day, and so on are so common that they are rather unsettling to read. All of this lore of curses and black magic makes for splendid urban legend stuff, but many in the profession swear that it's true. Despite the uncounted thousands of productions of the play that have gone off without a hitch over the centuries, many actors would still prefer not to tempt fate.

The curse of Ophelia?

It's not just *Macbeth* that potentially brings disaster on actors and companies. Over the centuries, some have claimed that actresses who take on the role of the mad and doomed Ophelia from *Hamlet* are beset with problems in their personal lives. Realistically, this is just a prime example of anecdotal correlation being mistaken for causation, because large numbers of players have acted in the role and come out just fine. Meanwhile, terrible and horrible things have befallen those who never set foot in a theater or read a word of "the Danish Play." But in the interest of perpetuating superstitious fears, here are few actresses who took on the part and suffered calamities later:

Susan Mountfort (*fl.* later seventeenth century): A noted actress of the later seventeenth and early eighteenth centuries, Susan Mountfort (or Montford) had played the role to some acclaim, but was later betrayed by her love and lost her mind. She was kept under constant watch, but in 1720 escaped and made her way to her local theater, where *Hamlet* was showing. When Ophelia was set to appear in her scene of madness, Susan rushed to the stage and displaced the actress playing her. One account from the time notes: "She was in truth *Ophelia herself,* to the amazement of the performers as well as of the audience—nature having made this last effort, her vital powers failed her and she died soon after."

Sarah Siddons (1755–1831): A popular Welsh actress who first played the part in 1785, she was also known for her portrayal of Lady Macbeth—thus bringing another whole potential curse down on her! She married young, but the marriage was unhappy and five of her seven children died. It's worth remembering, however, that infant and child mortality were still pretty high in those days.

Mary Catherine Bolton (1790–1830): She first played the role in 1813 and caught the eye of one Edward Hovell-Thurlow, Second Baron Thurlow. She later married him and enjoyed wealth and privilege, but of course it would not last. After the baron's death in 1829, she was inconsolable, and she died less than a year later at the young age of thirty-nine. But she did have fifteen happy years and her sons survived.

In the twentieth century, a whole series of actresses who played the character were noted as later having significant personal troubles, including Jean Simmons, Marianne Faithfull, Helena Bonham Carter, and Kate Winslet. The fact is that, unfortunately, anyone can have tragedies befall them, so it seems fairly silly and even in bad taste to link a dramatic role with personal misfortune, but people seem to love looking for explanations for things, no matter how ridiculous and far out they are.

And the list goes on and on . . .

As if all of these superstitions and metaphysical regulations weren't enough to make theater people completely neurotic and to offer plenty of discouragement for up-and-coming actors from even getting started, here are several more guidelines with mysterious origins. They are not universal, so consult your local theater for the most relevant and up-to-date list.

Real flowers, jewelry, and money should never be onstage; this at least has a practical origin in attempts to prevent theft. Mirrors bring bad luck (broken or not) and should not be onstage; this one also has a practical purpose (i.e., to reduce stage light glare). Actors should not clean their makeup cases, and should never use new stage makeup on opening night, and never use a rabbit's foot when applying it (!). Actors should always leave the dressing room left foot first, but visitors should always enter the dressing room right foot first. However, no one should visit backstage during a dress rehearsal or some ill fortune will attach itself to someone's clothing during the play. Never place hats or shoes on a chair or a table in the dressing room. Never offer carnations to an actor or actress, as it means that their contract will not be renewed. A play should not open on a Friday night. The Green Room should never actually *be* painted green (as we've seen, it's an unlucky color). No one must ever knit in the wings of the stage (exactly why one would be knitting as actors are running on and off stage in a frenzy between scenes is not clear). One can learn one's lines better by sleeping with the script under their pillow (if only this were true!). An actor should never speak the last line of a play before opening night, because this could bring about an early closure for the production. However, a bad dress rehearsal will mean a fine debut performance (it allegedly gets the bugs out of the system, and many musicians believe this, too; yeah, right). Finally, never bow to an empty theater; it's insulting, because one must earn that bow from a real audience.

It all seems to be far more trouble than it's worth.

5

Haunted Theaters

Ghost stories provide some of our most popular entertainment, even from an early age. Whether huddled around a campfire or staying up late at night with only a creepy flashlight for illumination, children love scaring the pants off each other and themselves with tales of vengeful spirits and cursed old mansions. Or maybe it's daring their friends to sneak into that abandoned old house on the outskirts of town, the one where legend says terrible things happened and the dead are still there. As adults, we often dismiss such things as foolish and superstitious, and yet we still retain a fascination for the subject, even if only in fiction; films, television, and books are filled with stories of spectral incursions, and ghosts have played key roles in stage plays and operas for centuries.

The psychology of why people believe (or want to believe) in ghosts is obviously way beyond the boundaries of this book, but people generally fall into three categories: believers, skeptics, or somewhere in between. Skeptics will scoff and put down stories of real-life encounters to overactive imaginations. Perhaps they seek logical explanations, such as low-pitched radio frequencies, which can induce strange reactions in some people who aren't even aware of what's happening. Believers will counter with any number of anecdotal accounts of how some spirits seem to communicate or manifest themselves in audible or tactile ways, or are obviously directly tied to the building where they died. In-betweeners watch this sparring from the sidelines and assume that it will never be resolved.

For purposes of this chapter, try being an in-betweener as we delve into some of the stranger and creepier examples of haunted theaters and halls in Europe, America, and beyond. Given the superstitious nature of so many in the theatrical profession, it comes as no surprise that there would be countless stories of theater hauntings and meetings with the other side. Since so many playhouses are old, it's inevitable that they would feature an abundance of creaky floorboards, knocking pipes, drafty halls, and dark, scary basements. These are places where the imagination can run wild; indeed, that's already their primary purpose. Obviously, there are literally thousands of examples and we can only look at a few here, but these stories should be more than enough to pique your interest, and maybe even send a chill or two down your back.

Theatre Royal, Drury Lane, London

Sometimes called England's most haunted theater, the Theatre Royal (known simply as "Drury Lane" to locals) stands on a site previously occupied by three other theaters, the first of which was built in 1663. That's a lot of time for terrible things to happen, people to die, and ghosts to arise. In one example, a fire in the early nineteenth century killed more than twenty people. The current building dates from 1812, and it seems that most actors who have spent time there have experienced one thing or another that defies explanation. There are the usual stories of people hearing doors opening or closing on their own, things being moved, and in one case, a television changing its channels spontaneously in front of two actors who were chatting about the Drury Lane ghosts. Others have been touched or even shoved from behind, but see no one when they investigate.

There are at least three ghosts said to wander the premises. The first is Joseph Grimaldi (1778–1837), who is credited with inventing the modern clown look, including the white makeup with a fake grin and wigs, the costume, and the antics. This alone would make him scary enough for many. In contrast to his clown persona, his real life was quite miserable—he suffered personal loss, lack of money (he was often defrauded by con artists), and several injuries. He once attempted suicide by ingesting poison, but only ended up with a bad stomachache for a few days. By the time he died, he was crippled by stage injuries and beset with alcoholism. It's entirely possible that the spirit of such a tragic figure might wander without rest at Drury Lane. Grimaldi's ghost has been known to kick actors, apparently angry at losing the use of his own legs later in life. Legend says that he requested to be beheaded after his death and that the request was honored (who knows why?!); as a result, a disembodied clown face is sometimes seen floating around the stage area. Well, that's not creepy at all; sleep well tonight, all of you coulrophobes!

The second ghost is that of another clown, Dan Leno (1860–1904), best known for his cross-dressing pantomime roles. He also suffered from personal tragedy, had a mental breakdown, and died an alcoholic at a young age. Leno apparently suffered from incontinence (maybe due to stage fright) and would mask the smell of his urine-soaked trousers with perfume. Many have claimed that the scent of lavender mysteriously wafts through the stage area from time to time; perhaps Dan is taking a stroll nearby, but one wouldn't think that a spirit needs to pee.

The third ghost is known as the "Man in Grey," and is most often seen in the upper circle as a man dressed in—logically enough—grey, wearing a powdered wig and an eighteenth-century tricorn hat. Unusually for a ghost, he often appears during the daytime, and has been observed by numerous audience members, actors, and theater staff over the years, sometimes even sitting in a seat before vanishing. The ghost's origins are mysterious, but one theory is that it is the spirit of a young actor who was murdered in the theater. Indeed, in the 1870s, when workmen were doing some renovation on the upper circle, they discovered a bricked-up room that contained a skeleton. There were scraps of grey cloth about it, and chillingly, a dagger sticking out of the rib cage. Was he a young actor or theater patron who was violently murdered and whose body was then hidden? Is he condemned to wander the upper circle of Drury Lane for all eternity?

The Adelphi Theatre, the Strand, London

Like many theaters, the Adelphi has also undergone reconstructions and rebuilds since it was founded in 1806, but the chief ghost that wanders its dark halls shuffled off this mortal coil in 1897. William Terriss was a well-respected Shakespearean actor, and was also noted for his swash-buckling roles—Robin Hood, for example. He met his violent end on December 16, 1897, stabbed to death by a disturbed young actor, Richard Archer Prince. Terriss had tried to help Prince in the past, finding him roles and even offering financial assistance, but Prince's increasingly erratic behavior and alcoholism meant that he was no longer employable. He was reportedly seen arguing with Terriss a few days before the killing, and on the night in question, he hid in the shadows near the Adelphi's stage door. He stabbed Terriss in the chest, side, and back. The murder caused something of a sensation in the London press, though Prince was found not guilty by reason of insanity and committed to an asylum, where he died in 1936. Famed Victorian actor Henry Irving (1838–1905) was appalled by what he saw as a too-lenient sentence and noted with bitterness, "Terriss was an actor, so his murderer will not be executed." He would also later receive a death threat from Prince, mailed from the asylum.

As might be expected, someone who died such a horrible and pre-mature death (Terriss was only fifty at the time) might be inclined to hang around for a while, and not too long after his death, reports of ghostly incursions began. Terriss had been involved with actress Jessie Millward, and one report claims that as he lay dying, he promised he would come back to her. Sure enough, people soon began to hear mysterious knocks at the door of Millward's dressing room and occasionally see a figure moving about in the area. Once, in 1928, another actress named June claimed that she was attacked by an unseen force while changing in that same dressing room. Was the spirit of Terriss unhappy that a different actress was using his beloved's room?

Other reports claim that Terriss's ghost has also been spotted in the nearby Covent Garden Tube station. Witnesses have confirmed seeing him milling about, after being shown pictures of the actor. One ticket taker swore that Terriss appeared to him, pushed his head down, and then disappeared; he refused to work at the station afterward. Accounts of his presence there have continued into the last decade; maybe he's ultimately planning on going somewhere else? The idea of him boarding a phantom underground train for his last journey into the great unknown seems wonderfully poetic and fitting.

St. James Theatre, Wellington, New Zealand

On the other side of the world in Wellington, Kiwi playhouses are no more immune to the haunts of the dead than their British counterparts. A particularly unsettling example is the St. James. It opened in 1912, and after several decades of successful runs (including silent movies, talking movies, live stage shows, and music), it fell into decline in the 1970s. Stories of ghostly activity didn't help the theater's fortunes, and it was closed in the late 1980s. By the late 1990s, however, efforts were made to restore it, and it now operates fully again, including hosting the Royal New Zealand Ballet. The ghosts haven't gone away, however.

The most famous is the spirit of Yuri, who in life was a Russian acrobat. The story says that he fell to his death on the stage during a performance; some even claimed that he was pushed by a jealous fellow performer. Whatever the circumstances, he does not seem to be a vengeful ghost. Yuri is credited with turning the theater lights on again overnight after everyone has left; apparently the single ghost light isn't enough for him. One theater worker, a projectionist, swore that Yuri saved him twice. The first time, when the auditorium lights went out, he went looking for the switch near the edge of the stage and was shoved back by an unseen force. He later realized that in the dark, he would have fallen into the orchestra pit had this not happened, and probably would have been injured. Of course, maybe Yuri turned the lights off to begin with? In the second instance, the same man was onstage with his young child when an overhead beam fell. Again, he was pushed backward by invisible hands, and he swears that he saw his infant son lifted up and carried nearly ten feet away from the danger before being gently put down.

More malevolent is the ghost known as the "Wailing Woman," and with a name like that, you know she's going to be creepy, annoying, or both. Legends say that this is the spirit of an actress who, while trying to make a comeback and restart her career, was booed off the stage. She was so distraught that she slit her wrists and bled to death, either in the dressing room, or at home. Many people have reported hearing wailing and sobbing echoing in the theater, and the ghost also seems to delight in hindering living actresses, especially those in a lead role. Several women have inexplicably sprained their ankles onstage; one fell off a ladder, and another (an opera vocalist) was beset with a head cold that appeared suddenly just before her performance. She lost her voice and couldn't sing.

Even more unsettling, the theater is said to be haunted by an entire boys' choir. The boys gave their last concert in St. James during World War II. They set off on a ship to go on tour afterward, but the ship apparently sank and the choir was never heard from again. Employees have heard ghostly singers in various places, but when they go to investigate, the sound seems to move to another part of the theater.

So, why is this particular location such a hotbed of paranormal activity? There are the usual urban legends about it being built on an old Maori burial ground, but no evidence has turned up to prove this, so no one really knows. A recent paranormal investigation television team encountered the usual equipment malfunctions and a problem with an elevator used to bring musical instruments in, which apparently happens frequently. Old Yuri might still be having some fun with them.

The Palace Theatre, New York

The Palace Theatre, opened in 1913, was once the ultimate prize for vaudeville performers in the United States. Would-be entertainers of every imaginable variety would flock to New York and ply their trade near the venue in the hopes of attracting the attention of talent agents and the theater owners, who might then offer them a place on the coveted Palace stage.

Over its century-long history, it has hosted everyone from Harry Houdini to Bob Hope to Judy Garland. Magic shows, pantomimes, plays, and musical concerts have all graced its stage, and it seems that many of the performers (and a few others) are reluctant to leave. Indeed, one medium who went to the location declared that there were more than a hundred ghosts on the premises! She reported that many were unhappy—they felt stuck and could not leave until they corrected specific wrongs from their lives.

So, who's still hanging around? The most notorious ghost is that of one Louis Bossalina. His last name was misspelled as "Borsalino" by the *New York Times* in 1935, and that name stuck. Louis was a member of an acrobatic troupe called The Four Casting Pearls. They were performing on August 27, 1935, in front of an audience of some eight hundred; there were no nets on the floor. Louis leapt from his stationary position, attempting a double somersault, chillingly known as "the death loop," but missed grabbing his partner's hands and plunged more than twenty feet to the stage. Amazingly, he did not die, but his performing days were over; his hometown paper, *The Reading Eagle*, printed an obituary for him on August 4, 1963.

Even though the fall hadn't killed him, his spirit has returned to the site and has apparently been trying to get the stunt right ever since. There have been reports of a ghostly acrobat who screams as he falls to the stage once again, never able to perfect that last acrobatic feat. Seeing or hearing this particular apparition is allegedly very bad luck that can mean that misfortune or even death will befall the witness within a year.

Other less ominous spirits include a man dressed in a brown suit who is seen passing by the manager's office, usually after closing. There are also a sad-looking little girl who peers down at the auditorium from the balcony and a boy playing with toy trucks, also on the mezzanine. One performer recently saw a woman in the orchestra pit wearing a white gown and playing a cello, who vanished during the show.

The most famous resident is said to be Judy Garland. Though she is not usually seen, many have reported feeling a strange presence by the door that was built for her entrances and exits, near the rear of the orchestra. It's as if she's lingering there, still waiting to go on for one last performance.

New Amsterdam Theatre, New York

This Broadway theater, built between 1902 and 1903, hosted the famous Ziegfeld Follies from 1913 to 1927, and has been home to many grand productions over the last century. It actually functioned primarily as a movie theater from the 1930s to the 1980s, though it also had a nightclub and hosted smaller productions.

It also is home to a particularly interesting ghost, that of Olive Thomas. Olive had been in the Ziegfeld Follies production in 1915 and was quite famous, being called the most beautiful young woman in New York City. At one point, she was even painted for the cover of the *Saturday Evening Post*.

Alas, as often seems to be the fate of young starlets, her personal life became marred with troubles. In 1916, she eloped with Jack Pickford. Jack's sister, Mary, became a world-famous actress during the silent era, earning herself the name "Queen of the Movies." She would later win an Oscar.

Jack wasn't as talented or fortunate. Despite his movie-star good looks, he was an alcoholic and drug addict, and his behaviors increasingly made no one want to work with him; after 1920, his film credits drop off noticeably. While he loved Olive passionately, their relationship was stormy and abusive, zig-zagging from huge fights to making up and back again.

Possibly in an attempt to rekindle their love (though also to scout some film locations), they went to Paris in 1920. On the night of September 5, they returned to their hotel, after an evening on the town. Details are sketchy, but both were drunk, and both may have taken cocaine. At some point after midnight, Olive took a large dose of mercury bichloride, which her husband may have been using to treat syphilis (it was a common treatment before antibiotics), and later died at the American Hospital. Though her death was ruled an accident, it's hard to imagine someone ingesting a significant amount by mistake. Perhaps they had another huge row and she decided to end it all, but Jack insisted that it was a horrible accident and that he had done everything he could to save her. Nevertheless, the press had a field day, speculating on everything from a distraught suicide over Jack's infidelities, to him murdering her for insurance money.

Whatever the cause, Olive did not seem content to rest in peace. She chose to make her after-life encore at the New Amsterdam Theatre following her death. Employees at the New Amsterdam insisted that she could not be dead, because they had seen her, dressed in her Follies costume, but strangely, carrying a large blue bottle. She was seen at various points up though the 1950s and then seemed to fade from view.

However, in the early 1990s, Dana Amendola, an employee of Disney, was put in charge of renovating the theater, which the Mouse Corporation had recently acquired and wanted to restore for its own productions. Amendola was woken up by a phone call, sometime after 2:00 a.m., from a panicked security guard at the theater. He claimed that he had been walking across the stage, when his flashlight shone on a young woman wearing a beaded dress and headpiece (exactly the kind worn by the Follies performers), and carrying a blue bottle. Shocked that anyone would be there at that hour, the guard yelled at her that she should not be in the building, but she simply smiled, turned, floated across the stage, and disappeared through the wall. The poor man was so shaken that he quit on the spot.

Amendola has since studied Olive's life and has recorded many other instances of her hauntings. She mostly appears after the audiences have gone home, usually to men, and usually in a flirtatious way. A few have reported hearing a young woman's voice say "Hi, fella!" She seems mostly benign, but a few things have ticked her off, most notably, when still-living former Follies performers have visited the theater for reunions. Amendola said that on one such occasion, sets began shaking, as if in an earthquake. Another time, the light bulbs on an office floor all burned out at the same time, though no fault was discovered in the electrical system. Olive apparently doesn't want the attention taken away from her.

Most recently, she was observed walking in midair. Some research revealed that the area in question was once the site of a glass ceiling used for promenades. It seems that Olive is not yet done with the New Amsterdam, and still enjoys putting on shows from time to time.

The Duke of York Theatre, London

The Duke of York's spectral claim to fame is quite unsettling. It involves both a forceful ghost and a jacket that has tried to strangle its wearers. The ghost is believed to be that of Violet Melnotte, who along with her husband, Frank Wyatt, oversaw the building of the venue in 1892, first calling it the Trafalgar Square Theatre, but renaming it in 1895 to honor the young man who would later become King George V. Melnotte, an acclaimed actress and capable manager, was heavily involved in the operation of the theater's business, perhaps a little too much for some. Even though she would lease out the building to managers and producers, she always seemed to exert control and have at least some final say over productions.

She died in 1935, and almost immediately, strange things began to happen in the building. Clearly, she was not done yet. Over the years, many have reported hearing loud knocking sounds in various locations, very specific and seemingly made to attract attention. One sound in particular is that of an iron fire door slamming shut, but this door was removed long ago. One theater manager claimed that a skeleton key materialized out of thin air at the place where the door had been located and fell to the floor in front of him.

Melnotte is not usually seen, but there have been reports of her at one of the bars, dressed in black and shadowy in appearance. Other stories have told of how the door to her favorite private theater box will open and close by itself, as if she is still entering to watch the latest production.

A carpenter claims that the ghost may have saved his live when he was working on scaffolding. While he was painting a portion of the stage wall, he saw that the wheels on the platform were not locked and had begun to roll away from the wall. He was high up and risked falling to his death if the scaffolding collapsed, but for some reason it stopped, at least for a moment, and he was able to grab a pipe and pull himself to safety before the whole thing came down. Did the former manager intervene and prevent him from joining her in the afterlife?

Whatever the ghost's intentions, there is a more disturbing legend associated with the theater, involving a haunted ladies' bolero jacket. There are several versions of the story, but here are the basics: the garment may have been designed and created in a costume house in the years before World War I, and someone at the Duke of York's wardrobe department acquired it many years later (perhaps at a market stall) for a 1948 Victorian costume drama called *The Queen Came By*. Another account says that it was in 1949 and the problems first began at the Embassy Theatre before the show moved to the Duke of York; such is the way with urban legends.

The female lead in the show, Thora Hird (also highly acclaimed for her numerous film and television roles), had the garment adjusted and fitted for her, but every time she wore it afterward, she would complain that it felt too tight. Other actresses, including Hird's understudy, Erica Foyle, tried on the jacket and also reported the tightness. In addition, the understudy noted feeling a sense of dread, as if the garment was maliciously trying to strangle her (Foyle apparently also saw the ghost of a young woman wearing the jacket). Often, those who put it on felt a sense that the collar was beginning to close up around their necks. When they removed the jacket, the fear went away almost immediately.

The producer's wife thought that this was all nonsense and volunteered to try it on. She felt nothing, mocked the others for their irrational fear, and removed the garment, only to see red marks on her neck, as if ghostly hands had been attempting to strangle her, too. After this, a cast member suggested that they hold a séance in the theater following the final show of the run, to determine what was going on. Apparently, the medium was able to contact the spirit of a young woman (some say an actress), who communicated to them that she had been strangled by an angry and jealous man (her boyfriend?) while near the theater. He may have forced her into a barrel of water and held her there until she drowned. Some accounts say that he then hid her body or threw her and/or the coat in the river; communications from the dead get a little garbled sometimes. His evil had somehow attached itself to the very fabric and now the jacket wanted to strangle anyone who wore it, especially women. However, a man tried the coat on shortly afterward and promptly fainted, so the curse seemed to affect everyone.

Maybe someone fished the jacket out of the river, cleaned it up, and offered it for sale, and so it ended up at the Duke of York. Regardless of how they acquired it, you would think the simple solution would be to discard the jacket, or burn it or something, but the story says that it was actually sold on to an American known only as Lloyd, who took it to Los Angeles. Apparently, both his wife and daughter experienced similar dread and feelings of being strangled when they tried it on, and were obliged to take it off after only a few minutes. The current whereabouts of the garment are unknown, but readers might want to be careful if they find themselves shopping in any vintage clothing stores in southern California.

All of this is wonderful campfire-story fodder, or perhaps a creepy tale to be told to young actors by the glimmer of the Duke of York's ghost light, but is any of it true? Who knows? And honestly, who cares? That's the fun of a good scare; it doesn't have to be real, and it's probably just as well if it isn't.

6

An Encore of Theatrical Oddities

ere to finish up—and as a form of light entertainment, a virtual
vaudeville, if you will—are some short, whimsical, and occasionally
awful vignettes from various points in theatrical history. Here is a grab-
bag of the grim and a potpourri of the peculiar, in no particular order.
They don't need an introduction, but think of them as finely crafted
afters to a good dinner, to be savored with a rich and dark glass of port.
Or just a bag of pork rinds to go with a cheap can of beer, whichever you
prefer.

David Garrick and the wigs both scary and silly

Garrick (1717–1779) was an English actor, manager, and playwright
noted for his Shakespearean roles, Hamlet and King Lear among them,
and for bringing a naturalist approach to his acting. This was something
of a novelty at the time, and Garrick did not escape criticism. One disapproving theater enthusiast listed some of his offenses:

> His over-fondness for extravagant attitudes, frequently affected starts,
> convulsive twitchings, jerkings of the body, sprawling of the fingers,
> flapping the breast and pockets; a set of mechanical motions in con-
> stant use; the caricatures of gesture . . .

It seems that in trying to act more naturally, Garrick was thought by some to have gone too far and seemed fake instead.

One of his more interesting effects was the so-called "fright wig," which was a headpiece that looked like a normal eighteenth-century wig, but could be adapted to pull the hair outward and simulate one being startled. This would probably look completely ridiculous to a modern audience, but it apparently was useful in conveying emotions of shock and fear at the time.

And speaking of laughs, there is the wonderful story of Garrick in the role of King Lear, performing the climactic scene wherein the foolish old king holds the body of his beloved daughter Cordelia, just before his own death. One of the great moments in tragedy was inadvertently disrupted by an unexpected sight from the pit. Garrick, while trying to deliver his lines, had to suppress a laugh, and as you well know, the harder you try not to laugh, the more difficult it becomes. He wasn't the only one, for soon other actors onstage were hiding their giggles, including the "dead" Cordelia. Ultimately, Garrick and his costar were compelled to leave the stage hastily in fits of laughter, bewildering the audience.

What would send an experienced actor into such a juvenile fit? A contemporary report describes it all in detail:

> A Whitechapel butcher . . . was accompanied by his mastiff . . . [who] got on the seat, and, fixing his fore paws on the rail of the orchestra, peered at the performers with as upright a head and as grave an air as the most sagacious critic of the day. Our corpulent slaughter-man was made of melting stuff, and, not being accustomed to the heat of a playhouse, found himself oppressed by a large and well-powdered Sunday periwig, which, for the gratification of cooling and wiping his head, he pulled off, and placed on the head of the mastiff. The dog, being in so conspicuous a situation, caught the eye of Mr. Garrick and the other performers. A mastiff in a church warden's wig was too much. It would have provoked laughter in Lear himself at the moment of his deepest distress.

The paper couldn't resist one final pun, noting that the play took place on "one very sultry evening in the dog days" of summer.

Joseph Grimaldi's awful discovery

Grimaldi, if you recall, is said to haunt London's Theatre Royal, or at least his floating and disembodied head is. But in life, he had a brush with something equally terrible. During one performance of the panto-mime *Harlequin and Mother Goose* at Sadler's Wells Theatre in London in 1807, a false alarm warning of a fire caused a panicked stampede, as audience members tried to get out of the building quickly, rather than in the "orderly fashion" that everyone is told to adopt.

Grimaldi was in the production, but was evacuated safely. Ulti-mately, twenty-three people died in the push to escape, even though there was no real danger. Grimaldi wanted to return to the theater after the incident to assess the situation, but he was unable to, owing to the large crowds still gathered outside. So he came up with another idea, which led him to a terrible discovery. According to a news article:

> He ran round to the opposite bank of the New River, plunged in, swam across, and, finding the parlour window open and a light at the other end of the room, threw up the sash and jumped in, a la Harle-quin. What was his horror, on looking round, to discover that there lay stretched in the apartment [presumably a side room of the theater] no fewer than nine dead bodies! Yes; there lay the remains of nine human beings, lifeless, and scarcely yet cold, whom a few hours back he had been himself exciting to shouts of laughter.

They were victims of a disaster that never happened.

The show ultimately ran for two years, but Grimaldi considered it to be one of the worst performances he had ever given and became de-pressed about his involvement in the whole thing; no doubt the feeling had been made worse by his grisly discovery.

Sol Smith and the theater of bones

American comedic writer and theater company manager Solomon Franklin Smith (1801–1869) once described a grisly, if interesting, feature about the location of a theater in which he was performing in Natchez, Mississippi. He wrote in his book, *Theatrical Management in the South and West for Thirty Years*:

> The new theatre in Natchez was situated at the extreme end of the main street, and in a grave-yard. Two hundred yards of the street leading to it had been cut through this "last receptacle of humanity," and every day, in going to rehearsal, our sights were regaled with the view of leg-bones sticking horizontally out of the earth ten or twelve feet above us, the clay having gradually washed away and left them thus exposed.

> The dressing-rooms for the gentlemen were under the stage, the earth having been excavated to make room for them. Human bones were strewn about in every direction. The first night, the lamplighter being a little "pushed" for time to get all ready, seized upon a skull, and, sticking two tallow candles in the eye-sockets, I found my dressing-room thus lighted.

Well, that's one way to do it!

Henry Miller and the Great Divide with his audience

Miller (1859–1926) was an English actor whose parents immigrated to Canada when he was young. He later pursued a theatrical career on Broadway with great success. One show, *The Great Divide*, enjoyed much popularity, but seems pretty bizarre and offensive now, being a Western about a young woman who avoids being kidnapped from her Arizona ranch by promising to marry the most decent-seeming of the three kidnappers. He agrees—and so bribes one of his buddies and shoots the other; and he was the *nice* one of the group! The next day, they get married, and after a series of seemingly endless melodramatic interludes, they wind up in Boston and she decides that she really loves him.

For whatever reason, this odd ode to Stockholm Syndrome did quite well onstage, though noticeably less so in Pittsburgh; maybe they were a little more forward-looking? In any case, Miller was offended by their lack of theatrical knowledge and good taste, but was magnanimously willing to give audiences there a second chance. He scheduled another run of the show, presumably to demonstrate to them what they had been missing.

During a performance, Miller was acting with his costar Margaret Anglin. He noticed that some patrons were getting out of their seats and leaving. Annoyed because he felt that once again this town was shunning him and his work, Miller stopped the scene and walked to the front of the stage, where he literally yelled at them to return to their seats. Calling the city an "over-sized smudge pot," he warned them that he would not suffer their insults a second time. Some of the audience sheepishly complied and sat down again, but others simply ignored him and continued their exit. This led to more yelling and swearing from the irate Miller. Finally, Margaret took hold of him and said, "Stop being a jackass, Henry, the theater is on fire!"

Presumably, Miller then made a humbled and hasty exit along with the rest of the cast and the entire lot of his so-called insulters.

Hedda Gabbler's overly noisy suicide

The play *Hedda Gabbler* by famed Norwegian playwright Henrik Ibsen was first produced in 1891, and was immediately the source of controversy, featuring a possibly disturbed female lead character who engages in rather horrible and manipulative behavior to obtain what she wants. Ibsen was interested in the study of mental illness, still in its infancy at the time, and his play was unsettling.

Hedda marries a man, the academic George Tesman, more for the stability the situation offers than for love. Hedda's former lover, Eilert

Løvborg, enters the story, and Hedda fears that he is after the same university positon that George seeks, but Eilert has written a bestselling book and is planning a sequel, which is all he cares about. Hedda is jealous of the fact that a former classmate of hers, Thea Elvsted, is influencing Eilert, and she resolves to disrupt their relationship. Eilert loses the manuscript for his new book while drunk, but George finds it. Hedda then goes to Eilert and tells him that, because he has lost the work (she does not reveal that George has found it), he should kill himself, and she offers him a pistol. She later burns his manuscript. Eilert does die, but George and Thea resolve to reconstruct the work from Eilert's notes. Soon, a certain Judge Brack comes to Hedda and reveals that Eilert died accidentally in a brothel, rather than killing himself, but that he knows that she gave Eilert the pistol. He threatens to reveal her role in ruining him and she knows that a scandal will engulf her. So she goes to her room and shoots herself in the head, her body being discovered by George, Thea, and Brack.

Well, that was cheerful.

One would think that such a dark contemporary tragedy would have no room for humor, and this is true, but we must always remember the possibility of things going wrong during an actual performance. In one showing of the play at Carnegie Mellon University in Pittsburgh (Pittsburgh again!), the actress playing Hedda went behind a screen that was lit, so that the audience could see her shoot herself in silhouette, a good visual trick. She put the fake gun to her head, pulled the trigger and . . . nothing. Someone had forgotten to load the pistol with blanks, so all that was heard was a click, several actually, as she tried again and again. Some enterprising actor backstage had the clever idea to pick up a stool and drop it to the floor loudly, which would give a sufficient "bang" to pass for the sound of a gunshot. Except that said stool was chained to a table to prevent theft, and upon picking it up and dropping it, the sound was of the stool, the rattling chain, and various plates and glasses all clanking at once and some falling to the floor and breaking; it sounded more like a bull in a china shop than a gunshot.

By now, the whole thing was causing those backstage to burst into laughter, and probably many in the audience, as well. One of the actors onstage attempted to salvage the situation when he exclaimed that Hedda had stabbed herself, as if this somehow made it better or less funny. In the meantime, the blank was found and loaded into the pistol, and Hedda was finally able to pull the trigger and die properly, much to the relief of all at hand.

The madness of the King in Yellow

The King in Yellow is a fictitious play invented by Robert W. Chambers (1865–1933) and described in a series of his short stories that were collected in a book of the same name and published in 1895. Chambers imagined this "forbidden" work as being anonymous and written in two acts. The first act was fairly mundane, while the second contained unspeakable hidden truths about the nature of the universe that could potentially drive the reader or viewer insane. The work serves as a backdrop to several of the stories and Chambers includes his own invented "excerpts" from the play, while carefully avoiding any of the lines that might provoke madness, of course.

The play's plot is only hinted at, but concerns at least three characters, Cassilda, Camilla, and the Stranger, the last of whom may or may not be the eponymous king. It seems that the first act details the final days of a crumbling empire in a distant, mythic world. At a masked ball, the Stranger enters, wearing a "Pallid Mask." When Camilla asks him to remove it, he responds that he wears no mask at all. This presumably sets up the mind-bending horror of the second act, wherein the civilization falls into ruin as unspeakable truths are uttered by the one who may be the king.

Chambers's stories are filled with creepy atmosphere; one story tells of a man who reads the play and becomes convinced that he will rule America as its monarch, but ends his days in an asylum instead. Another describes a man who dreams of a sinister church organist, only to awaken and find that death has come for him and the King in Yellow is whispering to him. Chambers created a suitable fictional background for the play, noting that it was translated into French, but that the French government seized it and banned it, fearing its effects. Chambers spent time during the 1880s and 1890s as an art student in Paris, and was witness to the changes that came along with the sometimes decadent *fin de siècle* culture, so the concept of a forbidden play being read or performed in secret locations fit in well with widespread interest in the shocking, the occult, and the damned.

The idea of a tome of forbidden knowledge was also found in the stories of American horror writer H.P. Lovecraft (1890–1937), creator of the infamous *Necronomicon*, a "translation" of a seventh-century Arabic book written in Damascus that describes the horrific unseen forces of his "Cthulhu mythos." Lovecraft admired Chambers's work and incorporated some of the ideas into his own stories, though it seems that he read *The King in Yellow* later in his career and it did not initially inspire him to create his own unique visions of cosmic horror.

This fantastical play has inspired many other short stories and a whole mythos of its own that modern writers sometimes combine with Lovecraft's dark universe and creations. One can see why Chambers's Parisian years were the likely catalyst for it. In the world of the Theater of the Absurd and the Grand Guignol, a sanity-shattering play that reveals hidden horrors to the unwary doesn't seem all that far-fetched.

The game show guest who saw it all

On February 9, 1956, ninety-five-year-old Samuel J. Seymour was a special guest on the CBS show *I've Got a Secret*. This was an early game show where celebrity panelists, as the title suggests, tried to guess the secret their guest was hiding, through a series of yes-or-no questions. And Seymour had a doozy of a secret.

The near-centenarian (he actually thought he was ninety-six) had been a wee lad of five when he was taken to a performance at Ford's Theatre on the night of April 14, 1865. To those scratching their heads as to the date's significance, this would be the evening that a disgruntled actor by the name of John Wilkes Booth shot and murdered Abraham Lincoln as the president watched the performance. Little Samuel saw it all, though he confessed that at the time, he didn't understand the significance of what had happened, or that Lincoln was dead. He was only worried about the man (Booth) who had jumped from the balcony in his attempt to escape. Seymour was the last living witness to this history-changing event, which made him quite the remarkable guest on a show normally given to somewhat lighter fare. In the end, the celebrity panel—which included Lucille Ball—was able to figure out his secret pretty quickly.

A legend says that about a week before his death, Lincoln had a dream in which he wandered through an empty White House, entered the East Room, and saw a coffin on a platform surrounded by mourners. When he asked a nearby guard who had died, he was told, "The president." It seems that his fate at the theater was sealed.

Exit Stage Left

*O*ur revels now are ended. You have braved the countless dangers of the theater, both onstage and off, and now only the pale ghost light flickers in the darkened hall of this book's finale. It's probably not surprising that an art form that requires so much investment of emotion and the ability to present every feeling imaginable would have a decidedly dark, if not outright bloody, history. Life imitates art, more often than we realize.

But regardless of the origins of drama, skits, plays, and interludes, we can no doubt agree that the presence of theatrical entertainment has enriched our history for thousands of years, and probably always will, as long as we crave good stories and the unique opportunity to see them unfold in front of us. There's a visceral thrill to a live performance that can't be matched by its digital counterparts. Even in the face of movies, television, and endless online streaming services, live theater thrives, and its creators have achieved fame throughout the world.

Indeed, the names of those theatrical greats live on, but not everyone has been so optimistic about their prospects for immortality. I'll leave you with the words of French playwright and humorist Alphonse Allais (1854–1905), who was once asked to speak about his profession:

> I have been asked to talk to you on the subject of the theater, but I fear that it will make you melancholy. Shakespeare is dead, Molière is dead, Racine is dead, Marivaux is dead—and I am not feeling too well myself.

243

Suggestions for Further Reading

So, you'd like to learn more, but where to start? There is a bewildering number of books, resources, websites, and assorted other theatrical goodies out there. Here is but a small list that may help you get started on learning more.

Online Resources

Drama Online. A treasure trove of theater information: plays and playwrights, genres, eras, videos, criticism, the art of acting, and much more. The catch is that the majority of it can only be accessed by subscription. The second catch is that individual subscriptions are not available, but many libraries and universities do subscribe, so ask yours if they do, and if they don't, bug them about it until they do (www.dramaonlinelibrary.com).

The WWW Virtual Library, Theatre and Drama. A free resource with links to sites and organizations all around the world, though some are broken or have expired. It contains links to everything from acting schools and audition notices to theaters, libraries, organizations, and online texts (www.vl-theatre.com).

World Shakespeare Bibliography. This site has over 117,000 resources available at the time of writing. If you're interested in researching in the area, it's a gold mine. This site offers individual annual subscriptions (www.worldshakesbib.org).

Also check out the *Folger Shakespeare Library* at: www.folger.edu.

And *Shakespeare's Globe* at: www.shakespearesglobe.com.

Approached with a bit of caution, Wikipedia can also be a useful starting point, if you remember that anyone can edit its content, and the more controversial the subject, the more likely that things will change often. Some references are poor and out of date, but it's worth a try to learn more about any of the topics discussed in the book, and entries often have useful bibliographies.

Books

A good number of general theatrical introductions are very long and very expensive university textbooks, so here are some more specific options that make for very good and informative reading.

Pierre Louis Ducharte, *The Italian Comedy* (New York: Dover, 1966). This classic from the 1920s may still be the last word on the Commedia, and certainly is the first place you should look.

Stephen Greenblatt, *Will in the World: How Shakespeare became Shakespeare* (New York: W.W. Norton, 2004). An excellent biography that also looks at the era as a whole. Very enjoyable!

Richard Hand and Michael Wilson, *Grand-Guignol: The French Theatre of Horror* (Exeter: UK, University of Exeter Press, 2002). A very good English-language study, which includes scripts for some of the plays, if you dare to read them!

Brad Schreiber, *Stop the Show!* (New York: Thunder's Mouth Press, 2006). A fun collection of theatrical anecdotes (mostly twentieth-century), covering costumes, stage sets, private lives, audiences, and other fun things.

James Shapiro, *Contested Will: Who Wrote Shakespeare?* (New York: Simon & Schuster, 2010). Oxfordians hate Shapiro, so read this and decide for yourself. A fascinating history of Shakespeare skeptics, putting advocates for both Bacon and Oxford in the context of their times.

Acknowledgments

This is my second excursion into the history of the weird and freakishly wonderful in the arts, and as before, several people deserve thanks for their help and encouragement.

Many thanks to my editor, Olga Greco, and to Skyhorse Publishing for being willing to take another trip into the realms of artistic madness. Olga's close reading and edits make my work better, and I'm very grateful for the input and support. Thanks again to my agent Maryann Karinch, who continues to be enthusiastic about such unusual subject matter. Various people agreed to read drafts of the work in progress, and their feedback was most appreciated. Thanks to: Allan J. Cronin, Joshua Lapan, Gilbert Martinez, Keith Spears, and Samara Metzler.

And again, my thanks and love to Abby, and to those house felines who somehow have a way of helping to make certain projects take longer than they should.

About the Author

Tim Rayborn was bitten by the acting bug at a young age. Unfortunately, he made a full recovery and went on to be a musician and writer instead. Still, he has dipped one or two toes into the world of theater since then, including improvisational work at historical recreations (having donned an Elizabethan doublet and slops on more than one occasion) and once playing a very well-roared lion in an intimate (i.e., a college class) production of the immortal *Pyramus and Thisbe*, as retold in *A Midsummer Night's Dream*.

He has a PhD from the University of Leeds in England and is devoted to history and music in equal measure, with a special emphasis on the medieval period and England in particular. He finds that theatrical presentations of early music are quite effective at bringing very old sounds to life in a meaningful way for our modern age. With that in mind, he plays dozens of obscure instruments and has been fortunate enough to gallivant around the world sharing little-known medieval music with bewildered audiences. He has appeared on dozens of recordings and has written at least five books that he'll admit to. Future projects include more of the same (why mess with what works?) and continuing to improve both his cat parenting skills and his knowledge of food and other epicurean delights.

For more information, see www.timrayborn.com.